THE STORY OF THE
LAKELAND DALES

The Nativity, embroidered by Ann Macbeth (1875-1948)

THE STORY OF THE
LAKELAND DALES

ROBERT GAMBLES

And the end of all our exploring
will be to arrive where we started
And know the place for the first time

T.S. Eliot

PHILLIMORE

1997

Published by
PHILLIMORE & CO. LTD.
Shopwyke Manor Barn, Chichester, West Sussex

ISBN   1 86077 033 9

Printed and bound in Great Britain by
BUTLER & TANNER LTD.
London and Frome

CONTENTS

LIST OF ILLUSTRATIONS

Frontispiece: The Nativity, embroidered by Ann Macbeth (1875-1948)

LIST OF MAPS

LIST OF COLOUR ILLUSTRATIONS
Between pages 84 and 85.

ACKNOWLEDGEMENTS

The author would like to thank the following for permission to reproduce illustrations: Mike Barker/Westmorland Gazette, 33; Rev. H.C. Barrand, 41; Barrow Public Library, 15; Geoffrey Berry/Kendal Public Library, 1, 11, 12, 20, 32; British Museum, Patterdale map inset; Burke's Armoury, 4; Townley Hall, Burnley, 16; Carlisle Public Library, 10, 23; H.S. Cowper (CWAAS 1894), 14, 39, Buttermere, Miterdale (CWAAS 1895) and Eskdale (CWAAS 1899) map insets; Cumberland Pencil Co. Ltd, 2; M. Davies-Shiel, 35; Ann Gambles, 7, 9, 25, 29, 34, 36, 42, 47; Peter Gambles, Ennerdale, Wasdale, Martindale, Langdales and Duddon Valley map insets; Robert Gambles, 18, Winster Valley, Lyth Valley and Long Sleddale map insets; William Grant, 21; Jane Gray, 40; Herdwick Sheep Society, Borrowdale map inset; Christine Isherwood/Cumbria Wildlife, chapter end-piece sketches; Kendal Public Library/University of Lancaster, 27, 31, 45; P.J. de Loutherbourg, Government Art Collection/Crown copyright, 37; Angus Mitchell, Copyright Glasgow Museums, frontispiece, 38; B.R. Moore & Co., 3; National Trust, Kentdale map inset; RCHM (England)/Crown copyright, 22; Sylvia Rigby, Vale of Lorton map inset; William Reading, 6, 8, 24, 26, 28, 43, 44, and the Vale of St John map inset; William Rollinson, Long Sleddale map inset; Ben Stephenson, 19; Tullie House Museum, Newlands and Langdales map insets; C.D. Turner, 17; Alfred Wainwright, reproduced by permission of Michael Joseph Ltd, 46; Westmorland Gazette, Kentdale map inset; Margaret Woods, 30. Ben Stephenson provided the colour plates except for plate I which was provided by Ian Brodie.

The lines from T.S. Eliot's poem 'Little Gidding' are reproduced by permission of Faber and Faber Ltd from 'The Four Quartets'.

The lines from John Clare's poem 'Stray Walks' are reproduced by permission of the Curtis Brown Group Ltd, London. Copyright Eric Robinson 1966.

PREFACE

One of the pleasures enjoyed by the author of a book such as this is to look back over the years spent in its preparation and to recall the many kindnesses encountered on the way. It has been heartening to discover such a fund of goodwill among so many Cumbrian folk towards anyone with a genuine interest in the history of the countryside in which they live. My thanks are due to all those who answered my enquiries with so much care and patience, and especially to those acknowledged authorities on the history of the Lake District who have so willingly and so generously given me the benefit of their learning and expertise. In particular, I would express my gratitude to Dr. William Rollinson, Dr. John Marshall, Dr. Angus Winchester, Mr. Mike Davies-Shiel and Mr. George Bott who have, over many years, given me invaluable guidance and encouragement. Anyone who has attempted research into almost any aspect of local history will appreciate the debt I owe to the Staff of the Public Libraries and of the County Museum and Archive Services who have responded to every enquiry with unfailing and awe-inspiring efficiency. In Kendal I have been fortunate to have the assistance of Christine Strickland whose formidable knowledge of the sources of Cumbrian history has smoothed the path on so many occasions. I also acknowledge gratefully the work of the authors of the books and articles I have consulted, all of which are listed in the bibliography or in the notes. The volumes of the Transactions of the Cumberland and Westmorland Antiquarian and Archaeological Society are a treasure chest which it has been a highly valued privilege to plunder in my exploration into the story of the Lakeland Dales.

I owe a special debt of gratitude to all those who so generously and energetically helped to provide the illustrations: to Ben Stephenson who travelled so far and waited so often on the whims of the Lakeland weather to take the colour photographs; to Ann Gambles who also defied the elements to secure her black and white photographs: to William Reading and to Margaret Woods who spent many patient hours seeking out and sketching some of the more obscure corners of the valley scenes; to these and to all those whose work in sketch, engraving or photograph has helped to enhance the text of this book, I wish to express my sincere thanks. Individual acknowledgement is made in each case and every effort has been made to acknowledge ownership of copyright of both illustrations and quotations; any omission is inadvertent and is regretted.

I also wish to record my warm appreciation of the sensitive encouragement of Marian Armstrong who, despite her many other commitments, undertook the word-processing and produced the final draft of the book, a task performed with her customary patience and meticulous attention to detail.

Finally, I acknowledge with deep gratitude the devoted companionship of my wife, Hannemor, who has explored the Lake District with me for so many years and has given so much invaluable advice, discerning criticism and constant support.

ROBERT GAMBLES

INTRODUCTION

In his *Guide to the Lakes* William Wordsworth asked his readers to imagine themselves poised on a cloud hanging midway between the summits of Great Gable and Scafell:

> 'We shall then see stretched at our feet a number of valleys, not fewer than eight, diverging from the point on which we are supposed to stand, like spokes from the nave of a wheel.'

In the observations which follow he is primarily concerned with the natural scenery of the valleys and describes only in 'general terms in what manner it is indebted to the hand of man', confining his survey to a broad discussion of antiquities, cottages, enclosures, bridges and places of worship. Our knowledge of the region's history has been transformed since Wordsworth's day as a succession of dedicated amateurs and skilled professionals have applied their enthusiasm and expertise to produce innumerable historical, archaeological, geological and botanical studies, each one adding new and fascinating detail to the tapestry which portrays the story of the Lakeland Dales. The volumes of the Transactions of the Cumberland and Westmorland Antiquarian and Archaeological Society alone suffice to show how much has been learned, while a steady outpouring of specialist monographs and dissertations, is a constant reminder of how much we have still to learn.

The chosen vantage point of this book is at a considerably higher elevation than Wordsworth's imaginary cloud and so makes possible a prospect of more than twice the number of valleys encompassed by his modest station. The *Guide to the Lakes* is written in impeccable prose and illuminated with the genius of the poet, revealing an unsurpassed ability and instinct to express the very essence of his subject. Here I have attempted to present a portrait of seventeen of the Lakeland Dales in a plain, unembellished manner which, it is hoped, will appeal to the general reader and the curious traveller keen to know something of the human story rather than the academic history of the Lakeland scene. Dr. William Rollinson in his *Life and Tradition in the Lake District* has superbly and comprehensively depicted the daily life of the dalesfolk in earlier times, their work and play, their food and medicine, their customs and culture, thus catching a way of life on the wing before it vanished for ever; I am, inevitably and gratefully, indebted to his work for many references in these chapters but my primary purpose has been to tell the story of the Dales rather than specifically to portray the lives of those who lived in them.

Why, for example, did the whole of Europe once come to Borrowdale for its pencils? Which Lakeland river was famous for its pearls? Who was Wonderful Walker? Where did the Roman Legions march along imperial Highway Ten? What is the story of Eskdale's little railway and Wasdale's strange way of counting sheep? Was the Vale of Newlands truly the birthplace of England's mining industry? Why was there a mighty blast-furnace by the silver Duddon and the largest smelting works in Britain on the banks of the Greta? Who was the King of Patterdale and who was the Queen of

Borrowdale? Who committed murder in Miterdale? In which valley were grazing rights awarded in a contest by candle-light? Who was the counterfeit coiner of Wasdale? What were diatomites and where were they found? What was a 'Bridewain'?

The answers to these and a hundred other questions will, it is hoped, add a little to the pleasure and understanding of all those who come to the Lakeland valleys 'with an eye to perceive and a heart to enjoy', and of all who seek not only the solace and the thrill of natural beauty and grandeur but also cherish a glimpse into the events, personalities, and social and economic changes which, over many centuries, have left their mark on the story of the dales and provided topics of conversation at the market, after church, at weddings and wakes and by the winter hearth.

There is so much to learn of the long and varied story of the Lakeland Dales: none of us will ever know it all.

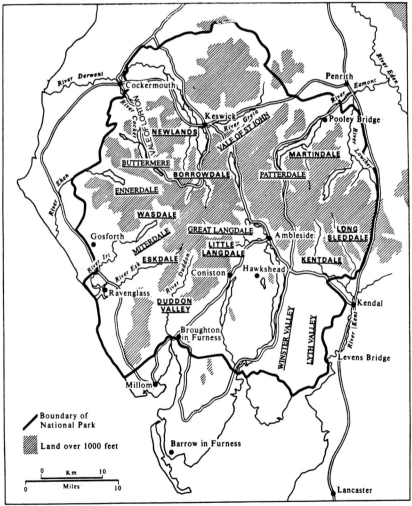

THE LAKELAND DALES

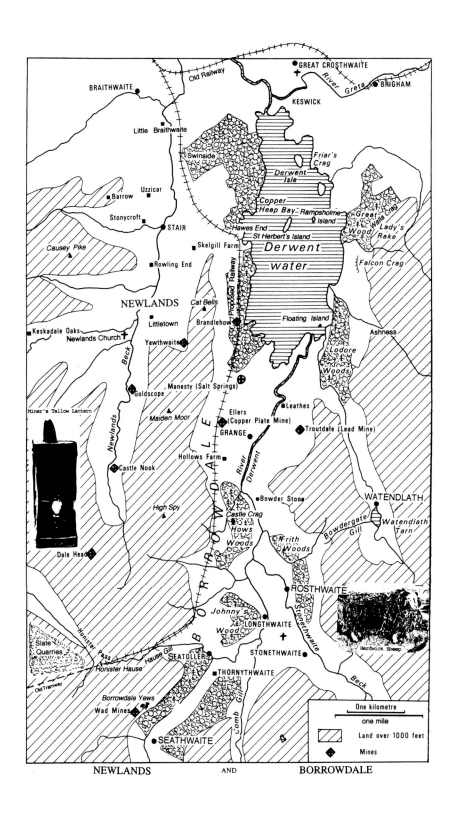

BRAITHWAITE

Old Railway

GREAT CROSTHWAITE

River Greta

BRIGHAM

KESWICK

Little Braithwaite

Swinside

Friar's Crag

Derwent Isle

Uzzicar

Barrow

Copper Heap Bay

Rampsholme Island

Great Walla Crag

Stonycroft

STAIR

Hawes End

St Herbert's Island

Wood

Lady's Rake

Causey Pike

Skelgill Farm

Derwent water

Falcon Crag

Rowling End

NEWLANDS

Cat Bells

Proposed Railway

Littletown

Brandlehow

Floating Island

Ashness

Keskadale Oaks

Newlands Church

Lodore Woods

Yewthwaite

Newlands Beck

Goldscope

Manesty (Salt Springs)

Leathes

Miner's Tallow Lantern

Maiden Moor

Ellers (Copper Plate Mine)

Troutdale (Lead Mine)

GRANGE

BORROWDALE

Hollows Farm

River Derwent

Castle Nook

Bowder Stone

WATENDLATH

High Spy

Castle Crag

Bowdergate Gill

Watendlath Tarn

Hows Woods

Frith Woods

Dale Head

ROSTHWAITE

Johnny's Wood

LONGTHWAITE

Stonethwaite

Honister Pass

STONETHWAITE

Slate Quarries

Hause Gill

SEATOLLER

Honister Hause

THORNYTHWAITE

Herdwick Sheep

Old Tramway

Borrowdale Yews

Comb Gill

Stonethwaite Beck

Wad Mines

SEATHWAITE

One kilometre

one mile

Land over 1000 feet

Mines

NEWLANDS   AND   BORROWDALE

1

BORROWDALE

A journey through Borrowdale is a journey through the history of the Lake District. Every historical and pre-historical influence which has shaped the life and landscape of the region may, in some aspect, be found in this most re-nowned of Lakeland valleys, justly acclaimed for its unique combination of rock, water and woodland, and notorious for its surfeit of summer visitors. A leisurely progress along the valley from the shores of Derwentwater to the quarried crags at Honister Hause will reveal not only some of the most captivating scenery in the entire National Park but also abundant and varied evidence of the changes brought about by many generations of human endeavour. Borrowdale as we see it today is the achievement of the constant and cataclysmic forces of nature aided and abetted by the puny but persistent efforts of mankind.

Readily and dramatically visible is the awe-inspiring scenic legacy of the Ice Ages, exposing some of the principal features of Cumbrian geology and creating the mighty crags which struck fear into the hearts of the first tourists and give delight to their modern successors; and strewn along the valley bottom are the farmsteads and pastures first cleared by the Norsemen, exploited by the monks of Fountains and Furness who followed them, and made prosperous by the yeomen statesmen who succeeded them in turn. The simple dignity of the cottages and farmhouses contrasts with the pretentious grandeur of Victorian hotels and mansions; the craftsmanship of the grey drystone walls and bridges is set against the untidy scars and relics of past endeavours to wrest mineral wealth from the mines and quarries; the pattern of lush green fields serves to enhance the joyful abandon of the Derwent as it foams over the rocky shallows or flows silently in deep jade pools. Old coach roads and ancient grassy tracks run side by side with a modern motor road; a multitude of footpath signs point the way for the hikers and fell-walkers along paths once known only to shepherds and local wanderers. Parish records, legal documents, personal memoirs and an avalanche of guidebooks tell us of land-ownership, local legends and folklore, valley customs and celebrations, natural disasters and human tragedies, and the changing fashions of tourism and scenic appreciation.

In our own time, Molly Lefebure has described Borrowdale as 'unique in its juxta-position of crag and foliage; rocks and birches cascading, intermingled, down deep fellsides'; John Ruskin declared that 'the scene from Friar's Crag is one of the three or four most beautiful views in Europe'; but a century before that The Reverend William Gilpin found the valley 'replete with hideous grandeur', the poet Thomas Gray was so overwhelmed by the horror of it all that he dared go 'no further than the farmer's at Grange', and Thomas Pennant saw 'all the horror of precipice, broken crag and over-hanging rock ... a composition of all that is horrible'. Not every 18th-century visitor allowed steep rock to go to his head, however: Dr John Brown, while conforming to contemporary fashion in describing 'rocks and cliffs of stupendous height hanging over the lake in horrible grandeur' with 'waterfalls tumbling in vast sheets from rock to rock in rude and terrible magnificence', was able to write eloquently and appreciatively of the many natural beauties of this 'Vale of Keswick'. His description of the view across the lake from Lodore is almost vintage Wordsworth:

> The natural variety and colouring which the several objects produce is no less wonderful than pleasing; the ruling tints of the valley being those of azure, green and gold, yet ever various, arising from an intermixture of the lake, the woods, the grass, and corn fields; these are finely contrasted by the grey rocks and cliffs, and the whole heightened by the yellow streams of light, the purple hues and misty azure of the mountains.[1]

The ambivalence of the Romantic writers towards the natural scenery of Borrowdale – an exaggerated 'fear' of the crags and a comfortable appreciation of their pastoral and lakeside setting – is nowhere better expressed than in the observations of Ann Radcliffe in 1795:

> Dark rocks yawn at the entrance, terrific as the wilderness of a maniac; and disclose a narrow pass, running between mountains of granite, that are shook into every possible form of horror. All above resembles the accumulation of an earthquake; splintered, shivered, piled, amassed. Huge cliffs have rolled down into the glen below, where, however, is still a miniature of the sweetest pastoral beauty, on the banks of the River Derwent; but description cannot paint either the wildness of the mountains, or the pastoral and sylvan peace and softness that wind at their base.[2]

Today, Borrowdale still polarises opinions; to many it is by far the prettiest and finest of all the valleys of Lakeland; to others it is teeming with tourists, congested with cars and the wettest place in all England. Perhaps Adam Walker, on tour from London in 1785, quaintly expresses both points of view: 'It requires no small resolution to persevere in a visit to Borrowdale ... but your courage will be rewarded by a scene of the wildest sequestration that perhaps ever excited human curiosity.'[3]

John Ruskin asked 'What sort of chisels were used to produce the largest piece of precious chasing or embossed work' which we see as the natural beauty of the Lake District? The simple answer to his question is 'Ice'; and in Borrowdale the process of chiselling was done on a dual geological structure of the two main types of rock which are found in the central area of the Cumbrian fells: the hard, craggy lavas of the Borrowdale Volcanics and the softer, smoother grits and shales of the Skiddaw Slates. An observant eye will have little difficulty in locating their meeting point in Borrowdale – on the east shore of the lake under Falcon Crag and near Hollows Farm to the south-west – and it is easy to see how they determine the nature of the landscape. Thomas Gray saw it clearly in 1796: 'Behind you are the magnificent heights of Walla Crag; opposite lie the thick hanging woods ... and Newlands Valley with green and smiling fields embosom'd in the dark cliffs; to the left the jaws of Borrowdale, with that turbulent Chaos of mountain behind mountain roll'd in confusion'.[4]

These contrasting scenes, originating from the basic geology of the valley, were given shape by the activity of the great glaciers which, on more than one occasion, ground their way through Borrowdale. It is now some ten thousand years since the last ice melted but the effects of this action are plain to be seen: the towering cliffs, the massive fallen boulders beneath them, the great 'Bowder Stone', transported by the glacier and abandoned for subsequent ages to wonder at; the ice-channel on the west side of Castle Crag, gratefully used by the builders of the old coach road and eyed optimistically by the engineers of the proposed Borrowdale Railway; the glacial moraines near Thorneythwaite and by the church at Rosthwaite; the beds of glacial lakes, now green pastures, between Seathwaite and Seatoller; the hanging valleys of Styhead Gill, Comb Gill and Watendlath.

Ice, however, is a fairly unsophisticated craftsman and it took many thousands of years for Nature and then, much later, Man, to refine this roughly chiselled landscape into the masterly sculpture we have inherited.

The inhospitable wilderness of shattered rocks, piles of boulders and debris, shallow lakes and universal swamp which was the immediate legacy of the glaciers was, in due time, clothed in forest and scrub, a scene of no great visual pleasure and utterly hostile to human settlement. It was not until the arrival of the Norsemen in the late 10th century that the Herculean task began of clearing the valley floor in order to create the first small farmsteads and cultivated fields. Before this date Borrowdale had certainly been visited by Celtic and Romano-British folk but it seems unlikely that there was any significant settlement. A few local place-names – Derwent, Comb Gill, Watendlath – are partly of Celtic origin and several axe-heads found in the valley are of pre-Roman date but this is slender evidence.[5]

A tiny hill-fort with triple ramparts near the road to Watendlath may provide more interesting artefacts when it is eventually excavated. But Castle Crag was almost certainly the site of an Iron-Age fort: it is so obviously an easily defended eminence and even today access to the summit is restricted to single-file passage. Some have claimed to see traces of ancient ramparts in the innumerable tumbled boulders scattered about the crag but if any once recognisable fort did exist here its useful remains have been almost totally destroyed by quarrying. Roman Samian pottery ware was certainly discovered here and may be seen in the Keswick Museum and, for the time being, this is the only archaeological 'proof' of the historical importance of Castle Crag to these elusive early settlers.

Our knowledge of a Roman presence in Borrowdale is, at present, imprecise: so ubiquitous were they in Britain, even in the remotest parts, that it would be remarkable

1   *Watendlath (engraving by T. Allom, 1833).*

if they had not found their way into this valley. A consignment of Borrowdale slate found among Roman remains at the fort of Oleanacum (Old Carlisle) near Wigton may indicate that the Romans were the first to exploit the quarries here. The general pattern of Imperial military engineering would strongly point to the construction of a fort at or near Keswick. No trace of this has yet been discovered but a recent study has helped to fill in the 'missing gap' in the Roman road between Penrith and Papcastle which, it now appears, ran close to the River Greta across the Vale of St John and headed directly towards Keswick.[6]

We are on rather more solid ground when we come to the Norse settlements. The evidence of place-names cannot always be taken as conclusive but a glance at the map of Borrowdale is sufficient to leave a powerful impression that the Norsemen were, indeed, the pioneers of permanent settlement in this valley as in so many others. The name Borrowdale is itself of Norse origin – Borgar dalr, the valley of the fort (almost certainly referring to Castle Crag). A clearing for a farmstead was a 'thwait' and towards the head of the valley we find Rosthwaite, Longthwaite, Burthwaite, Stonethwaite, Thorneythwaite and Seathwaite; an upland summer pasture or farmstead was (as in modern Norway) a seter – a name found at Honister or Honi's seter, Seatoller, Olvar's seter (or, possibly, the seter among the alders), and Seathwaite, the seter in the clearing. Landscape features everywhere here echo their Norse origin – fell, tarn, beck, how, force, gill, knott, ness.[7]

Norman conqueror succeeded Norse coloniser but the date 1066 has little significance here for it was not until 1092 that the rule of the new aristocracy began to be felt in these remote regions. Until then Borrowdale was part of the kingdom of Scotland, just within a frontier vaguely assumed to be across the central dome of Lakeland, and so does not appear in Domesday Book, much to the modern historian's regret. It was not until 1242 that the King of Scotland finally gave up his claims to lands in the new English counties of Cumberland and Westmorland, but from the time of William II's creation of the three great military baronies of Greystoke, Appleby and Kendal there was little doubt where the allegiance of these lands would in future rest.

It may seem strange that these troubled tracts of disputed territory should, so soon after their subjection to the rule of tough Norman barons, be handed over so readily to religious orders but in the course of the 12th century extensive grants of land were made for the foundation of Carlisle Priory, St Bees, Furness, Calder, Holme Cultram, Cartmel, Seaton, Shap and Armathwaite. Many of these belonged to the Cistercian Order whose rules demand that their houses should be situated in remote places far from human contact, and for this Cumberland and Westmorland were ideal. But this would not perhaps carry much political weight, however religious the Normans may have been, and it seems more probable that these lands were considered unlikely to produce the revenue the new overlords were coming to expect, or as W.G. Collingwood put it in his *Lake District History*: 'When early Norman lords had grants of perfectly wild country where the people were so rough that it did not seem likely that they would pay their rents, the natural impulse was to give a good piece to the priest.'[8]

Whatever her reasons, early in the 13th century Lady Alice de Rumelli, heiress to the vast estates of the Barony of Allerdale, disposed of great tracts of her lands to the Abbeys of Fountains and Furness, both of which acquired extensive holdings in Borrowdale. An unbecoming dispute developed between the two Abbots over the ownership of Stonethwaite, a prosperous vaccaria or dairy farm, an argument briskly settled in 1304 when the King confiscated the property and then promptly sold it back again to the Abbot of Fountains.

Under monastic supervision there now began in Borrowdale the first large-scale farming activity, with extensive sheep runs and dairy farms and the growing of crops of rye, oats and barley. The Furness monks attached sufficient importance to their farms in Borrowdale to establish a 'grange' there in which to store their harvests and from which to direct the administration of their holdings in the valley. They were keen and enterprising landlords and it is clear from the records of their Abbey that they developed to the full the economic potential of their domains, and this extended to the rigorous collection of rents and tithes. The independent dalesmen who were now tenants of these new and exacting masters, and who were also now obliged to make regular attendance at the church at Crosthwaite, must have found the blessings of the Christian Church at times hard to appreciate.

Most of the authors of the early guidebooks to the Lake District maintain that among the economic benefits of the Borrowdale estates were the revenues accruing from the sale of salt produced from the salt spring near Manesty: William Gilpin for example tells us that 'besides their tythe corn, they amassed here the valuable minerals of the country among which salt produced from a spring in the valley was no inconsiderable an article.'[9] There is, in fact, no evidence that salt was ever produced here and not even that most meticulous and comprehensive document, the Report of the Commission of Dissolution of 1537, makes any reference to it. The Great Deed of Borrowdale of 1615 mentions salt as one of the minerals included in the sale of land in the valley but gives no further details. It was not until the 18th century that the medicinal properties of this spring were publicised: in 1766 Thomas Short in his *Treatise on Cold Mineral Waters* asserted that the Manesty waters would ensure a 'rough, severe purge to a strong constitution', an aperient apparently of sufficient popular appeal to warrant the construction of a bath-house, open and free to everyone who felt the need for such drastic treatment. This has now vanished without trace.

Far more valuable an asset was the timber of the extensive Borrowdale woods which could be converted into charcoal for use at the important iron bloomery in Langstrath on Smithymire Island. It is not clear whether this was an enterprise of Furness or of Fountains Abbey nor do we know how much iron was produced. A similar bloomery was established, curiously, on Rampsholme Island almost in the middle of Derwentwater.

In their development of sheep farming and the woollen industry, in their dairy and arable farming and the field clearances this necessarily involved, in their charcoal and iron manufactures, in their exploitation of the woodlands for a variety of both useful and profitable industries (as the Commission of Dissolution sharply pointed out), the monastic foundations set the pattern for the future economic history of Borrowdale and of the Lake District as a whole.

The Borrowdale properties of Furness and Fountains were seized by the Crown at the Dissolution of the Monasteries and there soon began a period of intensive development of the mineral resources and a long series of legal disputes concerning the rights of tenant farmers. The creation of the Company of Mines Royal in 1564 and its impact on Keswick and on the Newlands Valley are outlined elsewhere (See chapter 2) but their mining operations also extended to the fells above Derwentwater and into Borrowdale itself. On the slopes of Cat Bells the Brandelhow Mine produced hundreds of tons of lead each year for 400 years, with crushing and dressing sheds and great waterwheels covering a large area down to the water's edge. Copper mines at Ellers, near Grange, proved to be so productive that Queen Elizabeth I wrested control of them from the Earl of Northumberland; this copper, like that mined in Newlands, was ferried across the lake on its way to the smelting works at Brigham and after processing it went to the Receiving

House in Keswick (now the Moot Hall) to be stamped with the Queen's mark. A small lead mine was also worked in Troutdale.

The Crown astutely held on to the mineral wealth of these valleys at the Reformation but, as elsewhere in the kingdom, for political and financial reasons the monastic lands were gradually sold off to Crown servants or to property speculators. Under James I the Borrowdale lands came into the grasp of William Whitmore and John Verdon who were the 17th century-equivalent of modern asset-strippers and before long they had arranged for the disposal of these properties – except the valuable wad or graphite mines – to 38 others with Sir Wilfred Lawson of Isel acquiring the most substantial holding. This rapacious landlord attempted to impose financial burdens on his tenants which resulted in a long period of litigation and a resounding declaration by the Borrowdale folk that such arbitrary 'fynes ansiently never were paid by our predecessors both upon the death of the Lord and on the change of tenant'. The Great Deed of Borrowdale was drawn up in 1615 to protect these long-established rights and customs.[10]

It was not long before Whitmore and Verdon saw an opportunity to sell off the wad mines and in 1622 these came into the ownership of several shareholders of whom, before long, the most eminent were, as two stones near the site of the mines informed all comers, John Banks Esquier and John Shepard Esq., the heirs to an enterprise which was shrouded in legend and mystery throughout the centuries of its existence.

The site of the Borrowdale wad mines is marked by the most famous trees in Lakeland, the Borrowdale Yews, famous as the only trees in the Lake District to be honoured by name on the Ordnance Survey Maps and as the subject of some of Wordsworth's less-inspired poetry:

> ... those fraternal Four of Borrowdale,
> Joined in one solemn and capacious grove;
> Huge trunks! and each particular trunk a
> Growth of Intertwisted fibres serpentine
> Up-coiling, and inveterately convolved.

Such tortuous verse matches the gnarled, weather-beaten appearance of these desolate trees one of which, the story goes, was violently uprooted in a great storm and under its roots was revealed the black mineral deposit which came to be known, variously, as graphite, wad, black lead, black cake, and plumbago. It was described by William Camden in 1582 as a 'kind of earth or hardn'd glittering stone, we call it Black Lead, with which painters use to draw their lines and make pictures of one colour in their first draughts'. This early reference foreshadowed what was to become in later years a famous local industry, for Borrowdale was the birthplace of the pencil and perhaps we, like William Gilpin in 1772, should feel 'a friendly attachment to this place, which every lover of the pencil must feel, as deriving from this mineral one of the best instruments of his art'.[11]

This was just one of the many uses found for this remarkable mineral. In 1709 Thomas Robinson noted in his *Natural History of Cumberland and Westmorland* that, 'It is a present remedy for the colic; it easeth the pain of gravel, stone and strangury; and for these and the like uses it is much bought up by apothecaries and physicians. The manner of the country people's using it is thus: first they beat it small into meal, and then take as much of it, in white wine or ale, as will lie upon a sixpence, or more, if the distemper require it ... Besides these uses that are medicinal it had many other uses which increased the value of it'.[12]

We learn from Robinson and other sources that the wad was in great demand for the fixing of blue dyes, for the marking of sheep, glazing pottery, preventing rust on metal, polishing iron, lubricating wheels and for casting cannon balls, round shot and bomb shells. It was also a precious commodity on the London market for the manufacture of crayons d'Angleterre, probably the most famous artist's drawing 'pencil' of all time.

Bavaria was the only other source of wad in Europe and, when export of the mineral from that country was banned, this and the steadily increasing range of its uses rapidly pushed up the price. The French metallurgist, Gabriel Jars, stated in the mid-18th century that Borrowdale was 'the only mine known in Europe for good pencils'. The deliberate curtailment of production by closing down the mine at certain periods also played a part in creating a scarcity and so further enhanced the price on the market. In 1788, for example, a consignment of 417 casks of Borrowdale wad weighing 70lbs each commanded a price of £43,785 or well over £3,300 a ton. It comes as no surprise to learn that the wad-miners and others considered it well worth while to take the risks involved in stealing and smuggling, but one wonders how seriously to take the claim of Joseph Budworth's workman who 'affirmed that he could get the value of £1000 worth in half an hour'. An exaggeration, perhaps, for the benefit of a curious visitor but even so there can be no doubt that a miner earning seven shillings a week could exchange a few ounces of wad in the *Bunch of Grapes* in Keswick for the equivalent of many months' wages. Borrowdale legend is full of tales of mysterious lights near the wad mines on dark nights and of secret journeys across the fells. The most famous of these smugglers was Moses Rigg whose name is preserved in Moses' Sledgate or Moses' Trod, the path between Wasdale and Honister Pass which crosses the slopes of Great Gable. He may have been responsible for building the 'Smuggler's Hut' hidden high in the cliffs of Gable Crag. Nothing more is known about Moses and the name may well have been a useful pseudonym for all those who aimed to make their fortune by stealing and smuggling wad to dispose of it in a ready market at Ravenglass or Whitehaven. At peak prices in the late 18th century a pack-horse load delivered in this way could fetch as much as the £1,000 referred to by Budworth's workman.[13]

So serious did this illicit activity become that miners were searched as they left the mine, security houses were built by each adit, and finally the whole power of an Act of Parliament (1752) was brought to bear to make the 'unlawful entering of any mine or wad hole of wad or black cawke, commonly called black lead, or unlawfully taking or carrying away any wad, etc. therefrom, as also the buying or receiving the same, knowing it to be unlawfully taken ...' a criminal offence with a punishment of transportation or hard labour for those found guilty. Even so wad smuggling continued so long as the price remained high enough to make the rewards worthwhile, and this was until the mid-19th century when imports of graphite from abroad forced the price down so rapidly and dramatically that within a few years the Borrowdale mine closed and the dark history of wad came to an end.

For over a century Borrowdale graphite was used in the Keswick pencil factories of which there were 14 in 1847. The most prominent of these was the Greta Pencil Works and Black Lead Mills of Messrs Banks & Co. who supplied lead pencils to all parts of the world and who achieved international renown when they were awarded the Prize Medals in the Great Exhibition of 1851 and also in 1862. By then Victorian technology had developed machinery which could bring Borrowdale wad and American cedarwood together to manufacture 10,000 Cumberland pencils every day in this one factory. The manufacture of pencils using Borrowdale wad ceased in 1906, some forty years after the miners had abandoned Seathwaite Fell to the sheep and the tourists.[14]

For much of the year the relics of the wad mines are almost entirely obscured by bracken and many of the visitors who throng Borrowdale in the summer months are

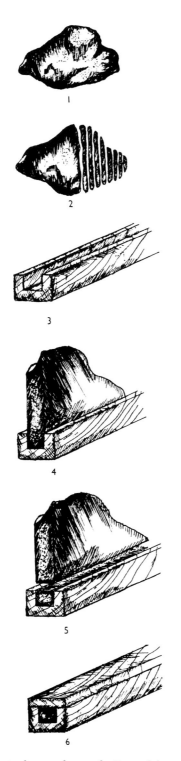

2   *Stages in the manufacture of a Borrowdale wad pencil*

unaware of their existence. By contrast, a mile or so away up the steep road to Honister are the very visible and impressive scars of Lakeland's best known slate quarry. The beautiful green slates quarried from the dark and forbidding crags at Honister are famous throughout the world. It is believed that the first slate was quarried here in 1643 and by the mid-18th century Honister was one of the most important of the many quarries then operating in various parts of the Lake District. Unlike the quarries at Coniston, Kirkby-in-Furness, Langdale, Tilberthwaite and Troutbeck Park which were able to transport most of their slate partly by water, the Honister slate had to be laboriously taken by packhorse over the high fells to the coast at Ravenglass and Drigg for shipment onwards. The 15-mile haul, from the quarry to Beck Head on the western slopes of Great Gable and down by Gavel Neese and Gable Beck to Wasdale Head and on to the coast, followed Moses' Trod and it is possible to find among the stones pieces of green slate which may tell of minor accidents as ponies and their burdens stumbled or slipped.

In the 1880s, at the height of the Victorian railway mania, such primitive means of transport were laughably antiquated and plans were drawn up for the construction of a Borrowdale railway. The proposed line would have branched from the recently opened Penrith to Keswick to Cockermouth Railway at Braithwaite and followed a route close to Newlands Beck and to the west of Swinside before swinging across to Hawes End by the shore of Derwentwater. From here it would cling to the slopes of Cat Bells and proceed from Brandelhow to Manesty and then on to Grange and Hollows Farm. The old coach road through the ice channel beneath Castle Crag and along the lower contours of High Scawdel had already marked out the next stages, a scenic route with wide views over the Derwent and the Rosthwaite meadows to the woods and fells beyond. Slate rather than scenery was the purpose behind this enterprise, however, and just before Seatoller the route turned round the crags to follow the contours straight to Honister Hause where the railway would share a terminus with the tramway which already carried the slate from the quarries down to the hause.

Formally designated the Borrowdale and Buttermere Railway, this line would clearly have facilitated the transport of Honister slate but it was a costly and risky undertaking and investors proved unwilling to provide the necessary finance to secure its construction. We can only speculate on the impact such a project would have had on the landscape of this most acclaimed of Lakeland valleys.[15]

This was not the end of the far from philanthropic efforts to provide the head of Borrowdale with better communications. In 1896 the first proposals were brought forward for the construction of a 'highway' or 'carriage road' between Seathwaite and Wasdale Head over Sty Head, the purpose of which was rather pompously declared to be to commemorate the Queen's Golden Jubilee, to emulate the glories of Rome and to ensure that the county's resources could readily be called upon at a time 'when this Empire will need all its resources in battle'. It was apparently in the national interest that the distance from Wasdale to Keswick should be not about forty miles but only seventeen. Again investors were slow to come forward and at its meeting in Keswick in August 1896 the Chairman of the Highways Board, perhaps influenced by the powerful rhetoric of Canon Rawnsley who had helped to found the National Trust just one year earlier, asked the members 'to do nothing more to the Borrowdale road to the end of time'. Later schemes to construct an electric tramway over Sty Head met the same fate and so, by good fortune, we have inherited a beautiful valley head and an area of wilderness which could so easily have been spoilt.[16]

Several early tourists and guidebook writers describe how in the 18th and 19th centuries they witnessed the awe-inspiring sight of the quarrymen bringing slate down the crags by man-handled sledge. James Clarke in 1787, having seen the workmen perform this operation, was incautious enough to try it for himself:

> The slate is laid upon a barrow, which is called a trail-barrow; it has two inclining handles or stanges between which the man is placed, going, like a horse, before the weight, and has nothing more to do than keep it in the tract, and prevent it from running too fast. Those who are dextrous will not sometimes set a foot on the ground for ten or twelve yards together; but the barrow will often run away with an unskilful person, which was my case when I made an attempt.[17]

An average stint for an experienced sledman was seven or eight sledges a day with a load of a quarter of a ton of slate on each descent. When this hazardous activity was replaced in 1881 by a gravitational tramway, tales were told of past heroics by such men as Joseph Clark of Stonethwaite who made 17 journeys in a single day and brought down five tons of slate, and Samuel Trimmer who for a wager of a bottle of rum made 15 descents in one day. Such feats serve to illustrate the calibre of the men who worked in these quarries from 7a.m. to 5.30p.m. for six days a week, spending the nights in huts near the quarry and returning to their homes in the valleys only on Saturday evening. During the week they communicated with their families by carrier-pigeon, a mail service which could usually ensure a reply within a matter of hours and proved so efficient that the Quarry Management on site adopted it to communicate with their headquarters in Keswick.

The green slate of the Borrowdale Volcanics, quarried at Honister, Coniston, Langdale and Kirkstone, had its origins in the volcanic ash expelled by the eruptions of the volcanoes in the central Lake District some 450 to 500 million years ago, and contain the green silicate mineral known as chlorite. The blue slate quarried mainly at Kirkby-in-Furness belongs to the Silurian shales which lie thickly over the volcanic layers and

3   *A slate-river at Honister Quarry, c.1910*

were formed from the sediments deposited on the bed of the Iapetus sea which covered much of the area some 400 to 450 million years ago. This basic difference in origin and mineral content accounts for the difference in colour and also for the different properties of the two slates. The green slates are of coarser texture and so less amenable to fine riving but they are more attractive in their shades of colouring and in the variety of ripple marks which have perpetuated the movements of the waters of the seas where they were formed. The planes of cleavage in the slate which are so important to the riving process are the results of massive upheavals of the earth's crust at a later date forcing the layers of particles into parallel directions and so determining the lines of cleavage.[18]

The mines and quarries brought a degree of hard-earned prosperity to Borrowdale where the yeomen farmers were already enjoying a higher standard of living following the expansion of agriculture in the 16th and 17th centuries. Here, as elsewhere, farmsteads were built or rebuilt on more generous and more comfortable plans, and domestic furniture and furnishings became more elegantly designed. Today Borrowdale has a rich heritage from this age and it is fortunate that so much of it is now under the expert care and protection of the National Trust which has a direct interest in such notable farmsteads as Ashness Farm, Hollows Farm, Chapel House Farm, Yewtree Farm and the hamlet of Watendlath, as well as a number of cottages.

When Thomas Gray made his famous visit in 1769 the only notable buildings here were these scattered farms of modestly prosperous yeomen, the solid stone cottages of humbler folk, the corn mill in Comb Gill, and the old chapel at Rosthwaite with the 'notorious' *Nokka House Inn* nearby, a much maligned hostelry which probably owed its 'notoriety' to the gossip of those who disapproved of the dice and card games which were played there and of the bucolic revels of the 'merry neets' which were held there. The coach road over Honister was not yet built; indeed, Gray was led to believe that access beyond Seathwaite was 'barr'd to prying mortals, only there is a little trackway winding over the Fells, and for some weeks in the year passable to the Dale's men'. This was the ancient packhorse route over Styhead which less than a century later the intrepid Eliza Linton was to travel in light-hearted mood by moonlight.

Mrs. Linton and her contemporaries demonstrated that it was possible to walk and climb in the Lakeland fells without 'the necessity for a fit of apoplexy half-way', and from the mid-19th century onwards there was no place in the guidebooks for exaggerated melodrama. John Murray's *Handbook to Cumberland, Westmorland and the Lakes* (1867) and M.J.B. Baddeley's *Guide to the English Lake District* (1886), the 'Bibles' of the late Victorian tourist, present detailed and comprehensive information on the history, topography, timetables, tours, walks, viewpoints and curiosities of interest to the earnest visitor. Thus, for example, a tour to the Bowder Stone would be enhanced by the knowledge that it was 62 feet long and 36 feet high, 89 feet in circumference and weighed 1,970 tons; that it fell in 'some great convulsion of nature' from the rock above – more correctly, it was deposited by a melting glacier – and that it was possible for two people to shake hands through the gap underneath its finely balanced base or to climb the ladder to its top to admire the view along Borrowdale. This wonder could be reached by a short walk from the comfort of the *Lodore Hotel* where a week's full board cost 120 shillings including breakfast, luncheon, afternoon tea, dinner and attendance. A tour on the lake would be enlivened by details of the islands: St Herbert's Island with its story of the 7th-century hermit and his friendship with St Cuthbert which ended when both died on the same day; Lord's Island and its drama of the Jacobite Rebellion and the subsequent capture and execution of the Earl of Derwentwater while his Countess made a romantic escape via Lady's Rake; Derwent Island and the extraordinary tale of Joseph Pocklington, who built there a mansion described by Norman Nicholson as 'laughably ugly', a large model of Castlerigg stone circle, a boat house looking like a chapel, a chapel which looked like a doll's house, and an ornate fort bristling with brass cannon which was to be the centre-piece of a mock sea-battle 'with dreadful discharge of musketry' echoing round the mountains and heard even as far away as Appleby! And finally, the Floating Island, a phenomenon which fascinated visitors and guidebook writers for over a hundred years.[19]

Derwentwater's floating island excited so much curiosity among the first tourists that it became the subject of much speculation concerning its appearances and disappearances, some of it bizarre and some based on serious study. In 1855 Harriet Martineau in a typically forthright comment revealed her impatience with it all:

> The floating Island ... has obtained more celebrity than it deserves, It is a mass of soil and decayed vegetation which rises when distended with gases and sinks again when it has parted with them at the surface. Such is the nature of this piece of natural magic which has excited so much sensation during successive generations.[20]

Miss Martineau would have been unable to write with such certainty without the work of Jonathan Otley who had studied the island closely between 1814 and 1828 and had put forward the explanation given so simply by Miss Martineau. Otley's work was later followed up by G.J. Symons who in 1888 published a detailed study of the island based on his observations in the summers of 1884 and 1886 and on his historical researches. The island had appeared 40 times between 1743 and 1888, always during a spell of warm weather and usually at some time between mid-June and mid-September, the longest period being in 1831 when it was afloat from 10 June to 24 September. His conclusions were cautiously stated but he believed the island consisted of a mass of peaty material mixed with forms of vegetation which gave off bubbles of marsh gas. As the mass was not anchored to the bed of the lake but only rested on a layer of diatomite, a sufficient accumulation of gas permeating the peat, assisted by the plant growth on the surface, would make the island lighter than water and so it would lift to the surface of the lake, sinking again when the gas had dispersed. The size of the island varied greatly: the largest recorded was in 1798 when it was 540 feet long and the smallest in 1813 when it was no more than 36 feet. Subsequent observations have not significantly changed Symons' theories. The island appears just to the north of the mouth of Watendlath Beck but, for obvious reasons, its presence cannot be guaranteed: it is, as a recent guidebook put it, more of an event than an island.[21]

A far more valuable asset to Borrowdale's rich natural heritage is the valley's famous woodlands. From Great Wood by the shore of Derwentwater to Johnny's Wood near Seatoller, Borrowdale 'has a greater extent of semi-natural woodland composed of native trees than any other Lakeland valley. Evidently virtually all these woods are planted and growing on the site of former forests exploited for timber and charcoal during earlier centuries, but as the replanting was largely with native trees, perhaps they show some approach in character to the original, natural woodlands of the district.'

The geological diversity of Borrowdale has resulted in the creation of different soil conditions and this gives to the woods a variety of trees and undergrowth which contributes greatly to their interest and beauty. On the wet, peaty soils we find an abundance of ash, birch and wych elm with tall shrubs such as bird cherry, hazel and holly; but most of the Borrowdale woods are on the hard, acidic soils associated with the local volcanic rocks and here, as in Johnny's Wood, the characteristic growth is the sessile oak, often stunted but occasionally of substantial height, with a sparse scattering of rowan, larch and birch. All these woodlands have a rich undergrowth with a remarkable variety of flowering plants and herbs but of special interest is the collection of ferns, mosses, liverworts and lichen. For those who are erudite in such forms of plant-life Dr. D.A. Ratcliffe has listed 10 species of fern, 40 mosses and liverworts and 106 different types of lichen, all of which find a congenial habitat on the damp, rocky terrain of these steep woods or on the trunks of the trees growing there.[22]

Joseph Budworth on his *Fortnight's Ramble to the Lakes* 200 years ago also noted the profusion of 'mosses and plants with which this neighbourhood abounds', adding that 'Those who have a taste for Botany ... may collect many things worth carrying away', a sentiment which would earn him little praise now. If he were to visit Lodore Falls today he would not find 'the largest strawberries I ever eat and innumerable raspberries'.[23]

Poets, novelists, artists, guidebook writers, curious travellers, historians and scientists have all found inspiration for their work in Borrowdale and left their impressions of their various experiences. But none has come near the lives of the ordinary dalesfolk, those few hundred people who spent all their years from the cradle to the grave in this valley enduring the travails and enjoying the pleasures of simple family life in a small community. Indeed, the patronising comments of John Murray's *Handbook* on the rough manners, lack of education, deplorable taste and dubious morals of the Lakeland 'peasantry' probably reflected the degree of understanding shown by the contemporary tourist of the native residents and the lives they led. Tales told of the rustic stupidity of the Borrowdale folk became part of the tourist patter and could be guaranteed to raise a superior laugh. By the time he returned home almost every visitor was able to relate a version of the story of the dalesfolk who built a wall round the valley in the hope that this would prevent the cuckoo from flying away and thus ensure perpetual summer; or of the local lad sent to collect a load of lime from Keswick who was alarmed when the sacks began to smoke in the rain and attempted to put out the 'fire' by throwing water over them thus making the situation worse.

For a truly genuine glimpse of life in Borrowdale in the 19th century we are able to turn to a source of a very different kind, an authentic voice. Sarah Yewdale was born in Borrowdale in 1768 and lived there for more than one hundred years. Her account of cottage life, the round of the seasons, the local customs and festivals, the people she knew, all told with that discerning eye for detail with which every rural raconteuse seems to be gifted, recreates the daily life of the valley community in a manner which no guidebook writer, sociologist or historian could ever hope to achieve. In the vivid language of the local dialect (see Glossary, p.163) this 'Queen of Borrowdale' describes how,

ivery body leeved o' their awn produce, an' war clad wi' haem-spun claeth ... a gay substantial stuff an' keept yan rarely warm i' winter ... There wasnt a farm hoose but ye med hae hard through aw t' lang winter neets t' whirring an' t' burring o' t' woo' an' t' line wheels, men a' woman, lads an' lasses aw as busy as inkle weavers ... We hed laale to deu i' winter beside waiten o' coos an' spinnen i' t' neets, an' sae t' huntsman's horn was a cheery soond amang us, an' nowt wokened t' echoes o' t' fells maer welcome. Bless ye, a've known t' day when mudders wi' barns o' their backs wad hae gaen a hunten.'

Sundays were special days, however, when,

we aw donnt up i' oor best an put on oor slender shoon an' war verra perticular aboot gaen to t' chapel. There was some o' t' auld Statesmen at wadent hae missed t' sarvice for nowt. They used to meet i' t' chapel garth i' gay good time, an' it aw t' news, an' mebbe hear ov a stray sheep or twoa. Maistly teu, their dogs com wi' them....If there was any seeal or owt public gaen on i' t' Deeal it was customary, i' them days, t' mak it known efter fwok had come oot o' t' chapel. Mebbe it wasnt reet, but fwok dudnt think it sae i' then auld times.

Christmas was celebrated in great style:

Cursmas was Cursmas than; a think t' fwok o' t' auld time enjoyed life maer than they deu noo, an' war aw far maer friendly yan wi' anudder. For a week afwore Cursmas-day ivery body begun to be busy, an' for aw that week there was sic scrows wi' killen o' sheep an splitten o' wood, an' beeaken o' pies, as niver war seen. Than o' Yule Iben a gae gart log was o' t' back o' t' fire, an' t' barreel was tapped, an' aw tidied up, an' t' fiddler wad cum an' a few gart fellows wid him, an' if fwok warent gaen to bed there wad be a dance, an' away agaen. It was a regular thing to brew in October for Cursmas. Iverybody dud sae, beeath rich an' poor, an' some brewet at seeam time for t' clippen. But when Cursmas was yance fairly set in, we dud nowt but feeast an' dance an' play at cards tul Cannelmas. In them days we allus had a fiddler i' t' Deeal, an' there was niver a feeast but there was a dance. What, barn, yan fairly ran through yan's sel at sic times, neet efter neet feeasten an' dancen till yan wad gae off asleep t' next day amang yan's wark. But there was nae pride an' differences amang us than: sarvants an' statesmen's sons an' doughters were aw alike, as weel they mud.

A valley wedding, too was a time for feasting and celebration and Sarah Yewdale gives a lively account of the day's events while regretting that times have changed: 'Some steeal off as they deu noo, an' gat weddit, an' niver a dog barkt, an' neabody t' wiser till aw was ower.' Not like it used to be when

there wad mebbe be as far as twenty or thirty gang to t' Kurk o' nagback t' bride sitten on a pillion behint t' fadder ... It was a verra cheerful seet to see them aw gaen doon t' rwoad in a lang string, on a fine summer mwornen. But there were sad fakes comen back, sec gallopen and clatteren, ye med hae thowt at aw Borrowdale was gaen mad; for ye see it was rackoned a gart thing to be furst haem fra t' Kurk ...
Efter t' dinner was ower fwok com in fra aw parts o' t' Deeal, an' t' bride sat in a chair i' t' pworch wi' a wood dish on her knee, an ivery body gev her summat ... But fwok gat ower prood to be beholden to yan anudder, an' Bidden Weddins went oot o' t' fashion. There used to be wosseln an' runnen an' lowpen i' t' efterneun, an' plenty to eat an' drink, an' nowt nae warse.

Sarah gives us a glimpse into a dale farmhouse of her time:

A Farmer's house dudnt leuk amiss wid its gart oppen chimley, full up t' rannel balk with hams an' flicks o' bacon an' legs o' mutton, an' a gart lang drusser i' t' far side o' t' hoose, wid rows o' breet pewder plates an' dishes. Nae, there is nae pewder plates noo, nut at they war offen used i' t' auld times, for maistly t' frying pan was set on t' middle o' t' teeable an' we aw helpt oorsels oot on't.

A simple folk perhaps but if anyone should have the idea that there was

> nut mickle larnen i' Borrowdale i' them days, a can tell ye, ye'r under a gart mistake....Theear
> was better scholars lang sen than ther ur noo twenty times ower. T'skeul was nearly allus towt
> be t' preest an' ivvery farmer's son was keept gaen tu t' skeul tull he war verra nar twenty. Many
> a man theer was in Borrowdale than, an' theear's a few on 'em left still, 'at larnt Latin an' could
> write a hand like copperplate an' deuaan t' hardest questions i' t' coonten beuk.

Even allowing for an old lady's exaggerations this does suggest quite a good standard
of literacy and numeracy and should be set against the picture of an ignorant and
illiterate peasantry as portrayed in some of the guidebooks.

On a touchingly familiar note Sarah, like the older folk in every generation, laments
the regrettable changes in the weather since she was young:

> for ye see winters war nowt like what they are noo. Frae November to Cannelmas we'd nowt
> but frost an' snaw, an' verra seldom dud t' snaw git off t' fell tops befwore Midsummer. A' can
> mind when it was a verra common thing to hev to tak t' geavelock to breck t' ice i' t' beck for
> t' coos to drink. What, a can remember when Darran was yance frozen over for thirteen weeks.
> But we've nowt o' that noo, nur sic fine summers. We've nowt but rain an' sic noo, snell wedder
> at a cannot put my heead to t' deur widdout gitten cauld.

Sarah Yewdale died in 1869 in her 101st year. And today we can echo her truly
heartfelt exclamation: 'Borrowdale changed! It's nowt like t' seeam spot'.[24]

The town of Keswick, Borrowdale's metropolis, has been omitted from this chapter. Its
story is admirably told in *Keswick: The Story of a Lake District Town* by George Bott (1994).

Tree-creeper

2

NEWLANDS VALLEY

Wordsworth averred that 'every valley has its distinct and separate character'. It is not easy to define precisely the distinctive character of the Vale of Newlands for this is a valley of contrasts: the empty solitude of the mosses, crags and lonely pastures above Keskadale is quite another world from the neat white-washed cottages, green enclosures and well-kept dry-stone walls near Littletown and Stair. A gem of natural beauty may be set next to an ancient spoil heap; nature reigns supreme towards the valley head but elsewhere the handiwork of man is everywhere. James Clarke was drenched and desolate as his carriage negotiated the storms and other hazards on the way to Newlands Hause while Joseph Budworth, resting comfortably at a farm below, enjoyed 'two bowls of whey' and watched 'two machines at work ... making butter for salting ... each of which could churn thirty pounds'. This pleasant pastoral scene does indeed contrast with the desolation of the upper valley but it shares with it the grandeur of the great crags and fells which enfold them both. The steep Newlands flanks of Cat Bells and Maiden Moor lead on to the long, long precipice of Eel Crags falling from High Spy; the heather-clad turrets of Scope End are matched by the mighty ridge of Robinson, and, hidden between them, is the boggy hollow of Little Dale described by Wainwright as 'a gorge thunderous with waterfalls that put many better-known ones to shame'. On the western side of Newlands lie the steep ridges of Knott Rigg and Ard Crags, the distinctive knob of Causey Pike and the modest but rewarding summit of Barrow, all with magnificent views across and along the valley and of the impressive array of mountain scenery on the other side. Yet none of this inspired that sense of horror which the first tourists suffered when confronted by the awesome crags of Borrowdale and it is in this, perhaps, that we might find the key to the 'distinct and separate character' of the Vale of Newlands. William Gilpin expressed this on his visit in 1786 when he commented that Newlands was 'totally different from the rude valleys we had yet met with ... Here, the idea of terror was excluded. The valley of Newlands was adorned with the beauties of Luxuriant Nature'.[1]

Just 250 years before Gilpin's visit John Leland, Librarian to Henry VIII, had found 'a poor lytel Market Town called Keswicke'. Poor by London standards, no doubt, but Keswick was even then a modestly successful farming and dairy centre with a Market Charter dating from 1276 and enjoying the patronage of the locally powerful family of Derwentwater. This simple medieval economy received an unexpected boost in the 14th century with the opening up of the 'New Lands' a few miles away across the lake. New farms – the 'Neulands' first referred to in 1318 – were formed following the draining of Husaker (Uzzicar) Tarn, a fairly large, shallow lake which had been created by the holding back of the waters of Newlands Beck by an embankment built to carry a causeway, possibly Roman. A document from the records of Fountains Abbey appears to suggest that this 'dam' was removed during the 13th century, thus releasing the water from the tarn. The name 'Newlands' or 'Noulandes' appears regularly from this time onwards.[2]

15

The yeomen who farmed these lands, with the Herdwick sheep as the foundation of their economy and modest crops of oats, barley and beans as the mainstay of their field produce, were fortunate to have the Keswick markets so close at hand, but they were not all the proudly independent and confidently prosperous minor gentry of historical romance. They were, for the most part, simple, hard-working tenant-farmers whose holdings were on quite a small scale and whose livelihood was often precarious when an unfavourable summer combined with a hostile environment to render much of their effort in vain. A few certainly prospered and, with their modest wealth and sturdily built stone farmhouses, aspired to a higher place in the social hierarchy, but these often owed their good fortune not to superior farming but to successful ventures in other fields – in mining, or quarrying, in trade or even in the law. Work in the mines and quarries also gave the humbler labourer additional employment to eke out the meagre living afforded by his farm. In almost every Lakeland valley, from the late 16th century onwards, such opportunities were opened up – and Newlands was the first to see the commercial exploitation of the mineral wealth which lies beneath the fells.[3]

On 1 August 1566 Thomas Thurland wrote from Keswick to the Queen's Secretary of State, William Cecil, a letter which must have brought great satisfaction not only to Queen Elizabeth but also to Robert Dudley, Earl of Leicester, and all the other shareholders in the Company of the Mines Royal. 'This week in Newlands', he informed them, 'a copper mine was found which they say is the best in England', a discovery which promised substantial rewards for the initiative taken two years before, when the Company was formed, with the Queen's blessing, to exploit the mineral resources of the country in order to obtain

> that true benefit wch her Ma[jes]tie & ye State might reap by making copper wch is in her Realme thereby to be provided of a competent Store for her necessary without being beholden to forrayne Princes her Neighbours ... [4]

and so that England might emulate those other lands where revenues had been so significantly enlarged by the profits of the mining industry.

In an increasingly hostile European situation and with poverty, unemployment and serious local shortages of food as major domestic problems, Elizabeth could not afford to ignore all these advantages which, it semed, might stem from the development of a native mining industry. Her father, Henry VIII, had appointed a Surveyor of Mines but had quickly discovered that his subjects lacked the particular technical skills required in the mining, smelting and refining of metals. Elizabeth proposed to remedy this deficiency without delay as she could no longer continue to rely on foreign sources for so vital a commodity as copper which was extensively used not only in the casting of cannon but also in the construction of ships and, in the domestic economy, was essential in the manufacture of cards and combs for the woollen industry on which the prosperity of the nation depended.[5]

Evidence is sparse concerning the earliest workings of the rich veins of copper in the hills adjoining these newly cultivated lands. A brief reference in the reign of Henry III (1216-1272) is followed by grants to German miners in 1359 and again in 1478 but there seems to have been no significant activity. Then in the short reign of Mary Tudor, Thomas Percy, the ambitious 7th Earl of Northumberland, whose lands had been sequestrated for treason under Henry VIII, secured not only the restoration of his estates but with them a royal patent to work any mineral deposits which might be found in the Newlands Valley. The canny Percy already knew, as he later confessed, that about 100,000lbs of copper ore had been extracted here just before the grant of Mary's Letters

Patent. It was unfortunate for him that only one year later his Catholic sovereign died to be succeeded by the Protestant Elizabeth who within two years of coming to the throne had invited a German mining company – Haug, Langnauer of Augsburg – to prepare a report on the prospects for Crown exploitation of mineral deposits in all parts of her realm.[6]

The Company of Mines Royal was duly set up in 1564 and incorporated four years later, 'the first company to be formed in England for the manufacture of an article [copper] as distinct from companies formed for trading purposes only'. So began an enterprise which, whatever its failures, was to be a landmark in England's industrial development and which was to bring to a quiet, secluded Lakeland valley the first large-scale mining industry the country had ever known. For more than three centuries the 'sweet scenery' of Newlands was to be littered with all the trappings of a mining

4 *Arms of the Company of Mines Royal granted in 1568.*

operation and the surrounding fellsides were to echo to the clatter of an industrial enterprise. The nearby town of Keswick became England's Elizabethan Klondike.[7]

At first, affairs appear to have moved very slowly and we find the Company's chief shareholder, Thomas Thurland, writing sharply to Cecil on May 1566 to the effect that if he will not answer his letters he will write no more though he be the Queen's Chief Secretary of State. The discovery of the rich copper vein a few weeks later stirred Cecil into action and before the end of October a Bond of 500 Crowns had been arranged in Augsburg for 20 German miners to be sent to England.[8]

Meanwhile the indignant Percy was challenging at Law the Crown's right to ride roughshod over his claim to the minerals on his lands. The result was one of the most famous lawsuits of the time. There were no more law-abiding monarchs in Europe than the English Tudors but rarely did the Law fail to give them what they wanted. Percy's hopes were forlorn. The outcome of his legal wrangle with the Queen established that in English Law all gold and silver belonged to the Crown even if they were found on the lands of the Queen's subjects; that all ores bearing gold, silver and base metal together also belonged to the Crown unless the value of the base metal was greater than that of the gold and silver; base metals alone legally belonged to the landowner. Orders were promptly issued to the Lord Warden and to the Justices of the Peace that 'the Almain miners' were to be given full protection against the hostility and violence with which the local populace had received them. The initial 20 soon became several hundred.[9]

The impact of so many German immigrants on the small community living in and near Keswick must have been quite dramatic. Large sums of money were lavished on the new Company's enterprises, exemption from taxes was freely granted, privileges to cut timber and peat were readily forthcoming, stone and slate for building were quarried at will, the acquisition of land for the Company's housing and industrial needs seemed to present no problems. All this aroused the envy and resentment of the local people, sentiments intensified by the steady flow of imported luxuries pouring into the town for German homes – oranges, lemons, peppers, red cinnabar, sugar, almonds, artichokes, cloves and salad oils; feather beds, taffetas, linen bedcovers; French and Spanish wines, Rhenish, Muscatel and Claret – opulence and affluence well beyond the poor and unsophisticated Cumbrian peasantry. Conflict was inevitable and there were unpleasant incidents, including one murder, and even 20 years later in 1587 the Sergeant of the Mines Royal was 'riotously assaulted, beaten and unlawfully stayed, in the open street'.[10]

The local girls were less apprehensive about these fascinating foreigners who had money to spend. Within two years 14 of them had married German husbands, and between 1565 and 1584 the Crosthwaite parish registers record the births of 176 children with German fathers. Many of the men had left wives and families at home in the Tyrol, Styria and other German provinces; the Company's account books record their return for holidays and the payments of money sent out at regular intervals throughout the year. There were, as one might expect, a few rogues among so many men: Wolfgang Prugger sent money to his wife in Germany, it is true, but he also married Elizabeth Toulson of Keswick; Jorg Deufferer had a wife and family in Schwatz, he also had a wife, Alice Bradley, in Keswick; Jorg Kolmanstetter's wife received only 24 out of the 36 kreutzer to which she was entitled, so the Company deducted a sum from his wages until matters were put right; Jorg von Syber was discharged from the mines for idleness but he was energetic enough to marry two local girls. These seem to have been the exceptions among a body of men who were hard-working, highly skilled, and good to their families.

Daniel Hochstetter, the Director of the Mines, soon became a well-known figure in the district and he and his family set up a permanent home in Keswick. The Hochstetters were an Augsburg family of some standing, among 'the richest merchants in Germany' according to Sir Richard Gresham, and socially the equals of the great banking families of Fugger and Welser. Daniel had made a name for himself as a mining expert by the 1550s and he was approached by that astute English financier, Sir Thomas Gresham, on behalf of Queen Elizabeth, to seek his services in developing the mineral deposits in England. His company (Haug, Langnauer of Augsburg) agreed with alacrity as they were in need of further capital development at that time, and in 1563 Hochstetter arrived to begin his survey.

After 18 months, during which Hochstetter had created a very favourable impression, he was convinced that there was a promising future for an English mining industry and by the summer of 1566 he and his wife, Radagunda, and their numerous children had left Germany for good and were enjoying the London Season before finally moving to their new home in Keswick. The family name was changed to Hechstetter and appears in this form in the local registers. Daniel died in 1581, Radagunda in 1610 and both were buried at Crosthwaite. Their 10 children, five boys and five girls, married into English families and their descendants include Thomas Tullie, Dean of Carlisle, Thomas Rawlinson, Lord Mayor of London, Daniel Hechstetter, Master of Carlisle Grammar School, and two Fellows of the Royal Society.

With immense energy and expertise Hechstetter extended the Company's operations. The Brigham smelting works were constructed near Keswick and were the largest in England and probably in Europe, 'so numerous that they resembled a little town' and a source of employment for several hundred men. Vast quantities of fuel were required for these works and more than 50 men were employed to transport peat from Skiddaw and from Flaskow Common; timber and charcoal were brought in from the forests for many miles around, even coal from Workington and wood from Ireland. Lady Katherine Radcliffe, wife of the Lord of the Manor, owned much of the woodland in the Keswick district and proved a formidable business-woman demanding exorbitant prices for the timber from her estate, 'marvellous unreasonable and sore to deal with' as one exasperated Company official complained. She also owned the land on which Brigham Forge was built and drove a hard bargain before agreeing to rent it to the Company.

The site of these works is today spanned by the controversial flyover of the A66 and bears little trace of the great industrial enterprise established there four centuries ago. It requires a positive leap of the imagination to re-create the sights and sounds of roaring furnaces, heaving bellows, pounding hammers, ringing anvils, groaning wheels and the shouts of many men through the clouds of smoke and hissing steam. From Daniel Hechstetter's Notebook we learn that between the years 1567 and 1584 more than 500 tons of high-grade copper were smelted at Brigham, an achievement which owed much to the drive and business acumen of Hechstetter himself who had overall responsibility for 16 mines and conducted all the correspondence with his home Company in Augsburg and with his principal shareholders in London as well as negotiating with numerous local suppliers and contractors, including the difficult 'Miladi Catherina Radclieff'. He also organised a steady traffic of goods and refined copper between Keswick and the port of Newcastle, no mean task on the appalling roads of that time.[11]

In all this business activity Hechstetter found the time to see that five shillings were paid 'to the workmen for singing on Three Kings' Day' and to arrange for all the workers to be given appropriate quantities of ale and wine on his birthday. The Company's account books and Mrs Hechstetter's household accounts help us to glimpse something of daily life in this little colony of German folk who made their home in this corner of the English Lake District:

> One warming pan to warm the beds ... one hundred oranges at 2/- ... feathers and cord for bedsteads ... one dozen tin spoons ... shoes and hay for horses ... 3000 slates to roof the mens' bath-houses ... manure from Miladi's stables to put on the garden on the Island (Derwent Island where several German families had settled) ... raising sunken boats after floods and storms ... loads of ore being run across the frozen lake ... archery on St George's Day ... mumming at Christmas ... [12]

All this was the background to the hazardous business of mining. While Hechstetter had his problems of management, and these soon included the withdrawal of Haug, Langnauer & Co. from all operations in England as they had exhausted their European credit, his miners were delving ever deeper into the Newlands fells which echoed to the clang of hammer on stope and feather,[13] the crash of falling stone, the constant plash of water and the shouts and curses of sweating workers toiling in the dim light of oil lamps and candles. Above ground was heard the ceaseless creaking of the water-wheels which raised the water, the ore and the waste from below, a steady background rhythm accompanying the thump and crunch from the stamping sheds and the crushing mills, and the shuffling of packhorses as they felt the weight of their kibbles or panniers being loaded with ore to be carried to the smelting works at Brigham. And all around lay the clutter and debris of an industrial site, now entirely vanished beneath overgrown and grassy mounds. By 1829 *The Cumberland Directory* accorded only a passing reference to these long disused workings and devoted more attention to the flourishing 'quarry of fine roofing slate at the head of the valley'. Attempts in the early years of the 20th century to re-open some of the veins in the Newlands coppermines came to nothing.

Hechstetter's company of highly skilled miners and mining experts had discovered workable veins at a number of sites along the valley; at Rachel Wood, Thornthwaite, Stoneycroft, Barrow, Dale Head, Castle Nook, Brandlehow, and, most famous of them all, Goldscope or as the happy discoverers christened it 'Gottes Gab', God's Gift – and

A—CRUCIBLE. B—BOARD. C—WEDGE-SHAPED BAR. D—CAKES OF COPPER MADE BY
SEPARATING THEM WITH THE WEDGE-SHAPED BAR. E—TONGS. F—TUB.

5   *Refining copper*

so it must have seemed, with its nine-feet thick vein of copper and a 14-feet thick vein of lead richly endowed with silver and a modest quantity of gold. Joy was apparently unconfined at the promise of good times ahead and the miners were inspired to romantic fancy as they thought up names for successive veins of ore: sackpfeiffen, vogelsang, weinreben – bagpipes, birdsong, grapevine – and an assortment of saints. These were halcyon days. In 1599 the Coniston mines came into full production and the six furnaces at Brigham were working at full capacity, making exhaustive demands on the fuel resources of the entire area. When local supplies ran out timber was brought from the Vale of St John, from Isel Park near Cockermouth, from the Windermere area and from as far afield as Furness while 30 tons of coal were purchased from 'Mr Corbin (Curwen) at Worckington'. Leland's 'poor little market town' at Keswick, placed at the very heart of the operation, had never known such prosperity. Work and good wages were to be had for the asking; goods to buy had never been so plentiful; both townsfolk and dalesfolk shared in the economic boom the Newlands mines had brought. The Elizabethan industrial miracle seemed to be a dream come true.

All was not as well as it seemed however. The high hopes of the early years of discovery had led to extravagant expenditure, over-capitalisation, excessive privileges and exemptions, and an over-generous rate of wages, with inadequate consideration for the long-term production costs and fluctuations in the market. The realities of the Company's financial problems were closing in and Keswick's golden years were coming to an end. Historical tradition maintains that 'the smelting houses and works were destroyed and most of the miners slain' by troops of the Parliamentary Army in 1651 but there is no evidence to substantiate this. Certainly the whole enterprise came to a sudden and disastrous end in the mid-17th century and the Hechstetters abandoned mining and turned their talents elsewhere.[14]

Whatever the cause of the failure of the operation – and no entirely satisfactory explanation has yet been given – the collapse must have cast a deep gloom over the Hechstetter home newly-built in comfortable Jacobean style and proudly displaying the family crest. The outlook for the Newlands mines was bleak. Thomas Denton in his Perambulation of Cumberland and Westmorland in 1667-68 observed that everything was in ruins, a state of affairs confirmed a few years later by the Reverend Edmund Sandford.[15]

Occasional fortune seekers, lone prospectors or desperate men, made forays into the
abandoned workings to extract minute quantities of ore but the only organised efforts
to revive the industry were a short-lived Society of Royal Mines Copper set up mainly
by a group of Dutchmen in the reign of William III and an ill-fated enterprise early in
the 18th century by the Duke of Somerset whose workmen managed to destroy over 50
tons of ore from Goldscope Mine by incompetent smelting. This marked the end of the
road for serious mining in Newlands until the Victorian entrepreneurs brought new skills
and technology to the scene.

The mine speculators returned to Newlands in the 1840s when a vein of cobalt was
discovered in an unpromising position between Scar Crags and Sail. At great expense,
crushing, smelting and dressing machinery was set up and a tramway built from
Stoneycroft, but no more than a few ounces of cobalt were ever produced, an enterprise
soon abandoned and described as being 'the worst mining investment in the whole of
the district'. The mineral vein was, ironically, rich in arsenic.[16]

In the course of the 19th and even the early 20th centuries most of the Elizabethan
veins were opened up again and vigorously exploited until the cost of winning the ore
became prohibitive and uncompetitive. Goldscope yielded 400 tons of lead each year for
12 profitable years between 1852 and 1864; Brandlehow produced 300 tons per annum
during the same period and more at great expense later on; Yewthwaite offered up 420
tons each year late in the century and even Barrow's 240 tons over five and a half years
were considered worthwhile. Thornthwaite was finally abandoned in 1921 having yielded
over 20,000 tons in its final lease of life. The old mine at Stoneycroft Gill was quite
unproductive and became better known for the smelt mill at Stair nearby where ore was
brought for smelting not only from the Newlands mines but from as far away as Greenside
lead mine, 10 miles over the Sticks Pass, a costly and arduous haul.[17]

It was, perhaps, the revival of mining operations in the 1850s which discouraged the
Victorians from building their country mansions and tourist hotels in the Newlands
valley as they did in neighbouring Borrowdale. In this respect, as in so many others, the
contrast between the two valleys is notable. Nor can Newlands boast of famous men who
made their homes there: even the tradition that the Cromwellian General, Thomas
Fairfax, lived at Stair House has no foundation in fact. The initials, 'FF', above the door
with the date 1647, are not those of Thomas's father, Ferdinando, but belong to Frances
Fairfax, a local lady of property whose marriage is recorded in the register at Crosthwaite.

The guide-books of the Romantic Age of Lakeland tourism have little to say about
the industrial history of Newlands. The scars and the decaying ruins spoiled the essential
picture of wild, untamed grandeur and the pastoral idyll of life on the valley farms. John
Murray's *Handbook* admits that at Rowling End 'the scenery is very striking' but then
steers his readers firmly away from the area and in a welter of adjectives rivets their
attention towards Newlands Hause where the turn in the road 'opens up one of the
grandest scenes in the Lake District ... a rare scene of pastoral beauty imbued with
mountain sublimity', thus echoing Wordsworth's sentiment that this view 'is scarcely
equalled in Cumberland'. Thomas West expressed a rather more dispassionate opinion
of the upper reaches of Newlands: 'Above Keskadale', he wrote, 'untamed Nature holds
her reign in solemn silence amidst the gloom and grandeur of dreary solitude'; and
James Clarke even complained of the whimsical ways of the weather in these parts as
well as deploring the lack of civilised conveniences:

> I do not admire this journey through roads where a carriage can hardly travel amidst deserts. In
> many places the traveller cannot even meet with shelter from the storms which sometimes come
> on extremely sudden ... the rain came as suddenly and with as little ceremony as the shower

6   *Stair House*

which Xantippe is said to have discharged upon the head of her husband. I had not time to look about me – the day had been perfectly clear, and I never so much dreamed of rain until it came PERPENDICULARLY upon my head.[18]

On the road to Newlands House which Clarke founds so tedious may be seen a relic of Newlands ancient forest – Keskadale Woods, a hallowed spot for naturalists, the highest natural piece of woodland in the country and one of the few surviving relics of the primeval forest. At an altitude of between 1000 and 1400 feet the Keskadale and Birkrigg oaks are, not surprisingly, fairly small with a girth of about three feet only and a height of no more than 17 feet. Even this is remarkable when one considers all the factors militating against their mere survival – the temperature and wind force, the steepness of the fellside, the stony scree to which they cling, the difficulties of regeneration as sheep constantly graze among them, and the widespread destruction of almost every other tree around during the centuries of mining and of charcoal manufacture. The margin of survival must have been small indeed. Among these oaks grow an abundance of mosses and a variety of fungi, and a few pairs of brave chaffinches choose these damp and ancient woods to make their nests.[19]

There are many 'stations' from which to view the mountain scenery and the green pastures of the Vale of Newlands but none better than the path followed by Lucie in Beatrix Potter's *Tale of Mrs Tiggy-Winkle.* Here, high on the western slopes of Cat Bells, we can follow Lucie's steps from Skelgill Farm with a splendid view towards the south end of the valley – beautifully shown in Potter's illustration – until with Littletown Farm 'right away down below' we can, like Lucie, drop an imaginary pebble down the chimney.

Newlands Valley Fungi

3

BUTTERMERE VALLEY

From a boat 'on the bosom of Crummock Water' William Wordsworth surveyed the Vale of Buttermere and was overwhelmed: 'In no other spot is the mystery of the Mountains so irresistibly felt as an omnipresence.'[1] On the one hand is the great towering bulk of Grasmoor, then the steep pyramid of Whiteless Pike and the brooding hump of Robinson; far ahead looms the dark menace of Honister Crag balanced by a splendid view of Fleetwith Pike. On the other hand the waters of the lake lap against the craggy flanks of Mellbreak, and beyond the track to Scale Force the sharp ridge of Red Pike, High Crag and High Stile cuts the southern sky. To Thomas West this was 'the most extraordinary amphitheatre of Mountainous rocks that ever eye beheld';[2] and enclosed within it lie the twin lakes of Crummock and Buttermere, the former graced with an attractive shore-line, tiny islands and deep, clear water; the latter with its hanging woods and its famous fringe of pine trees and dark reflections of the peaks around it always a fascinating study of water-colours – the deep velvet blue of indigo, the smooth velvet green of emerald, the dark troubled clouds at sunset. Here, as elsewhere in Lakeland, the primary agent in the sculpting of this 'sublime piece of natural scenery' was ice: great glaciers, massive in weight and volume, grinding their way down from the heights, cutting out channels in their flow, pulverising resistant rocks which barred their way, gouging out the valley floors where lakes now lie, leaving here and there high corries where lonely tarns were formed and from which foaming waterfalls now plunge in sparkling cascades or in ribbons of liquid silver. The work begun by ice was carried on by water which for 10,000 years has slowly and inexorably fashioned the landscape. The rich pasture land between the two lakes is water-borne sediment deposited on a rock sill which was originally the bed of a single large lake. It was these dairy meadows which gave Buttermere its name – the lake by the butter fields, a name bestowed by Anglian settlers who penetrated into the valley probably sometime in the late seventh century.

By which route they first came to Buttermere we do not know but whether they set eyes on the valley from Honister Hause, Newlands Hause or Rannerdale Hause they must surely have been delighted with the prospect before them: well-watered land, lakes for fish, woods for game and timber, and protected by a formidable natural barrier against any attack. Indeed, it is said that these natural defences enabled Buttermere to claim to be perhaps the only place in England never to have been subjugated by the Norman kings.[3]

By the time of the Conquest much of the Lake District had been colonised by Norsemen and, as most of the place-names near Buttermere indicate, they had established their farmsteads at Lanthwaite, Rannerdale, Dalegarth, Gatesgarth and Brackenthwaite, all names of Norse origin as are Hassness, Burtness, Scarth Gap and Sail Beck, this last possibly the site of the only known Norse water-mill in England. In these mills the axle was not horizontal but vertical and at its lower end, submerged in the water, was a series of vanes which required a fast flow of water to turn them as they were

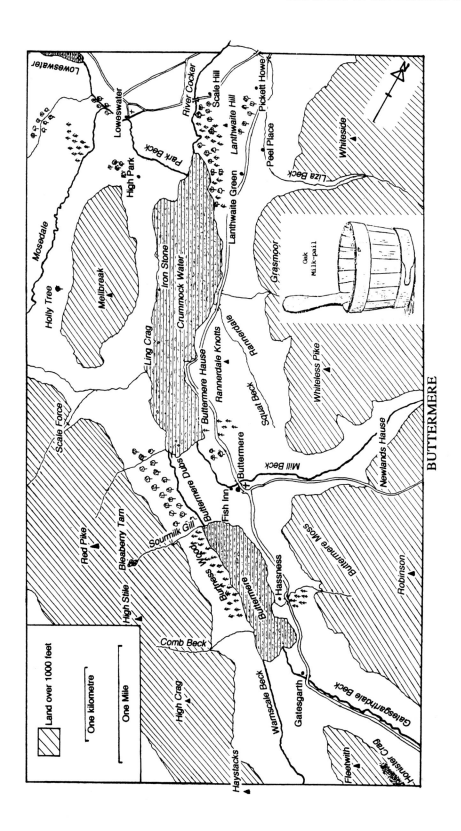

fixed directly, via the axle and through the lower millstone, to the upper millstone which they turned. This unusual corn mill continued to operate until 1735 and the spot where the rock was cut to construct the mill could, until recently, be seen near the *Bridge Hotel.* In 1936 Nicholas Size postulated that the carvings in the rock formed part of the segment of the circular rotation of the wheel and put forward the suggestion that the original mill was probably built by Norsemen.[4]

If the Norman overlord Ranulf Meschin was, in fact, decisively repulsed here, then these were the men to do it. A realistic account of 'The Battle of Rannerdale' is given by Nicholas Size in his book, *The Secret Valley*, with a convincing description of how the Normans were outwitted, out-manoeuvred and put to flight by Earl Boethar's stalwart little army. There is hidden behind Rannerdale Knotts a little valley, filled with bluebells in the spring and now quite deserted. This is where 'the battle' took place and where until some 200 years ago there was a tiny hamlet and the chapel of The Blessed Mary Magdalene, both referred to in the Percy muniments of 1508 but now no more than grassy mounds.

The medieval chapel of Rannerdale was ruinous when the first tourists arrived in Buttermere, preceded by the intrepid writers of the early guide-books who blazed a trail into the wilderness, scouring the countryside in search of the picturesque, the spectacular, the dramatic and the idyllic.

Among the earliest of these writers was Father Thomas West, who published his *Guide to the Lakes* in 1778 with a list of viewing 'stations', some of which are still well-known. One of those which is less popular today than in Victorian times is Lanthwaite Hill near the foot of Crummock Water, a small eminence commanding a truly outstanding view over the lakes and towards the Buttermere fells and easily comparable with all the 'classic' viewpoints. A few years after West's visit the Rev. William Gilpin agreed that the scenery was 'grand and beautiful' but considered the much-praised cascade of Sourmilk Gill to be 'an object of no beauty';[5] although he did find the valley to be 'fruitful and luxuriant', the inhabitants 'cheerful and healthy', and the food 'luxurious'.[6] James Clarke was here in 1789 and, like Thomas Gray twenty years before him, was a fearful explorer who considered 'the rocks and mountains about Buttermere ... truly awful and romantic' and he clearly preferred the fish from the lake which he pronounced to be 'the best fish of any (Ulswater [sic] only excepted)!'[7] The Honourable Mrs Murray (Sarah Aust), 'the first Lady of Quality to cross Honister Pass' (a feat she performed in 1794), also found the food in Buttermere quite acceptable. The alehouse where she stayed provided 'admirable ale, bread and cheese, and, perchance, a joint of mutton'. She was less relaxed about the bed-linen, however, 'but, with the help of my own sheets, blankets, pillows and counterpane, I lodged there a week very comfortably'. Thomas Gray also enthused about the mutton from the local fell sheep which he claimed 'nearly resembles venison'.[8]

Among Buttermere's trail of visitors in the 1790s was Joseph Budworth, a writer of miscellaneous articles for the *Gentleman's Magazine.* His *Fortnight's Ramble to the Lakes* is a lively, observant journalist's description of places and people, with accounts of his visits to the theatres and the more dramatic scenic spots, details of local customs and recipes, and curious tales of his encounters with local characters. So, in the Vale of Buttermere he recommends the ale which Mrs Murray found so much to her liking: 'If you are fond of strong ale, I must tell you Buttermere is reckoned famous for it.' He writes with true journalistic flair of the spectacle of Scale force which he declares has a perpendicular drop of 200 feet,[9] 'a musical abyss' where he was 'lost in admiration' at 'one of the most inimitable scenes that ever enriched the fancy of man'. But it was his meeting with Mary

Robinson, the daughter of mine host at the *Fish Inn*, which proved to be the most momentous occasion of his visit to Buttermere, having consequences far beyond Budworth's innocent observations, bringing embarrassment and some remorse to him, national notoriety to Buttermere, and personal shame and tragedy to Mary Robinson.

Budworth was so captivated by the country beauty of the innkeeper's daughter that he penned and published such a rhapsody on her charms that within a very short time the *Fish Inn* and Mary of Buttermere became a tourist attraction and all the world was beating a path to her door:

> Her hair was thick and long, of a dark brown, and though unadorned with ringlets did not seem
> to need them; her face was a fine oval, with full eyes, and lips as red as vermilion; her cheeks
> had more of the lily than the rose ... When we first saw her at her distaff she looked like an angel;
> and I doubt not that she is the reigning lily of the valley.
>   Ye travellers to the Lakes, if you visit this obscure place, such you will find the fair MARY
> OF BUTTERMERE.[10]

Among those drawn to Buttermere by Budworth's story was a lone traveller journeying in some style and announcing himself as The Honourable Alexander Augustus Hope, M.P. and younger brother to the Earl of Hopetoun. Once installed in rooms at the *Fish Inn* he was captivated by the beauty of Mary Robinson and set his sights firmly on her seduction. The young country girl was soon beguiled by the suave urbanity and calculating attentions of this persistent suitor and she was eventually induced to marry him. The ceremony took place on 2 October 1802 in the church at Lorton and so widely known was Mary's fame as a paragon of feminine beauty that the marriage was reported in the London press where it was read by acquaintances of the real Colonel Alexander Hope who knew that he was certainly not in Buttermere at that time. A warrant was issued for the arrest of the imposter who promptly abandoned his bride and fled, leaving Mary in her shame and distress. He evaded arrest for some time but in the summer of 1803 he was brought to trial at Carlisle Assizes under his real name of John Hatfield. There he was exposed as a plausible seducer, bigamist, imposter, forger and bankrupt who had for years led a life of deception, fraudulently sponging off any willing victim, and had deserted his real wife and three daughters who lived on the charity of their relatives. Evidence at his trial revealed the full extent of his villainy and aroused universal hostility to him and universal sympathy for Mary Robinson. In returning a verdict of guilty the jury left no doubt that, in their eyes, he was being sent to the scaffold less for the offence of forgery than for the iniquity of his conduct towards Mary of Buttermere.

The scars of her bitter experience were healed for Mary by a happy marriage to a local farmer, Richard Harrison, and they made their home at Todcrofts near Caldbeck. Her death in 1837 was reported in the London *Annual Register*: 'the far-famed and much talked of "Mary of Buttermere" or, as she was more commonly termed "The Buttermere Beauty".'[11]

The home of the Maid of Buttermere became a popular attraction for Victorian tourists embarking on one of the more adventurous outings organised from the hotels in Keswick. This was the 'Buttermere Round', a day's expedition by coach through some of the most dramatic scenery in England. There were several alternative routes, each arranged to approach the Buttermere valley by one of the passes which made access by road at all possible. The shortest tour was by way of the Newlands valley and Newlands Hause, a route not at all recommended by James Clarke who, at least in 1787, found the roads distinctly uncomfortable to travel on, and, although he conceded that 'the prospects among these mountains are everywhere grand', he hardly thought them 'worth the excessive labour of the journey'.[12] On the other hand, Wordsworth considered 'the

7   *Buttermere Church*

descent of the Hause ... most magnificent' and the scenery 'scarcely equalled in Cumberland', while Murray's *Handbook* assured its readers that they would see 'a rare scene of pastoral beauty combined with mountain sublimity'.[13] During the heart-stopping descent from the Hause to Buttermere they could enjoy a fine view of the recently erected church, tiny and superbly sited on its rocky knoll, 'so perfect', wrote Norman Nicholson, 'that it might have been built for a film set'.[14] Priests at Buttermere were more likely to be hedge-parsons than film stars, however, for we learn that so poor were the rewards of the office that the incumbent was allowed 'clog shoes, harden sack, whittle gate and guse-gate' by his parishioners, that is to say, a pair of clogged or ironshod shoes and a coarse shirt once a year, free board at each parishioner's house for a certain number of days, and the right to pasture his geese on the common land.

Far more guaranteed to ensure a frisson of excitement was the route through Borrowdale and over Honister Hause. To journey through the Jaws of Borrowdale might not be quite the horrifying experience conjured up by Thomas Gray but it was still an adventure into the wilderness far removed from the civilised comforts of the *Royal Oak* in Keswick, and, although a coach road had just been built over Honister, only two-horse coaches could negotiate it, and in parts it was so steep and rough that it was usual for the passengers to have to walk, or even push the coach. It is not difficult to imagine the exclamations of relief when the summit was eventually reached, nor the gasps of awe and dismay as the route of descent came into view. Before them lay a desolate wasteland of boulders and shattered rocks through which their road plunged under the great precipice of Honister Crag, a scene described by Wainwright as 'a place without beauty, a place to daunt the eye and creep the flesh'.[15] Bracing themselves for the ordeal, they would read their Murray and learn that from this mighty crag was quarried 'the finest roofing slate in the kingdom', and those who dared would scan the cliff for any sign of the quarrymen 'hanging like summer spiders from the eaves of a house', their presence betrayed by the clicking of their hammers as they chipped away at the dizzy rock-face.[16]

Rejoining their coach the tourists would follow the waters of the beck steeply downwards for two rough and anxious miles, until near to Gatesgarth Farm the relentless crag receded, and there before them lay Buttermere Lake nestling in its green and lovely valley and reflecting in its waters the image of the magnificent fells which surrounded it. On the nearest shore was a grassy sward, a shingly beach and a comforting group of pine trees. They had passed from darkness into light: this they could now enjoy with happy relief: the experience of Honister could be reviewed more calmly later on.[17]

And so to lunch at the *Fish Inn* followed perhaps by a boat trip across Crummock Water to Ling Crag and a brisk walk along the causewayed path to Scale Force. Their guide, like tourist guides of all ages, would entertain them with embroidered anecdotes about Mary of Buttermere, the golden eagles which nested above Burtness Comb, the Mellbreak Foxhounds or the great water-spout which, on 9 September 1760, fell over the Grasmoor Fells and created such a flood that the little Liza Beck was transformed into a mighty river and swept away bridges, houses, trees and entire woods, stripping away the very soil down to the naked rock and covering many acres round Brackenthwaite with a vast bed of stones and gravel several feet deep.

Such was the Buttermere Round, perhaps the most memorable of all the Lakeland tourist excursions of the Victorian Age. We should be grateful that after a century of steadily increasing pressure from 'development' of all kinds we, too, can enjoy the unrivalled beauty of the Vale of Buttermere unspoilt by unseemly modern disfigurement. We owe a great debt to a number of individuals and organisations who in the 1930s, before the National Park was established, made great efforts to save Buttermere from the developers. Notable among these benefactors were the historian, G.M. Trevelyan, the National Trust and Balliol College, Oxford. It was in the peace and quiet of Buttermere that the Cambridge economist Professor Arthur Pigou, in his study at Lower Gatesgarth, first formulated the principles and structure of the Welfare State, perhaps Britain's most important political achievement of the 20th century.[18]

J.M.W. Turner's famous painting of Buttermere perceptively depicts that special quality which gives this valley a unique distinction among all the Lakeland valleys, and that is the depth and subtle variations of colour and light created by the combination of water, rock, high peaks, woodland and a constantly changing sky over a vast natural amphitheatre. Artists have found it irresistible, for, as W.G. Collingwood wrote, the Buttermere valley was 'made in heaven for summer evenings and summer mornings: green floor and purple heights, with the sound of waters under the sunset or lit with the low north-eastern sun into pure colour above, and the greyness of the dew upon the grass'.[19]

Great Spotted Woodpecker

4

THE VALE OF LORTON

The Reverend William Gilpin little knew what a priceless gift he was bestowing on all those who have followed him in describing the natural beauty of the Vale of Lorton. In essence little has changed there since he penned his much quoted lines in 1772 and none of his successors has had the temerity – or, indeed, found it necessary – to try to improve on the succinct simplicity of his description or on the exquisite aptness of his choice of words:

This vale, unlike all the past, presents us with a landscape entirely new. No lakes, no rocks are here to blend the ideas of dignity and grandeur with that of beauty. All is simplicity and repose – Nature in this scene, lays totally aside her majestic form and wears only a lovely smile.

This Vale, which enjoys a rich soil, is, in general, a rural, cultivated scene; though in many parts the ground is beautifully broken and abrupt. A bright stream pours along a rocky channel and sparkles down numberless cascades. Its banks are adorned with woods; and varied with different objects; a bridge, a mill, a hamlet; a glade overhung with wood; or some little sweet recess; or a natural vista through which the eye ranges between irregular trees along the windings of the stream.

Except the mountains, nothing in all this scenery is great, but every part is filled with those engaging passages of nature which tend to sooth the mind and instil tranquillity.[1]

Lorton Vale is still very much as Gilpin described it; even the growth of Cockermouth at the northern end has never overwhelmed its character as a modest market town; the mountains which close in to the south may now echo to the sound of a thousand fell-walkers but they are still the grazing grounds of a thousand sheep; the summit of Lanthwaite Hill may no longer be the chosen venue for decorous Victorian picnics but it still offers – for very little effort – one of the most spectacular panoramas of mountain scenery in the whole of the Lake District.

It was from these mountains which dominate the head of Lorton Vale that, twice in modern times, the unpredictable and violent forces of Nature have shattered the quiet and customary tempo of pastoral life in the fields and farmsteads of Brackenthwaite.

On 9 September 1760, 10 years before Gilpin visited the scene, a tumultuous thunderstorm broke over the heights of Grasmoor precipitating an enormous volume of water which soon swelled the Liza Beck, between Grasmoor and Whiteside, into a raging flood of immense and destructive power. This swept down into the valley taking with it a battering ram of loosened rocks and boulders which uprooted trees, demolished barns and scoured away soil and gravel down to the naked rock. Ten acres of farmland were laid waste and covered with a deep bed of stone and debris but, remarkably, the hamlet of Brackenthwaite itself escaped the fury of the waters which were diverted by the outcrop of rock on which the houses and farms were built and surged onwards and downwards to pour in a muddy flood into the River Cocker. Gilpin believed the devastation to be so complete that, as he put it, 'no human art can ever again restore the soil'. He under-estimated the healing power of nature, for today hardly a trace of this disaster remains.[2]

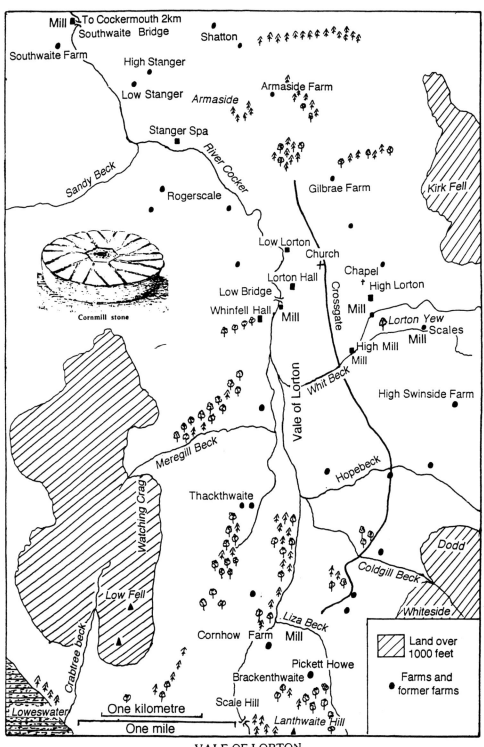

Mill ⬛ To Cockermouth 2km
Southwaite Bridge
Southwaite Farm
Shatton

High Stanger
Low Stanger   *Armaside*
Armaside Farm

Stanger Spa

Sandy Beck   *River Cocker*

Rogerscale

Gilbrae Farm

Kirk Fell

Cornmill stone

Low Lorton
Church
Chapel
Lorton Hall   High Lorton
Low Bridge
Whinfell Hall   Mill   *Crossgate*   Mill
Lorton Yew
Scales
High Mill   Mill
Mill
Whit Beck

Vale of Lorton

High Swinside Farm

Meregill Beck

Hopebeck

Thackthwaite

Watching Crag

Dodd

Coldgill Beck

Low Fell ▲

Whiteside

Liza Beck
Cornhow Farm   Mill

Pickett Howe

Brackenthwaite
Scale Hill

Crabtree beck

One kilometre
One mile

Loweswater

Lanthwaite Hill ▲

Land over
1000 feet

Farms and
former farms

VALE OF LORTON

Nature again disturbed the peace in this part of Lorton Vale on a fine summer day in August 1908. Hay-making was in full swing in the fields of Cornhow Farm when men and horses were startled by a loud rumbling and a mighty roar from Whiteside, the steep fell nearby. A great column of 'smoke' poured out and a cascade of huge boulders came hurtling down the fellside. After a while the air cleared and all fell silent: the subterranean forces which once helped to form these hills had stirred briefly in their sleep and have not spoken since. It is, perhaps, wise to tread softly on the path over Whiteside to Hopegill Head.[3]

Men seeking new lands to settle and cultivate have never been deterred by such unpredictable and infrequent manifestations of Nature's powers of destruction and it seems improbable that the possibility of such occurrences ever entered the minds of those Norsemen (and perhaps a few Angles) who created the first small farmsteads in the forest which covered all the land between Buttermere and Bassenthwaite, and from Cockermouth to Honister Hause, and was known to a later age as the Forest of Derwentfells.

The extent of Norse settlement in the Vale of Lorton is indicated by the predominance of Norse place-names throughout the valley: Lanthwaite, Brackenthwaite, Littlethwaite and Thackthwaite all originated in Norse clearings in the forest; Whit Beck, Hope Beck, Blaze Beck and Liza Beck are all Norse stream names; and Armaside was the property of the Norseman, Hermundr. The name of the valley itself is derived from a Norse river-name 'Lora'. The irregular field patterns and scattered farmsteads found throughout the Vale of Lorton – with the exception of the later straight strip enclosures seen near High and Low Lorton – also point to a typical Norse colonisation. It seems reasonable to deduce that permanent settlement began with the arrival of the Norsemen from Ireland and Western Scotland in the 10th century.[4]

Legend would have us believe, however, that a community had established itself at Lorton long before this. Following the devastating Viking raids on Northumbria in 793 and into the ninth century the monks of Lindisfarne made it their dedicated task to ensure that the body of St Cuthbert should not fall into heathen hands. Harassed by Viking raiders, they carried their sacred burden further and further westwards resting at intervals at temporary sanctuaries. One such place of safety was Lorton where, we are told, the Saint's body was placed in a chapel in 'a little tower'. This suggests a fortified stone structure of the kind which would be found only in a permanent settlement such as a monastic community or a tribal chieftain's stronghold. If this tradition is soundly based on historical fact it would place the date of this Lorton sanctuary at least a century before the Norse colonisation.

Any trace of the 'little tower' has disappeared but a later tradition associated with Lorton would seem to strengthen the belief in its existence. In the centuries just before and just after the Norman Conquest the Kings of Scotland had a valid claim to Cumbria which was then described as the land 'inter Angliam et Scotiam', and in 1089, King Malcolm III and Queen Margaret stayed at Lorton Tower in the course of a royal visit to this part of their Kingdom. This, too, bears the stamp of historical credibility and if it could be verified would prove conclusively that Lorton was also a place of some importance many years before the existing 15th-century pele-tower was constructed.

The medieval rooms at Lorton Hall with their usual labyrinthine complexity, although offering something less than domestic comfort even in the 16th century, were admirably suited to the construction of priests' hiding holes and escape tunnels, a facility which so many isolated country houses found useful during the Elizabethan conflict between the Government and the catholic families of Northern England. One visitor on the run was

8   *Lorton Hall*

Charles Stuart who in the years following his disastrous defeat at the Battle of Worcester
in 1651 fled to France but returned to England from time to time to secret rendez-vous
in his long struggle to restore the monarchy. Lorton Hall is believed to have been one
of the venues for these conspiratorial gatherings. Shortly after Charles attained his goal
and was crowned King Charles II Lorton Hall acquired the striking classical Caroline
frontage which lends it a certain distinction today.

During these Tudor and Stuart years the owners of Lorton Hall were the Winder
family, one of the three families who had substantial possessions in Lorton Vale in the
reign of Henry VIII. In common with so many other families of minor gentry in the
England of the late 17th and 18th centuries the Winders sought financial fortune in the
rapidly developing commercial world of that time, and, also like so many others, within
a few generations they lost interest in the remote country estates from which they came.
Winders were deeply involved in the East India Trade, in the Caribbean, in Spain and
in the lucrative profession of Commercial Law in London. By the late 18th century their
Lorton connections were entirely lost.[5]

Lorton Church lies just across the meadow from the Hall. It stands on the site of a
much older foundation which is first referred to towards the end of the 12th century and
like its modern successor was dedicated to St Cuthbert. This was the church where Mary
Robinson, the Beauty of Buttermere, was lured into marriage by the infamous and
bigamous imposter, John Hatfield. This was in 1802 and the old church was then in a
sad state of decay. Soon afterwards it was replaced by the present Gothic Revival
structure which has earned few compliments. It certainly lacks any architectural merit
and its stained glass is brusquely dismissed as 'indefensible' by Nikolaus Pevsner. The
kindest words written about it are those of Edmund Bogg who just one hundred years
ago described it as having 'a modest tower with tall pinnacles and battlements and its
grey pebbled walls stand out prominent from the green environments and background
of dark fells': a diplomatic evasion of the true fact that this is the least interesting of all
the Dales churches.[6]

It is impossible to determine whether so remote a valley was visited by the early
Christian missionaries such as St Kentigern and St Ninian who set up preaching crosses
in many known places throughout Cumbria. The only clue might lie in the name of an
ancient road which runs along part of the valley and has always had the name of
Crossgate – the road by the cross – and it is possible that the 12th-century church of

St Cuthbert may have been built on the site of a preaching cross since this road passes close by.

Certainly later Christian evangelists found a response in Lorton Vale. In 1652 George Fox found an eager flock ready to hear the message of Quakerism when he came here to preach by the famous Lorton Yew which threatened to break under the weight of all those who found a vantage point in its branches; just one hundred years later John Wesley's followers built a new Methodist Chapel and the great man came to preach in it – as he did on two subsequent occasions in the course of his travels in Cumbria.

9   *The Lorton Yew*

The Lorton Yew has featured in almost every guidebook for more than 200 years and is believed to be some 2,000 years old. In 1898 Edmund Bogg declared it to be 'only a wreck of its former glory' and claimed that 'in its pride and strength the trunk measured 24 feet in circumference'. Bogg may well have indulged in some exaggeration on both counts for today the tree looks healthy enough, by no means 'a wreck', and its girth is probably little more than half of Bogg's estimate, although the spread of its branches must be all of 50 feet (15 metres). This venerable, gnarled and twisted tree was described by Dorothy Wordsworth as the 'patriarch of yew trees' and inspired her brother to compose a typically ecstatic poem in its honour:

> There is a yew tree, pride of Lorton Vale
> Which to this day stands single in the midst
> Of its own darkness as it stood of yore ...
> Of vast circumference and gloom profound
> This solitary tree! a living thing
> Produced too slowly ever to decay;
> Of form and aspect too magnificent
> To be destroyed ...

But destroyed it almost was! In 1855 it was actually sold for £15 to a Whitehaven cabinet maker who was on the point of cutting it down when, as Bogg tells us, it was saved by a gentleman from Cockermouth who persuaded the axeman to stay his hand. We should be profoundly grateful to this anonymous 19th-century environmentalist that we are able to stand in the presence of 'a living thing' which has flourished here for 20 centuries. It was a young sapling at the end of the first century when the Roman legions were building their fort at Papcastle a few miles to the north, and was already more than 1,000 years old when the Normans built their own fortress at Cockermouth.[7]

It is unlikely that before the 12th century Cockermouth was more than a small hamlet at the junction of the Rivers Derwent and Cocker with a history more closely linked to the old Roman settlement at Papcastle than to the Vale of Lorton. In 1150 the Normans abandoned the remains of the Roman fort and established their power base at Cockermouth Castle. Early in the 13th century, in 1221, William de Fortibus secured a market charter for his new town, and before the century ended Cockermouth had also been granted a number of coveted privileges which finally set the seal on its medieval urban status and commercial prosperity. These included not only the right to send two

10   *Cockermouth Castle*

members to Parliament (a privilege the town appears to have taken very casually as it returned no M.P. at all between 1300 and 1640) but also the right to regulate prices of all commodities within the town. By the end of the 16th century Cockermouth had eliminated rival markets at Ireby and Crosthwaite, and when Camden visited it in the reign of Elizabeth I he described it as 'a mercate town of good wealth' with a weekly fair in addition to its Monday Market. A century later on the occasion of the Herald's Visitation it claimed to be 'ye best Market Towne in this part of the country ... adorned with a stately Castle, a Fair Church, two good stone bridges, a fair house and many other fine buildings'. The Herald also noted that Cockermouth could boast five families worthy to bear arms as against only two in Carlisle and one each in Kendal and Penrith.

Industrial developments in the 18th and 19th centuries added to Cockermouth's prosperity. The ample waters of the Cocker and Derwent provided the power for many mills: ancient corn and fulling mills were now joined by others manufacturing woollen textiles, hats, gloves and high leather boots, paper and bobbins; there were also barkmills, sawmills and mills for dressing flax. The population doubled between 1785 and 1851 thus ensuring plentiful labour and a local market for many of the goods they produced. The introduction of a network of stage-coach services offered yet further opportunities to a town situated on the main route to Whitehaven, at that time the most important port after Bristol and Liverpool on the West coast of England. Many hostelries in Cockermouth took advantage of this new development in transport, among them several coaching inns of high repute including *The Globe, The Sun, The George and Dragon,* and *The Appletree.*[8]

Pre-eminent among the local industries which serviced these establishments was Jennings' Brewery which continued to produce its renowned ales long after the watermills had had their day. The Jennings family came from High Swinside Farm in the Vale of Lorton and their first brewery was at High Lorton where the old flax mill was converted into a malt-house. It now serves as the Village Hall.

The waters of the Cocker and of the many becks feeding into it had provided power for Lorton Vale's numerous mills for many centuries. All trace and record of some of them have disappeared but it is known that there were corn mills at Lorton Bridge and Southwaite Bridge, two fulling mills at Brackenthwaite as early as 1437, a thresh mill at

Scales, a corn mill and a fulling mill at High Mill (apparently in ruins in 1478), a further fulling mill at Tenters, and the linen mill at High Lorton. The existence of at least four fulling mills and a field called 'Tenters' suggests that, for a time at least, Lorton had a flourishing textile industry which no doubt had a ready market in nearby Cockermouth, while the rapid growth of the local population provided a secure outlet for all the food the farmers could produce.

All mills were hot, dusty and noisy places to work in and the working week often exceeded 75 hours: usually 13 hours a day with an early finish at 4 o'clock on Saturdays. For a large part of the year these workers were rarely out in the daylight and only on Sundays were they free to enjoy the fresh air.[9]

A popular Sunday expedition for the mill-workers of Cockermouth and Lorton was along the banks of the Cocker and across the fields to drink the waters at Stanger Spa to cleanse their stomachs of the unhealthy dust they had endured all week. For the spring at Stanger was no ordinary spring: its waters had the same medicinal properties as the famous aristocratic spa at Cheltenham. With a high impregnation of marine salts it was strongly aperient and was highly recommended for disorders of the skin and the digestive tracts. The walk in the fresh air and a powerful draught of Stanger water would certainly have had more beneficial effects than any treatment contemporary medicine might have had to offer.

The reputation of the spa at Stanger spread far beyond the Vale of Lorton. Only sparse documentary evidence survives but it is known that bottles of the water were dispatched regularly to many parts of the world and that a local entrepreneur established a service which sold the water for six pence a bottle. By 1816 its reputation was such that it achieved a reference in D. and S. Lysons' 'Magna Britannia' where a chemical analysis of the water is given. The well is described as a 'Holy Well' but it is not possible to say whether this indicates that it was used in medieval times, or even earlier, or whether the name is an invention of a later romantic imagination. Although the site today is in some state of dereliction there still remain the walls of the handsome stone building which sheltered visitors, with seats for them to rest on, the niches for the drinking vessels and the neatly dressed stone surrounds of the well itself. Very few of the many visitors who come to admire the pastoral scene of Lorton Vale are aware of this unusual part of the valley's historical heritage and most of those who walk the public footpath which leads to it pass it by as just another derelict barn.[10]

Almost every Lakeland valley has at least one character in its history who has found a place in what used to be called *The Book of Worthies*. Duddon has Wonderful Walker, Wasdale has Will Ritson, Eskdale has Tommy Dobson; Jonas Barber is famous in the Vale of Winster, Bernard Gilpin in Kentdale, Sarah Yewdale in Borrowdale. The sad figure of Mary Robinson haunts the story of Buttermere; the ghost of Lanty Slee is never far from Langdale; the notorious Mounseys, King and Queen of Patterdale, have long been laid to rest. The Vale of Lorton produced a true Man of the Mountains, a pioneer rock-climber and explorer of the high fells, eager to share his discoveries and his joy in the airy pathways to the crags with all who were willing to follow him.

This was J.W. Robinson of Whinfell Hall. He was born into a Quaker family in 1853 and grew up in an age when many now familiar routes on the more precipitous crags were first being attempted, and when walking the fells for pleasure, rather than merely to gather in flocks of sheep, was first regarded as an appropriate pastime for Victorian gentlemen and, indeed, for a surprising number of intrepid Victorian ladies. Robinson is described as having 'a well-built figure, sandy side-whiskers, an extremely bald and shining head and merry blue eyes' and his diary lists between thirty and forty ladies whom he escorted to the top of Pillar as well as innumerable men. It was he who pioneered the Pillar High Level Route, probably the finest walkers' highway along the craggy precipices of the Lake District; few who go there can fail to be moved by the tribute to Robinson which forms part of the memorial cairn built along the now well-worn path. Robinson also discovered the mysterious stone hut high on the forbidding north face of Great Gable variously known as The Smugglers' Hut or Moses' Hut. He also achieved fame for his pioneering fell-walk in 1893 when he completed within 24 hours a 70-mile expedition covering the summits of Great Gable, Scafell, Scafell Pike, Great End, Bowfell, Helvellyn, Blencathra and Skiddaw. This presented a challenge to succeeding generations, taken up many times and with a record of success which would give no-one greater pleasure than John Wilson Robinson himself. 'There has never been a more complete Lake District man. It was his home, his place of work and his place of pleasure.'[11]

Robinson's passion for the lonely crags and fell tops would have been looked upon as mildly eccentric by most of his fellow dalesfolk, only a few of whom had either the leisure or the inclination to join him; but he was a well-known figure in the Vale, always wearing the same Norfolk jacket of yellowish-brown Harris tweed, twill knickerbockers, brown stockings and nailed boots, and a hat of the deer-stalker variety with ear-protectors and a peaked 'neb' fore and aft.[12]

He would certainly have been among those to receive an invitation to those popular valley occasions known as 'bidden weddings' and 'bridewains'. The former were held at the home of the bride's parents and guests were invited individually, although generally everyone in the valley was included. These were convivial celebrations but somewhat less rumbustious than those at a 'bridewain' where the festivities were held at the new home of the bridal couple, and country folk for miles around were invited by the posting of printed handbills. Keswick Museum has an example of such a notice advertising the marriage in 1807 of Joseph Rawlings and Mary Dixon of High Lorton. All 'Friends, Acquaintances and others' were invited and they were assured that every effort would be made 'to accommodate the company and render the day agreeable'.

Just what this involved is genially described for us by John Stagg, the 'Cumberland Minstrel', in his dialect poem 'The Bridewain'. This was a day of 'truly rural festivity ... and convivial merriment' and once the church ceremonies were over it was, indeed, 'On with the dance! let joy be unconfined' as high spirits and bucolic exuberance echoed across the fields, filling house, barn and garth with the clamour of lusty country folk relaxing in uninhibited glee.

Festivities began with a headlong and disorderly race, on horseback or on foot, from the church to the bridal house where the winner received a riband of victory from the bride. The fiddlers who had led the procession to church were now busy tuning their fiddles in the barn while in the kitchens willing hands were at work preparing vast quantities of homely food and fresh-brewed ale for hungry and thirsty guests, some of whom had travelled far.

Those who were able to resist the temptations of free and unlimited liquor joined in the other entertainments which the invitation had promised. Some competed in energetic activities such as running races, the winners receiving a pair of mittens, or wrestled for a belt, while others organised horse races.

The children and the less athletic played 'hitch, step and loup' (hop, step and jump) or penny-stones, the game known as pitch and toss with stones instead of pennies. Some of the older folk were content to enjoy so much company, happily exchanging valley gossip and laughing together at the antics of those who took part in the gurning contests.

This old Cumberland pastime, often known as 'gurning through a braffin' or making a grimace through a horse-collar, was once popular at all country gatherings, the prize being awarded to the face which was judged to have been contorted into the most convoluted grin: 'a daft divertion' Stagg thought!

A much more serious custom at a bridewain was the contribution which all guests were expected to make to the bride's dowry. John Stagg describes how the bride, all flustered, sat on a small wooden stool with a pewter dish on her lap and, as the wedding guests gathered round, 'crowns and half crowns thick as hail' were poured into it. Generous sums of up to £100 could be collected on these occasions, a considerable sum at a time when a farm labourer could be hired for no more than £12 per annum.

And so,

> Wi' fiddling, dancing, cracks and yele
> The day slipt swiftly ow'r

and the time arrived when the bridal pair were put to bed.

At this point the older and more staid guests set off homewards but for the young and for those unable and unwilling to leave so much good ale unappreciated, the night was just beginning. The dancers in the barn stomped on with even more enthusiasm as the fiddlers and their music became more fuddled as the hours passed by. Much lively horse-play went on in the haystacks and lads and lasses could be found in all 'the nuiks and crannies'. As for the drinkers, they, too, revelled all the night until, as dawn approached, all those who were still awake and capable made their way home. One of these was John Stagg himself who tells us that

> I homewards fettl'd off myself
> Just as the sun was peeping.[13]

It was perhaps in the hushed stillness of the day following a bridewain that Edmund Bogg came to Lorton and, with permissible licence, declared that, 'No place can exceed in soft pastoral charm and sweetness the lovely Vale of Lorton...as smoothly and velvety as a well-kept garden. All is beauty and repose'.[14]

Lords and Ladies

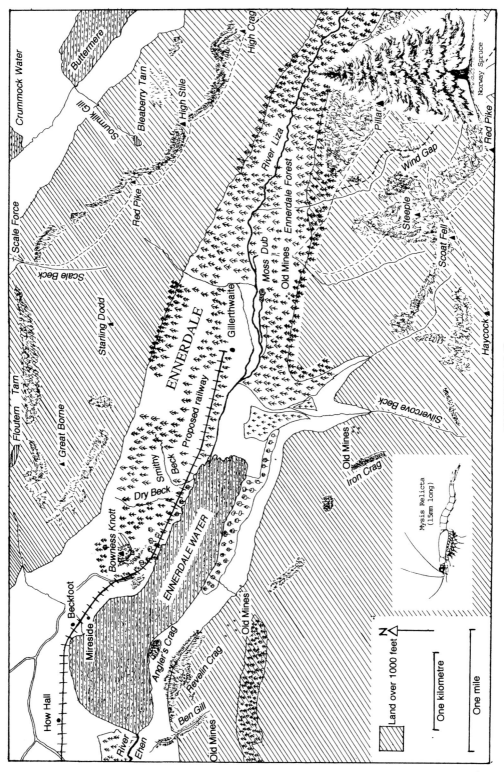

Mysis Relicta
(15mm long)

Land over 1000 feet

One kilometre

One mile

ENNERDALE

How Hall

River Ehen

Beckfoot

Mireside

Bowness Knott

Dry Beck

Smithy Beck

ENNERDALE

Starling Dodd

Great Borne

Floutern Tarn

Scale Force

Scale Beck

Red Pike

Red Tarn

Bleaberry Tarn

High Stile

High Crag

Buttermere

Crummock Water

Soumilk Gill

Gillerthwaite

Proposed railway

River Liza

Moss Dub

Ennerdale Forest

Old Mines

ENNERDALE WATER

Angler's Crag

Revelin Crag

Ben Gill

Old Mines

Old Mines

Iron Crag

Silvercove Beck

Old Mines

Pillar

Wind Gap

Steeple

Scoat Fell

Haycock

Red Pike

Norway Spruce

5

ENNERDALE

In 1864 Eliza Lynn Linton, a shrewd and observant traveller, visited this wild and forbidding valley and wrote:

> Ennerdale is the least known and, at the present time, the least likely to be visited of all the lakes
> ...Until Ennerdale has the benefit of carriage ways along its banks, it will remain comparatively
> a terra incognita to the tourist world, save those who can brave a rough pass and those who care
> only to gape away an hour at the foot ... quite contented with the belief that they have seen
> Ennerdale.[1]

Extensive conifer plantations may have transformed the appearance of Ennerdale so that it is no longer Collingwood's true Icelandic country and would, indeed, be totally unrecognisable to Mrs. Linton, but there is still no 'carriage way' along the valley and it is still the least frequented of all the principal Lakeland dales. Those who come here are still hardy walkers or those who are content to spend an hour near the foot of the lake, uplifted and perhaps inspired by the awesome grandeur of the mountain scene before them.

It could so easily have been quite a different picture. Soon after Mrs. Linton's visit plans were prepared for the construction of a railway along Ennerdale, with the primary object of exploiting the iron deposits which were being worked on remote fellsides but also with an eye to the development of the valley as a tourist attraction. The Lake District Defence Society mounted a fierce opposition to such an enterprise but those who had, by this time, convinced themselves that railways were England's gift to all the backward parts of the world, found a powerful ally in the *Pall Mall Gazette* which went so far as to publish a 'Poetical Lamentation on the Insufficiency of Steam Locomotion in the Lake District':

> Wake, England, wake! 'tis now the hour
> To sweep away this black disgrace –
> The want of locomotive power
> In so enjoyable a place.
> Nature has done her part, and why
> Is mightier man in his to fail?
> I want to hear the porter's cry,
> 'Change here for Ennerdale!'

The proposal came before Parliament in the early 1880s and it was only narrowly defeated after a stirring speech by James Bryce, the eminent statesman, jurist, historian and climber. There would be no railhead at Gillerthwaite.[2] The acquisition of much of the land on both sides of Ennerdale's River Liza by the Forestry Commission in the 1930s almost certainly prevented the subsequent 'development' of the valley and the construction of roads along it. Not that James Bryce and the Foresters had quite the same purpose in mind: Bryce wished to preserve the open grandeur of a wild and lonely mountain fastness; the Commission wished to establish a vast enclosed forest of conifers blanketing the fellsides, excluding the public and eliminating almost all farming activity. As a sanctuary from the 'swarms of pleasure-hunters' so much feared by Wordsworth, Ennerdale has, indeed, been preserved but only by the obliteration of much of the valley's natural, pristine beauty.

The coniferous disfigurement of Ennerdale was universally condemned. The regimented battalions of spruce and larch which marched uninterrupted for more than five miles along the valley and the hard, bureaucratic edges of the fellside plantations up to 1,200 feet (giving Pillar and Steeple the semblance of a tailored skirt) aroused such hostility to afforestation of this kind in the Lake District that the Forestry Commission was compelled to enter a series of agreements with the National Trust and the Council for the Preservation of Rural England which strictly controlled future plantations.

It would be wrong, however, to believe, as many still do, that forests and woodlands are alien to the valleys and fells of Lakeland. The landscape, as we see it, with the fellsides almost bare of trees and the valleys adorned mainly with small copses, would

11   *Ennerdale Water: Winter*

have seemed strange to those who lived here no more than 500 years ago. For at least 2,000 years man has cleared the primeval forest to extend the area of cultivated land, to create grazing for cattle and sheep, to provide fuel for home and industry or timber for buildings and boats; but it was not until the 17th century that most of the great forests had gone. Ennerdale itself was deep in the vast forest which covered much of the land from Eskdale northwards as far as Cockermouth, and, like the Forest of Inglewood beyond that again, was a seemingly limitless source of oak, ash, birch and hazel for the gargantuan appetite of the numerous industries which fed upon it. The writing appeared on the wall for Ennerdale Chase in 1578 when a Notice of Sale offered '22674 oke trees' at sixpence a tree, and mining for iron ore began on Revelin Crag and Bowness Knott with a bloomery or smelting furnace in the woods between Dry Beck and Smithy Beck. Ten years before this all the tenants on the land owned by the Percy family in the valley had been confirmed in their right 'to great timber for fire-houses and barns', a sure sign that agriculture was prospering and more land was needed for farming.

Ennerdale Chase was renowned as a deer park until the 17th century and in 1675 it was said that in the tiny remnant of the original forest known today as The Side there were 'hartts and staggs as great as in any part of England'. This small plot of deciduous woodland still remains to remind us of the rather different type of forest which covered the valley a few hundred years ago — a pleasant mix of those 'native deciduous trees' which Wordsworth believed should 'be left in complete possession of the lower ground', it being 'impossible, under any circumstances, for the artificial planter to rival the beauty of Nature'. In defence of the Forestry Commission's emphasis on planting conifers it must be said that, commercial considerations apart, on soil so impoverished by so many years of leaching and erosion after the earlier destruction of the woodlands, only conifers would flourish and, in time, restore sufficient stability and fertility to enable more demanding species to become established once more. This point was well put by Dr. Winifred Pennington:

> The Forestry Commission do not plant these trees from sheer contrariness as some of their opponents would almost suggest, but from economic and ecological necessity.

It was the aesthetics of the planting and the insensitivity of the public relations which generated most of the criticism.[3]

Among the casualties of the afforestation of Ennerdale were places which had been farmed for many centuries. This valley, in common with almost every other Lakeland dale, has many names of Norse origin, although there are also a number of place-names here of clearly Celtic origin suggesting an earlier British presence. Woundell, Dub and Ehen are Celtic but Ennerdale itself is Norse as is the River Liza and farm names such as Routen, Mireside, Beckfoot and Gillerthwaite, while most of the surrounding fells bear Norse names — Bowness, Latterbarrow, Herdus, Scoat Fell, Haystacks — as does lonely Floutern Tarn.

The earliest physical remains of human settlement in Ennerdale are to be found by Smithy Beck where the foundations of more than a dozen stone-based structures have been investigated and pronounced to be the site of either an early medieval farmstead or, possibly, a group of Norse shielings. Gillerthwaite would appear to have been the most substantial farm in the valley by the 13th century for in 1334 it is recorded as an important vaccary or large, enclosed cattle farm. A sizeable flock of sheep was also maintained there for we learn that the farmer was constantly in trouble for allowing his stock to stray inside the boundaries of the Forest and was frequently fined for this breach of the strictly enforced Laws of the Forest.[4]

When the Forest was 'disparked' (probably in the late 16th century) and the enclosed pastures and crops of oats and barley were ravaged by the freely roaming deer, the harassed farmers took a terrible revenge. The deer were run into a trap of scythes and pitchforks where they were painfully impaled and almost the entire herd was destroyed. The few which escaped found refuge in the woods along The Side, one of the last sanctuaries of the red deer in Cumbria.[5] These savage events were long past when Thomas West came this way in the 1770s and was totally enraptured by the scene at Gillerthwaite. In his *Guide* he wrote ecstatically of this 'verdant island whose romantic situation must be seen. The genius of Ovid would have transformed the most favoured of his heroes into a river and poured his waters into the channel of the Liza, there to wander by the verdant bounds of Gillerthwaite, the sweet reward of patriotism and virtue.'[6]

Such sentiments thus expressed would have received a brusque response from the local dalesfolk toiling long hours each day to make a decent living. The very remoteness of their farmsteads made self-sufficiency a necessity for survival: everyone would be required to lend a hand – in the barns and byres, in the milking parlour and in the dairy, at lambing time and shearing time, at haysel and harvest, at spinning and weaving, and all the other multitudes of household and farming chores – even, it would seem, including the tending of the bees, for Mrs. Linton tells us that 'Every summer and autumn hundreds of hives are brought up to Ennerdale and set on Revlin, for the bees to get strength and sustenance before winter-time'.[7]

There was little time to spare for these busy folk to dream of the rewards of patriotism and virtue, a questionable activity at best and verging on delusion when the forces of Nature could at any time unleash an orgy of destruction on their fragile lives:

> a water spout
> Will bring down half a mountain
> a sharp May storm
> Will come with loads of January snow,
> And in one night send twenty score of sheep
> To feed the ravens.[8]

The routine of daily toil and the hazards of living so close to the unpredictable whims of Nature made the dalesman's views of the grandeur of the scene around him somewhat less rhapsodic than those of the tourists and the guide-books they carried with them. They cared little that Pillar was 'the most handsome crag in Lakeland';[9] to them it was first and foremost a dangerous hazard for wandering sheep requiring a constantly maintained drystone wall to make it safe.

Another hazard familiar to the Ennerdale farmer throughout the centuries was the menace of wild animals and savage dogs. The greatest ravager of all, the wolf, had become extinct in England by the 16th century but the medieval shepherd often had to guard his flock day and night. Ennerdale, at the heart of the great forest of Copeland, would certainly have had its share of wolves but these have long been forgotten, unlike the 19th-century 'Wild Dog of Ennerdale' which is still part of the folk-history of the valley and the surrounding fell country. 'T girt dog' terrorised the neighbourhood during the summer of 1810 covering many square miles in its marauding career, often killing seven or eight sheep in a single night and leaving many others badly mauled. Its toll of victims soon reached such proportions that a concerted effort was organised to bring the slaughter to an end but the cunning beast, a cross, it is said, between a mastiff and a greyhound, proved remarkably elusive and possessed of mighty stamina. Rare sightings came to nothing as it shrugged off the hunt and vanished into the landscape, to resume its savagery after nightfall many miles away. For five months it ran berserk among the terrified sheep until it was at last brought down and killed by a great gathering of local men with guns and dogs.[10]

Equally notorious in their day, but for quite different reasons, were the Ennerdale Patricksons, the only family in the valley who might have aspired to the title of 'gentry'. Indeed, one writer, recalling perhaps the Mounseys of Patterdale, once described them as 'Kings of Ennerdale' thus denoting their pre-eminence in the district. They first appear in the reign of Henry VIII and in the course of the next 200 years they acquired numerous properties and interests, married astutely and multiplied prolifically. They established themselves in four substantial estates and secured control of several commercial enterprises, the most unusual of which was the pearl-fishing rights in the Rivers Irt and Ehen. Thomas Patrickson obtained a Charter incorporating the Company of Pearl Fishers in 1693 and succeeded in developing a lucrative market among London jewellers, selling for hundreds of pounds pearls which he employed local people to gather for a few pence, a profitable enterprise well-known in the days of Elizabeth I when John Hawkins held the patent. It is difficult now to assess the true quality of these Cumbrian pearls: they are known locally as the horse-mussel and their pastel colour has been compared unfavourably with the more famous pearls from the Orient. In Roman times Pliny considered them to be very inferior baubles but Julius Caesar regarded them highly enough to adorn a breast-plate he presented to the temple of Venus Genetrix, his divine ancestress. Mary, Queen of Scots, owned a much-valued necklace of 52 Cumbrian pearls and, according to tradition, St Edward's Crown itself is also set with these unlikely products of the rivers Ehen and Irt. The poor folk who waded waist-deep to search for them appear to have had a less exalted view of their value: to them an 'Irton Pearl' was a bride who was known to be not quite as pure as appearances would suggest. It may have comforted the less than perfect young lady to know that the Cumbrian pearl-mussel, Margaritifer margaritifera, has a life-span of about 100 years, one of the longest-lived of all vertebrate animals.[11]

The Patricksons seemed well-set to achieve the social status coveted by so many prosperous yeomen in Tudor and Stuart times and they were, in fact, awarded a coat of arms in 1592 but they then proceeded to bring about their own undoing. In an age noted for its litigiousness the Patricksons were inordinately litigious: 'they were always at law with someone; it seems to have been their main occupation'. The catalogue of their law cases which included a large number against one another, is a remarkable cautionary tale of a family steadily ruining itself by its inability to resist an obsessive urge to go to law. If delusions of petty grandeur had not blurred their judgment they might well have heeded the advice of Francis Bacon, the Lord Chancellor, that 'Laws were like cobwebs where small flies are caught and the great brake through'. The Patricksons of Ennerdale were only small flies and they were well and truly caught. As, indeed, they were when they involved themselves in the Civil War in the Royalist cause and paid the penalty in heavy fines which left them in severe financial straits and entangled in yet more law suits. Prolonged litigation ended in Thomas Patrickson being sent to prison, with all his goods and cattle seized, a somewhat stiffer sentence than that imposed on his ancestor, Margaret Patrickson, just a century earlier, when she lost one of her forays into the courts and was fined 12 pence for using 'indecent words'. The years before, the years in between and the years following are full of the ruinous law-court adventures of the Patricksons.[12]

Ennerdale and its lake are powerful and magnificent but there is here little of that gentle softness found in other valleys; the scene is awesome rather than seductive.

Ennerdale, as Wordsworth put it, has a 'lake of bold and somewhat savage shores', and as the scene unfolds beyond the lake it becomes even bolder and more savage, a sight to thrill the hearts of all who seek out the high, austere and lonely places. Above the steely waters and beyond the dark mass of forest loom the great ridge of Red Pike and the formidable crags of Steeple, Scoat Fell and Pillar, with the seemingly invincible ramparts of Great Gable, the Scafells and Kirk Fell as a final dramatic barrier.

The grandeur of Ennerdale's mountain scenery is the fortuitous outcome of the junction and interaction of varied geological features. The principal rock formations of the Lake District are all found here: the Borrowdale Volcanics, the Skiddaw Slates and various igneous intrusions, and to these are added Ennerdale's own granophyre, a pink granite, a hard acid rock, resistant to erosion. This has metamorphosed the softer rocks around it to form an imposing array of ridges, crags and coves, all creating a quality of delicate and harmonious beauty which is yet further enhanced when the evening sun shines across the lake. Thomas West was so overwhelmed by the scene that he believed it to be the work of some Great Designer with an artist's eye and an architect's vision: 'The extent of the water is particularly calculated with the height of the adjoining mountains to produce the most astonishing reflection from the surface'.[13]

Twentieth-century industrialists and water engineers have taken a more worldly view of Ennerdale Water. Next to Wastwater this is the 'purest' lake in the district with very low levels of the nutrients needed to support any significant plant or animal life. The high quality of this water has proved irresistible to the expanding industrial and urban demands of West Cumbria and a number of assaults have been made on it over the past half-century. On each occasion battle was joined with the massed ranks of Conservation

12   Ennerdale Water

and, although an initial scheme to make the lake a reservoir won approval, the effects were minimal. Subsequent proposals were far more drastic and on these occasions total victory went to the National Park and to the forces of Conservation. The campaign claimed one sadly lamented casualty: the *Angler's Hotel*, a hostelry beloved by generations of walkers, climbers and anglers, and sited on the lake-shore with a truly spectacular view across the water to the mountains, was demolished in the face of a threatened immersion which in the end never happened.[14]

The purity of the water in the lake may attract human interest but it has no attractions for many forms of life which are abundant in most other lakes. Planktonic diatoms and flatworms, sure signs that the waters they inhabit have been 'enriched' by plant nutrients such as phosphates and nitrates, clearly find Ennerdale Water most inhospitable but 'game fish', the true angler's favourite, find it very congenial. Brown trout, salmon, char and stickleback live an unharassed life here in the company of *Mysis relicta*, a strange shrimp-like creature, probably left behind in these waters by the melting ice: Ennerdale is now its only home in England.

Eliza Linton would never have made her home here. She found Ennerdale 'wilder even than Wastdale; more lonely and austere if less sublime; at the head wonderfully noble, with a majesty of mountain unusual. But it is not lovely, taking that word to mean an admixture of softness with grandeur; not even when "on the lake", which is such a soft and lovely experience everywhere else.'[15]

The imposition of a dark, brooding forest of conifers adds an acid emphasis to her judgment: Ennerdale is not warm and hospitable; it wears the cold aloofness of wounded majesty.

Alder Catkins

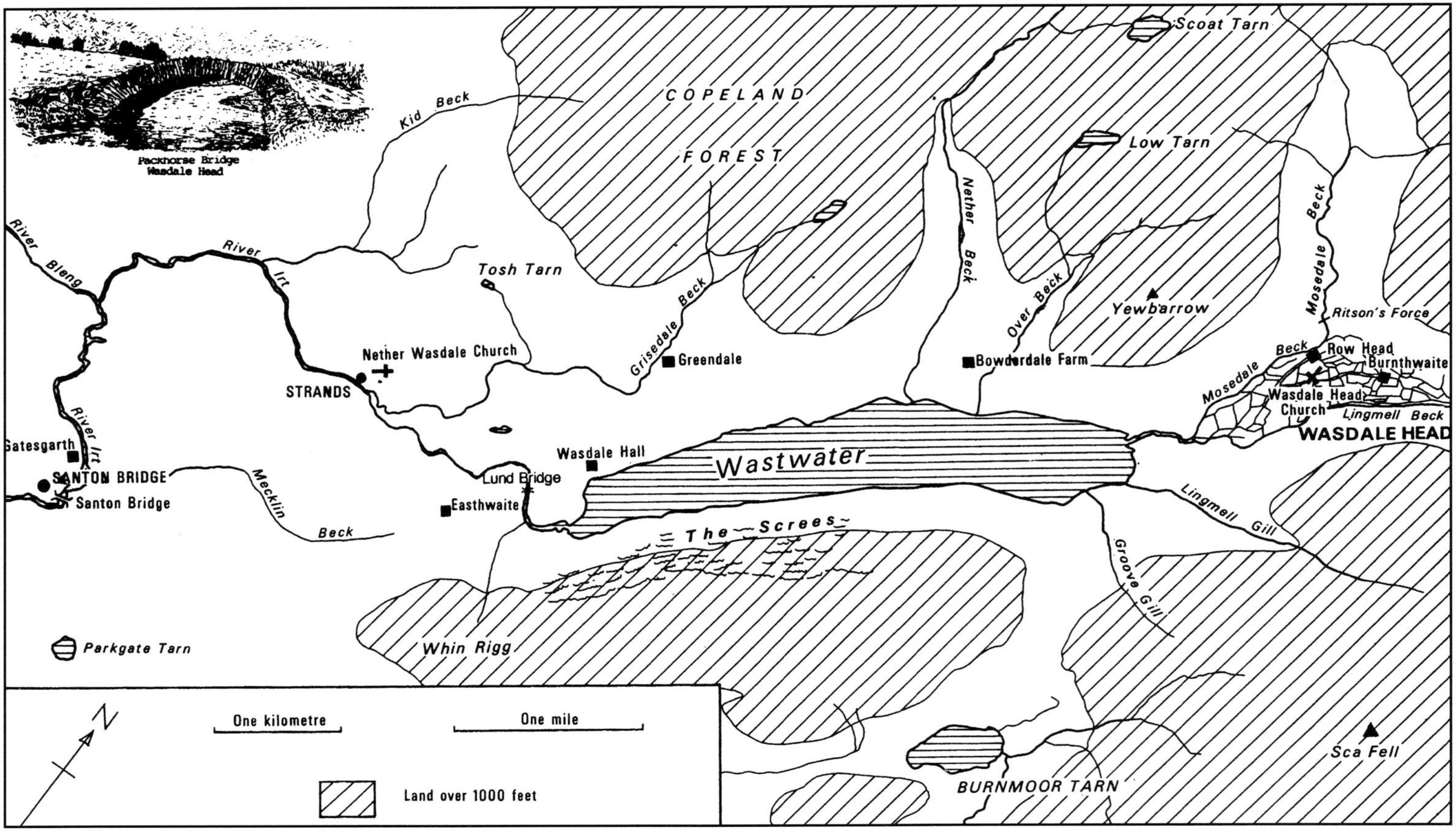

WASDALE

Scoat Tarn

Mosedale Beck

Ritson's Force

Row Head

Burnthwaite

Lingmell Beck

Wasdale Head
Church

WASDALE HEAD

Beck

Mosedale

Sca Fell

Lingmell Gill

Low Tarn

Groove Gill

Yewbarrow

Over Beck

Bowderdale Farm

BURNMOOR TARN

Nether Beck

Wastwater

COPELAND

FOREST

The Screes

Grisedale Beck

Greendale

Whin Rigg

Tosh Tarn

Wasdale Hall

Lund Bridge

Kid Beck

Nether Wasdale Church

Easthwaite

River Irt

STRANDS

Mecklin Beck

One mile

Parkgate Tarn

Gatesgarth

River Irt

SANTON BRIDGE

Santon Bridge

One kilometre

Land over 1000 feet

River Bleng

N

Penthouse Bridge
Wasdale Head

6

WASDALE

Poised on his imaginary cloud midway between Great Gable and Scafell, William Wordsworth exhorted the readers of his *Guide to the Lakes* to turn due west and 'look down into and along the deep valley of Wastdale, with its little chapel and half a dozen neat dwellings, scattered upon a plain of meadow and corn-ground intersected with stone walls apparently innumerable, like a large piece of lawless patchwork, or an array of mathematical figures'.[1]

There are no golden corn-grounds in Wasdale now but a modern fell-walker, surveying the same scene from the more conventional viewpoint of the Westmorland cairn on Great Gable, will find that the last 200 revolutionary years have brought very little change. The seasonal rash of tents and the procession of mechanical ants along the lakeshore are features of modern tourism which many will deplore but there is some consolation to be found in the knowledge that Wasdale Head is still truly the end of the road – thanks to the decisive defeat of a late 19th-century proposal to construct a road over the Styhead Pass to Borrowdale. There is no alternative here but to put on one's boots and walk and relish the exhilaration of the moment when, like Frodo and Sam in *The Lord of the Rings*, we 'turn our faces to the mountain and set out'.

Great Gable is no Mount Doom, however, nor is our journey to it fraught with all the hazards of the land of Mordor. The pleasant pastures, sheltered farmsteads and colourful patches of woodland, all set in a landscape of rocky hummocks, irregular mounds, untidy boulders and the 'sweet disorder' characteristic of a glacial moraine, make the approaches to Wastwater through Nether Wasdale a disarming experience which serves only to intensify the impact of the first glimpse of the mountain scene. The thousand-foot plunge of the Wastwater screes, breathtaking at any time but a true *coup de théâtre* at sunset, is a dramatic curtain-raiser to the stage set by nature for England's highest mountain and deepest lake:[2] Whin Rigg, than which 'no mountain in Lakeland, not even Great Gable nor Blencathra nor the Langdale Pikes can show a grander front'; Yewbarrow, from whose modest summit 'all four of Lakeland's 3000 footers can be seen'; Kirk Fell, 'the patron fell of Wasdale Head'; Great Gable, 'the favourite of all fell-walkers'; Great End, 'awe-inspiring in its massive strength'; and the Scafells with their 'sublime architecture of buttresses and pinnacles soaring into the sky', a great cathedral where a man may 'lose all his conceit ... and realise his own insignificance in the general scheme of things'.[3] And just as in a great cathedral we may admire the vast architectural conception as a whole or seek out the detail of the stone-mason's skill, worship with others or find solace in private prayer, so in Wasdale we may stroll in the valley and lift only our eyes to the hills or take up the challenge of an arduous but rewarding climb, join the throng on the popular paths or find solitude by a singing beck or on a rocky knoll.

Wasdale is only a few miles from the sea and it is therefore probable that the Norsemen who arrived from Ireland and the Western Isles during the 10th century were the pioneer farmers in Wasdale. The strongest evidence for this is the overwhelming predominance of Norse place-names in the district: near the lake we may find Easthwaite, Burnthwaite, Lund, Grisedale, Netherbeck, Overbeck, Bowderdale and Lingmell Gill, all of indisputably Norse derivation. Place-name evidence alone may be misleading, however, and we should always bear in mind the possibility that these Norse settlements may have replaced earlier primitive Celtic field systems, and that they, in turn, were modified by what W.G. Hoskins described as 'the characteristic field pattern of medieval colonisation'. Even so it is impossible to ignore the fact that Norse influence on the place-names and on the local dialects of central Lakeland is so profound that it is difficult not to accept the reality of a deep penetration and settlement of the remote valley heads such as Wasdale by the Norsemen.[4]

The first historical document of real importance relating to Wasdale is the 'Survey of The Estates of Henry Percy, Earl of Northumberland', compiled in 1578. This states clearly that at that date there existed at Wasdale Head a common field in which 17 tenants held between three and 10 acres of arable and meadow as well as 'a great parcell of the Lord's wast called Forest male being as they alledge a common onlie proper to themselves'. The Survey tells us that of 46 tenants in Nether Wasdale only six had holdings in the common field, suggesting that most of these farms were the compact units of medieval encroachment on the private Forest of Copeland which had gone on steadily since the late 13th century. The striking patchwork of the enclosed fields in this part of the valley contrasts markedly with the intriguing irregularity of those at Wasdale Head with their huge cairns of boulders piled up in the corners of the clearances and the astonishing thickness of the boundary walls.[5]

The pattern of agriculture in all these fields has changed fundamentally over the years. The increase in population during the 16th and 17th centuries demanded a 'change in the balance between the importance of stock and crops' and the development of 'a more flexible form of farming with greater arable bias'.[6]

We learn from the Account of Sarah Fell of Swarthmoor Hall that in the late 17th century a wide variety of cereals and vegetables was cultivated in South-West Cumbria, while the tithe maps show that much land here which is now pasture or overgrown with bracken once grew crops such as peas, beans and potatoes as well as rye, oats and barley – the 'corn-grounds' of Wordsworth's day.[7]

Important as these changes in agriculture may have been – and the food harvest was always of over-riding concern for on its success life itself depended – however thick the valleys might be with corn, before they could laugh and sing as the psalmist exhorted, the upland farmers had to make sure that the fold was full of sheep, for wool, too, was his bread.

Sheep have been at the very heart of Wasdale life for a thousand years. The breed of sheep most commonly found on the Lake District fells is the Herdwick but other breeds such as Swaledales, Rough Fells and Teeswaters are also well established in the dales. The Herdwick, with its characteristic white face and legs, its leonine ruffle round the shoulders and its coat of thick coarse wool, once regarded as 'the worst wool in the realm' but now appreciated for its natural colour and used in the manufacture of carpets and cloth, has long been renowned for its ability to withstand harsh conditions. It is able to survive on a diet of tough grass, heather and holly bushes and to defy days of burial in deep snowdrifts: the records of the Herdwick Sheep-Breeders Association refer to a flock of 97 Herdwicks buried under 15 feet of snow in the winter of 1947 and all but two emerged none the worse for their ordeal. The Herdwick also has an uncanny awareness of the boundaries of its native pastures – its 'heaf' – 'a valuable instinct first discovered by the people of Wasdalehead', according to James Clarke who adds, with dubious accuracy, that they wished 'to keep this breed as much as possible in their own village'. No doubt these Wasdale folk had the same discriminating appreciation of the Herdwick's tasty mutton which led to its choice for the Coronation Feast of Queen Elizabeth II in 1953.[8]

The origin of the Herdwick breed is still uncertain. Tales of 40 sheep swimming ashore from the wreckage of the Spanish Armada in 1588 may safely be discounted. Equally improbable is the fable of this particular animal wandering into Britain across the land-bridge from 'Europe' before the formation of the Channel. The records of the Abbeys of Fountains and Furness provide clear evidence that their sheep-farms were known as 'Herdwycks' and accounts of the migrations of the Norsemen in the 9th and 10th centuries indicate that they took their stock with them. Recent genetic research seems to confirm that our Herdwick sheep may be 'the sole survivor of a hairy Norse sheep that came from the North'. It is highly probable that in the end biological science will bring Norsemen and their Herdwicks to Wasdale together.[9] Some support is given to this theory by the similarity in terminology and in the system of markings used by sheep-farmers in both Cumbria and Scandinavia. This may, perhaps, tell us more about the origin of the shepherds than of their sheep but it may have some bearing on the latter also.

Every sheep carries with it two identity cards: a smit-mark or 'pop' in the form of a letter, stroke or circle marked in a red or a black dye; and a lug-mark which is a precise and unmistakable shape clipped from the sheep's ear, or, occasionally, branded on the horns. In Wasdale the dye, or 'ruddle' as it was called, was obtained rather precariously from the ironstone which gives the Wastwater Screes their attractive pink colouring, the source of their sunset radiance. Local boys risked their lives to collect these rocks which, we are told, when immersed in water and rubbed, 'produced a deep red paint which hardly any exposure to weather can wash away, especially when stained upon an oily substance like wool'. Borrowdale graphite was used to produce a black dye.[10]

The lug-mark was a more permanent proof of ownership. The word is derived from the Norse 'log' meaning 'law'; records of the meetings of the early Scandinavian 'Things' or Assemblies leave no doubt that, among the Norse communities, the lug-mark was regarded as the only lawful means of identifying ownership of sheep: smit-marks could obviously be lost when the fleece was clipped. The law was strictly enforced. Punishment for unlawful cropping of sheep's ears was severe – outlawry or death. Only the Head of the Commune had the right to

Lugmarks - a page from the 'Shepherd's Guide', 1819.

1 Fold bitted	2 Slit	3 Cropped or stoved	4 Forked
5 Shearhalved	6 Halved	7 Key bitted	8 Punched
9 Ritted	10 Twice ritted	11 Sneck bitted	12 Stove forked

13 *Sheep lug-marks*

crop the whole ear, a privilege later given to the Lord of the Manor; lesser mortals did so at their peril. So important were these lug-marks in the business of sheep farming that it is surprising to discover that not until 1817 did the first written guide to them become available. Before that date they were handed down from generation to generation as part of the essential lore of the shepherd's calling. Joseph Walker of Martindale compiled his 'Shepherd's Guide' for his own valley and district and it was not long before others followed. Soon afterwards there appeared the classic encyclopaedia of smit-marks – Gate's *Shepherd's Guide for Cumberland, Westmorland and Lancashire*, a pictorial and descriptive compilation giving each farmer's name and farm accompanied by a detailed description of the lug-mark and the smit-mark with an illustration of a sheep with ears appropriately clipped and fleece appropriately dyed:

> Edward Nelson, Gatesgarth, Buttermere, Fleetwith Stock, under key-bitted near, two strokes over couplings, wethers black on head, twinters red.

> William Dixon, Halls, cropped near ear, and a small slit in the under side, a small slit in the upper side of the far ear, and a redstroke across the fillets and down to the tail head.

Such precise information made identification easy but all depended on a thorough knowledge of the terminology, a knowledge gained only by experience and tutelage. A few commonly used lug-marks may serve as an example:

Bitted	=	a triangular piece clipped from an ear
Key-bitted	=	a rectangular piece clipped from an ear
Punched	=	a circular hole clipped through an ear
Slit	=	a straight slit clipped from an ear
Cropped	=	the removal of the top part of an ear
Forked	=	a triangular slit clipped from the top of an ear
Ritted or	=	one (or two) narrow rectangular piece(s) clipped from an ear[11]
Twice-Ritted		

Another intriguing sheep-farming tradition in Cumbria was the remarkable system of numbers used for 'sheep scoring' or counting, a tabulation long fallen into disuse among shepherds but enjoying a vogue as a curiosity for tourists. Sheep were counted in groups of 20 and when that number was reached the shepherd raised one finger; five fingers represented 100 and this was signified by placing a pebble in a pocket. Simplicity does not immediately strike one as the most commendable feature of this assortment of words, fingers and pebbles but each valley seems to have adopted it and evolved its own variation. All may have a common Celtic origin as philologists have established a close affinity between the numbers widely used in Cumbria and those found in the Welsh, Cornish and Breton languages. Mysteriously, however, there appears to be no link with the Norse languages, thus providing another unresolved dilemma in tracing the early history of men and sheep in Lakeland.

In the following example of sheep-counting numerals it will be noted that the rhythm of the words suggests a group of five as the basis of the system of 20:[12]

Yan	Sethera	Yan-a-dick	Yan-a-Bumfit
Tyan	Lethera	Tyan-a-dick	Tyan-a-Bumfit
Tethera	Hovera	Tethera dick	Tethera Bumfit
Methera	Dovera	Methera dick	Methera Bumfit
Pimp	Dick	Bumfit	Giggot

Lonely shepherds' huts and isolated sheep-folds, short protective walls built on the very edge of precipitous crags, and many miles of drystone walls to enclose pastures and define ownership are all reminders that many man-made features of the Lakeland scene owe their existence to the needs of the shepherd and his sheep. A well-built drystone wall is an impressive tribute to the skill and craftsmanship of the waller and, like every other Lakeland dale, Wasdale has some fine examples. But there are no architectural splendours here: it is as if the towering fells would countenance no rivals and man conceived his own plans on an appropriately modest scale. Solid stone cottages and farmsteads, thick-walled and compact, were carefully sited to gain shelter from the storms; the famous packhorse bridge at Wasdale Head combines simplicity with elegance; the neat stone houses and hostelries of Nether Wasdale merge comfortably into the landscape while its simple dales church is unpretentious and unadorned except for some fine panelling brought from York Minster. The tiny chapel at Wasdale Head is one of the smallest churches in the country and is almost hidden by a group of ancient yew trees. It is believed to pre-date the Reformation although the first written reference to it is dated 1550. Until the Victorian enthusiasts restored the fabric in 1892 it was probably a very primitive place of worship indeed, with no glazing in the windows, few if any seats, an earthen floor occasionally covered with rushes or bracken, and perhaps no more than a large thorn bush to keep out the sheep. Just 20 years ago electricity replaced the ancient oil lamps here, and at the same time the church acquired its dedication, appropriately enough to St Olaf, the Norseman who in the 10th century converted his kingdom of Norway to Christianity. The mountain setting of this tiny church is poignantly emphasised by the gravestones which record the deaths of those who have lost their lives on the surrounding crags, and by a small stained glass window portraying Napes Needle, a memorial to members of the Fell and Rock Climbing Club who died in the First World War.

There can be few churchwardens who carry their staves of office with such affection as those in the church at Wasdale Head. For these staves are superb examples of the wood-carving craftsmanship for which Wasdale is renowned. The head of a Herdwick ram on one stave is matched by the head of a ewe on the other, both skil-

14 *A knitting-stick made by Walter Bibby for his sister.*

fully and beautifully carved. This craft has a long history in Wasdale and in the days when most items of clothing were made at home many housewives proudly wore in their belts knitting sticks which had been exquisitely carved by their menfolk. Many of these have survived and those from Wasdale are especially admired. The fine display of shepherds' crooks and walking sticks which may be seen at the annual Wasdale Head Show is proof that this local skill is as incomparable as ever.

Wasdale has a number of fine houses built by successful entrepreneurs who amassed a fortune in the world of 19th-century commerce but none is quite so intriguing as Wasdale Hall, a half-timbered, pseudo-Elizabethan residence built close to the lake-shore at the foot of Wastwater. It was built in 1829, with additions in 1839, by Stansfield Rawson, a Yorkshire banker whose dream − or so it would seem − was to set himself up as an Elizabethan country gentleman, and in this he undoubtedly achieved a high degree of success. His Tudor-style hall with its mullioned windows and oak panelling was set among woodlands and shrubberies with a fine view of the lake and the screes. Rawson planted over 300,000 trees on his estate, commendably mainly broad-leaved for, as he commented, 'there seemed to be nothing but larch and Scotch fir' here. He had little success with a grand scheme to develop orchards of apples, pears and damsons, but he did establish a well-stocked kitchen garden, the derelict remains of which may be glimpsed in the nearby lane known as Garden Lonnen. His heirs sold the Hall in 1864 to John Musgrave, a thrusting businessman little liked in the valley and best-known for his plans to construct a road over Styhead to Borrowdale where he had mining interests. In 1959 the estate was acquired by The National Trust and 10 years later the Hall became a Youth Hostel. Much of the carved oak still remains but the stained glass installed by Rawson was removed to Sizergh Castle.[13]

Such thrusting and ambitious men as Rawson and Musgrave were alien to Wasdale and their impact was comparatively short-lived. The worthies of Wasdale are of quite a different ilk, local men for the most part whose fame rests not on their wealth or social status but on strength of character. Only the Fletcher family achieved the ranks of the gentry and, having gained his knighthood in the turmoil of the year 1640, Sir Henry Fletcher promptly died fighting for the Royalist cause at the Battle of Rowton Heath. Two hundred years later, a descendant by marriage of the Fletchers acquired a more original sort of fame. This was Will Ritson, huntsman to Wasdale Hall, mine host at *Row Foot* (now *Wasdale Head Hotel*), raconteur, wit, fox hunter, wrestler, sheep farmer, friend of poets and academics, guide to the fells for bishops, professors and young scions of the aristocracy; a legend before his death in 1890, his fame endures more than a century later. At Rowfoot and at nearby Rowhead Ritson entertained a succession of 19th-century notables including William Wordsworth, Thomas de Quincey, Samuel Taylor Coleridge, John Wilson, Adam Sedgwick, Arthur Quiller-Couch and many eminent rock-climbers of the day such as W.P. Haskett-Smith and the Abraham brothers of photographic fame. Inevitably such a place found its way into the literature of the period, perhaps most famously in A.E.W.

15   *Wasdale Hall, c.1900*

Mason's *A Romance of Wasdale*. Ritson's innumerable tall stories are constantly quoted and a few of them appear in a small book of anecdotes entitled *Lakeland Memories* published by Ritson's climbing companion, George Seatree. Ritson has two memorials, one, appropriately, within a few steps from his lifelong home – Ritson's Force in Mosedale – and the other, more ambiguously, in the 'World's Greatest Liar' contest held annually in Wasdale. Ritson once won such a competition by announcing that he did not consider himself qualified to enter because, like George Washington, he could not tell a lie!

In more recent times Josh Naylor of Borrowdale has brought fame to himself and to Wasdale by his extraordinary achievements in the competitive world of fell-racing and long-distance mountain running, a record of successes which has demonstrated a high degree of dedication and stamina and notable strength of character.

An intriguing but far less praiseworthy figure from Wasdale's past is an unknown individual of considerable enterprise who frequented the valley towards the end of the 15th century. Who he was we may never know but he deserves a place, however dubious, in the Wasdale story.

In 1865 two blocks of Borrowdale wad or graphite were discovered close by the River Irt in Nether Wasdale. These proved to be the two halves of a mould bearing the obverse and reverse impressions of five English coins – a silver groat and a silver half-groat from the 1480s and three silver pennies from the reign of Henry VII. Experiment revealed that these moulds could cast acceptable copies of these common coins of the time. But all genuine English coinage was hammered or milled, not cast, and so we must assume that someone had created for himself a simple but effective means of producing fraudulent coin of the realm. The moulds bear the words '*Civitas Eboraci*' and so were clearly intended to be forgeries on the important provincial mint established at York. It would be interesting to know how successful the Wasdale forger was in his nefarious activities and if he remained undetected. Where did he obtain his supply of silver? How and when did his moulds come to be abandoned in this spot? Above all, who was he? It seems fairly certain that he must have been a man with some knowledge of the world of commerce, with access to quantities of silver and wad, and, presumably, with the right contacts to offer a profitable and safe outlet for his products. The Victorian archaeologist, R.S. Ferguson, pointed a finger at a renegade monk from Furness Abbey as a likely candidate. Certainly the monks of Furness were familiar with the properties of Borrowdale wad for its earliest known use is in the lines drawn by scribes in the Abbey's Coucher Book in 1412. The Wasdale mould belongs to the same century and was found only 20 miles away from the abbey, no unusual journey for these widely-travelled brethren visiting their many estates in the district.

One wonders if his rewards were as ample as those of that other astute speculator, Thomas Patrickson of Ennerdale, who sold a single consignment of Wasdale pearls to a London jeweller for the astonishing sum of £800, a small fortune at the time. According to Eliza Linton the Irt pearl fishers were still active in the 1860s. The jewellery trade still considered these nacreous gems with their fine polish and pale pastel tints to have a special appeal to their customers.[14]

Wasdale was discovered by the outside world some time after other, more accessible, valleys had become accustomed to guidebook writers and the tourists who followed them. Even Wordsworth makes only passing reference to it, albeit an appreciative one: 'no part of the country is more distinguished by sublimity' he wrote but warned that it is only for the 'Traveller who is not afraid of fatigue'.

Those who did make the effort to reach this remote dale came prepared to shudder at the 'horrors' of the terrifying crags. For some the experience was rather more than

they could comfortably bear. The formidable Eliza Linton herself was evidently over-
awed by it all and found here nothing but despair:

> Even in the sunshine Wastwater is desolate – perhaps more so than in the gloom. For you cannot
> help contrasting the loneliness of the place, its deathly silence and cut-off and cornered kind of
> life, with the brightness lifting up the heart of the world elsewhere.[15]

Clearly the austere beauty of Wastwater was not universally appreciated. Thomas
Wilkinson in his *Tours to the British Mountains* found mainly 'sternness and sterility' here
and warned intending visitors that 'If beauty is the leading object of their search, they
need not go to Wastwater'.[16]

Wastwater can, indeed, be as desolate and deathly silent as Mrs. Linton found it.
When the clouds sit heavily and apparently immoveable, and the mist veils the fells in
a damp and clammy shroud; when the surface of the lake is leaden and sinister and even
the purl of the beck seems muted and still; then it is hard, indeed, to lift up one's heart
and hear the music of the mountains. Wastwater can be savage, too. When the thunder
ricochets from crag to crag and the lightning flickers along the scree; when the roaring
wind combs the waters of the lake into a tempestuous frenzy or, for an awe-inspiring
moment, tears aside the cloak of mist to reveal a looming and exaggerated peak; when
the cold fury of the driven rain lashes one's face like hail and heeds not the label on
one's guaranteed waterproof; then the sublime beauty of Wasdale seems no more than
a poet's romantic dream.

The magic of Wastwater with its subtle variations of shade and colour, its challenging
defensive walls of crags and fells, its glittering screes and mirrored reflections, may not
be casually viewed: one must wait upon a felicitous converging of meteorological per-
mutations – 'Majesty always stipulates the times when audiences may be granted'.[17] At
those times the inspired artistry of nature's crowning achievement in Lakeland is a
wonder to behold: a flash of sunlight on the broad bosom of Scafell, a sudden glimpse
of the cloud-topped towers, the westering sun to set the screes on fire; and at the centre
of the tapestry, Wastwater itself, placidly reflecting a perfect image, but always cold,
pure, forbidding and irresistible – 'the most Scandinavian of all the lakes'.[18]

Peregrine falcon

7

MITERDALE

If there is still a 'secret valley' in Lakeland it must surely be Miterdale, the valley of the River Mite. For much of its length it is inaccessible to cars; its two points of entrance are discreetly inconspicuous; it has no tourist facilities or advertised accommodation; it has no popular walkers' route to the high fells. Officially, its very name has disappeared, subsumed by Eskdale. Yet for those who wish to enjoy the rare experience of true peace and solitude with only the sound of the singing river and the wind stirring in the trees, Miterdale is a glimpse of Paradise. The pastoral scenes near Low Holme and Low Place blend with copse and woodland in a delightful vignette of all that is best in Lakeland valley landscape, complete with grazing sheep and a lively birdlife flitting among the juniper and gorse or hovering in the sky above. At the head of the valley, beyond the long-deserted and lonely ruins of ancient farms, lie the bare and open moorlands in a crag-encircled amphitheatre over which looms, dramatically, the great bulk of Scafell, dominating the scene like a solitary giant from Jotunheim. It is as if Nature has deliberately created a stage-set for some great act of theatre: 'almost too good to be true' as H.H. Symonds put it, with 'some air of artifice about it or of "scenery" as if it was made for the display of something – probably the dance of the fairies?'[1] The heavy hand of the Forestry Commission has, for the present, sadly diminished the natural charm of the head of Miterdale which in 1960 Alfred Wainwright described as a 'surprising little place of rocks and trees and waterfalls around a green glade',[2] an idyllic spot oppressively overshadowed by the gloom of encroaching conifers but still a haven of quiet seclusion.

It is not easy now as one contemplates the silent and overgrown ruins of Miterdale Head to imagine these as busy farms and a bustling inn. There were six tenements here according to the 1578 Survey – Low Place, Bakerstead, Browyeat, Sword House and two held by the farm at Miterdale Head. It is impossible to say how long before this date these farmsteads had been occupied; the earliest historical references appear in the manorial records of 1294 and 1332 which indicate a well-established farming community at that date. A process of amalgamation of holdings began in the 17th century and by 1758 Sword House had been absorbed by Miterdale Head while Low Place, having already taken over Browyeat, extended its land in 1771 with the purchase of Bakerstead. (The last family to live at Bakerstead were the Pharaohs and the last documentary reference to them occurs in the burial registration of the funeral of Sarah Pharaoh in 1799.[3]) By 1835 the owner of Low Place, John Nicholson, had acquired all the original 16th-century tenements, and the desertion of the farmsteads which had begun with the abandonment of Browyeat in the late 17th century was soon complete.

The ruins of Sword House have been identified as those of the former *Nanny Horns Inn*, once a hostelry on the major communications route between Keswick and Ravenglass, a route known to all as The Highway, a tough, hard road along which sturdy packponies carried wad, wool and slate to the quaysides at Ravenglass and brought sugar, rum, salt

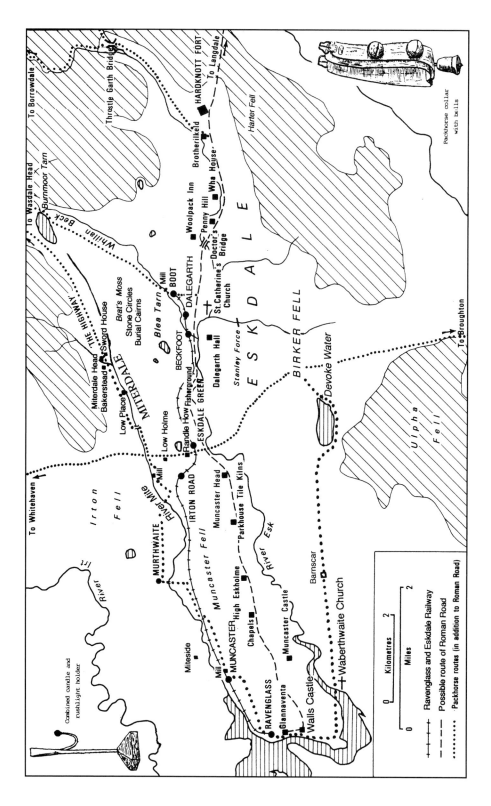

Combined candle and
rushlight holder

Packhorse collar
with bells

MITERDALE AND ESKDALE

and tobacco on their return. Randle How, the small rounded hillock between Miterdale and Eskdale Green, was the meeting point of many such routes, a busy terminal familiar to all travellers who passed this way, including John Wesley who came here on his spring journey through Cumberland in April 1761.[4] For all these travellers and packhorsemen the *Nanny Horns* meant warmth, rest and refreshment after the long and often arduous trail from Wasdale Head over the bleak moors below Scafell. We may safely assume that the inn and, no doubt, the other farmsteads hereabouts did a thriving business providing food and shelter for both man and beast. The humdrum daily life of the small community was also surely brightened by the gossip exchanged with the passing wayfarers and by sharing in the bounty of smuggled goods which regularly seemed to find a way past the excisemen at Ravenglass. If stones could speak we might hear such tales among the ruins of Miterdale as would hold children from play and old men from the chimney corner; and none would hold them in greater awe than the story of the murder at the *Nanny Horns.*

****

It was late one evening in early autumn. There had been few travellers during the day and the inn was quiet. The young housewife was alone with her baby; her husband had left in the early morning to go to a distant market and she knew that he would not return until the following day. This was the season for rush gathering and she had spent the afternoon in the marshy ground nearby selecting sound, strong stems with a firm pith. Now she was busy, as the evening light flooded into the kitchen, peeling the ripe sieves[5] and preparing to make rushlights ready for the darker evenings soon to come. A cauldron of mutton fat simmered over the fire, and into this she smoothly dipped the drawn piths allowing the hot tallow to cling and set, thus forming the candles which had provided light for farm and cottage for more than a thousand years. Singing softly to herself as she moved quickly and expertly about her work she gathered up the first batch which were now dried and ready: one she placed with pride and pleasure at its correct angle in the rushlight holder, the rest she stored in the rush-bark hanging on the wall near the window. As she gazed through the window at the evening sky she was startled by a sudden loud barking from the dogs, unexpected at this quiet hour, and, as she moved to still their noise lest they wake the sleeping child, she saw a lone figure approaching along the moorland track. It was rare for anyone to arrive so late in the day, and a solitary traveller too, and she watched with some anxiety as the stranger drew near. With a slight gasp of relief she eventually made out that it was at least a woman at her door, even if this increased her wonder that a woman should be wandering the lonely moors alone at this hour. She noted that her gaunt and weather-beaten features were heavily swathed in a country-woman's shawl, her ill-fitting clothes were soiled with mud from the marshes and her head was bent low with hunger and fatigue. She had lost her way, she explained in a faint, tired voice, and had wandered the moors for many hours with nothing to eat since early morning. Could she have a bite to eat and a seat by the fire for a while?

It was not long before the warmth from the hearth and the hot crowdy soup made the woman drowsy and, seemingly too exhausted to talk, she stretched herself out on the long hearthstone and fell into a deep and noisy sleep. The farmer's wife returned to her candle-making, quietly peeling her rushes as a dusky twilight fell upon the cosy farmhouse kitchen.

After a short while she went to attend to the pot of simmering tallow and as she glanced down at the snoring woman she clutched her hand to her breast and stared in fear and disbelief at what she saw. The heavy shawl had slipped away to reveal not the face of an elderly woman but the hard, unshaven features of a man, made more repulsive by his gaping mouth and the sounds which came from it. Panic-stricken and fearing robbery or violence to her baby or herself, the desperate girl seized the ladle full of boiling fat and poured it down the yawning throat ... again and again and again.

On his return the next day the husband found his wife distraught and hiding with her baby in the byre; and on the kitchen floor the corpse of a man scalded and choked to death with boiling tallow and dressed in woman's clothing.

The body was buried and nothing was said but out of this the legend of the ghost of Miterdale was born.

Shortly after these events took place a newspaper report described a violent quarrel between two seamen on a Whitehaven quayside in which one had been stabbed to death and the other had escaped into the hills. An isolated farmhouse had been broken into and a woman's clothing and shawl had been stolen ...

Perhaps a rough kind of justice had been exacted in Miterdale.[6]

****

The rewards of farming in this remote valley head can never have been more than just enough to provide the basic needs of everyday life and, particularly in years of poor harvest, even the task of ensuring sufficient winter food and fodder must have involved a hardship we can now scarcely imagine. And, right to the end, these struggling tenants of the Barons of Egremont were subject to various ancient medieval dues and tolls which must occasionally have seemed especially irksome. Indeed it is in some respects quite remarkable how closely the manorial court regulated the lives and the agricultural economy of these farmers. A document of 1587 records that the uplands beyond Miterdale Head were to be used for summer pastures only for 'all geld goods', that is for bullocks, heifers, horses and other stock without young; that each farmstead should use clearly named and specified cow pastures adjacent to its own enclosed land; that the high fells should be divided into individually named heafs; and that sheep should be driven only along specified driftways. Neither were the boundaries of the lord of the manor's deer park left in any doubt. All decreed in the interests of sound agricultural practice, perhaps, and probably reluctantly accepted as such, and certainly less resented than the curious medieval payments for which each tenement was liable even as late as 1860: 'Greenhew' was a toll exacted for the right to cut underwood in the forests for flails, scythe and pitchfork shafts, poles and posts, swill-wood and besoms, and also for leaf-cropping the ash trees to feed milking cows; 'Doortoll', a somewhat mysterious tax, seems to have been related to services due within the lord's forests and to the maintenance of the Lord's foresters, an imposition apparently peculiar to the Forest of Copeland.[7]

The many profound changes which were slowly transforming the countryside and improving the quality of life in the early 19th century, and were gradually affecting much of the population of Britain, had scarcely touched the families in Miterdale and it is truly not surprising, that perhaps after much deliberation, they decided that a way of life which had changed little in half a millennium was no longer acceptable. The old houses were finally abandoned to fall into ruins, Miterdale Head being the last to survive, and a thousand-year-old community came to an end. It is a strange irony that this depopulation of Miterdale probably saved it from all the excesses inflicted on so many other valleys by metalled roads and provision for the car-borne tourist.

This was not the first time that a long-established human settlement near the River Mite had been disrupted. Several thousand years earlier a community of Bronze-Age folk lived on what are now bare and windswept moors surrounding the source of the Mite above Burnmoor Tarn on Tongue Moor and Brat's Moss. Their simple homes, fields and pastures have long since vanished under the blanket of peat-bog and all that remains of this ancient civilisation is an impressive array of five stone circles and numerous burial cairns. The largest circle has a diameter of over 100ft. (31m) and has 41 granite stones enclosing five burial cairns which contained stone cists with deposits of burned bones and staghorn. The other circles are somewhat smaller but have many of their stones still standing and all are constructed as perfect circles. It is not the archaeological detail which overwhelms the visitor to these mysterious relics but the breathtaking vantage point where they lie. To the north-west rise the formidable bastions of Illgill Head and Whin Rigg; to the north-east loom the towering crags of Scafell and Lingmell; to the east are the mountains of Eskdale, a line of miniature Alpine peaks; and to the south, seen between the fells, is a view to the coast and the Irish Sea. It is a dramatic setting which seems to endow this remarkable cluster of circles and cairns with a mystical quality. The nature of the ceremonies and rituals which took place here remain an enigma but there can be little doubt that some 3,500 years ago this place was of immense importance in a culture of which we know almost nothing.[8]

A short distance away in a hollow below Burnmoor Tarn the River Mite has its rather unimpressive beginnings. It is tempting to believe that it was one of the Bronze-Age Britons who in a light-hearted moment gave the infant Mite its name which is said to be derived from a British root-word 'meigh' meaning 'to urinate' or 'to mizzle', a reference perhaps to the tentative nature of the river's course in its early stages. Within a mile a score of tiny supportive becks help to shrug off this unflattering image and the remaining eight miles of its journey to the sea are full of variety and interest. Bubbling and singing over its rocky bed it tumbles through an attractive glen passing by the ruins at Miterdale Head, the renovated building at Bakerstead, and the still active sheep farm at Low Place where in 1579 William Nicholson had 'a tenement, an orchard, and a croft adjoining' which contained three acres and a half and 'a little pighill'[9] of half an acre together with three acres of meadow in two enclosures called the How and the Foxhole. He also had a meadow called Lyme Croft, a garth called Skalegarth, part of a close called Nether Field and some common land. Four hundred years later the 1840 tithe map records exactly the same holdings for the Low Place farmstead. Except for a short period earlier this century when Low Place was temporarily abandoned, this ancient settlement has farmed the same lands by the Mite certainly since the 16th century when the present house was built and probably for very many years before.

Here, as at Low Holme the next farm down the valley, generations of farmhands would have been familiar with all the arduous tasks involved in tending large flocks of sheep, not least the former custom of 'salving' to rid the animals of the various parasites which torment them. The 'salve' was an obnoxious mixture of rancid butter and tar and each sheep had to be vigorously massaged for 20 minutes or so. Three dozen sheep required 16 pounds of butter and one gallon of tar and kept one man exhaustingly occupied for three long days. This unpleasant chore began to disappear in the mid-19th century when Bigg's sheep-dipping apparatus became more widely known. Resistance to change meant that salving was still practised on some Lake district farms until 1905 when dipping became compulsory. Most farmers by then had been persuaded to use the new method by the simple fact that the cost of dipping was considerably less than that of salving, and the cleaner, dipped fleeces were far more marketable than the tarry, pungent fleeces which had been so thoroughly anointed.[10]

An old hogg-house at Low Holme reminds us of another ancient tradition of sheep-farming which also disappeared in the 19th century. An early report of the Board of Agriculture refers to the custom in Eskdale and Miterdale of keeping the hoggs (yearling sheep) in the hogg-house all winter, feeding them on hay and driving them to water once a day, but 'this practice is now laid aside and they winter them upon the enclosed grounds'. Tending sheep still has its days of hard and intensive labour with uncertain rewards but no-one would wish to return to the constantly demanding and often nauseating routines of former times. Viewed in its historical and veterinary perspective the sweet, cuddly prancing lamb of the spring meadows is seen in a less endearing light: it is as well we can enjoy its innocent charm as it gambols among the rocky outcrops of Miterdale.

The Miterdale landscape is to a large extent determined by an intrusion of igneous rocks known as Eskdale granite notable for its delicate pink colour derived from the veins of haematite within the rock. The iron ore deposits were once laboriously mined; charcoal for the bloomery smelting furnaces was made at the pitsteads now hidden among the trees of Porterthwaite Wood.[11]

The scenery produced by this geology is seen most obviously in the attractive knolls and hollows characteristic of both Eskdale and Miterdale and especially in the low fells which separate the two valleys. Many of the farm buildings and drystone walls are constructed from this softly coloured stone which is widely esteemed as the most appeal-ing of the granites found in Britain. The eye-catching spectacle of the rose-coloured walls of Muncaster Castle in the sunlight readily confirms this. The great round, roseate boulders found in the local field walls distinguish this western edge of the Lake District as clearly as the rugged slates or grey volcanic masses belong to High Furness and Borrowdale. The weathering and shaping of all these stones is the result of the action of water and ice, and the granite of Eskdale and Miterdale has endured both. For each of these valleys once had its own glacial lake, hemmed in between the vast glaciers to west and east. Muncaster Fell was an island separating Lake Eskdale from Lake Miterdale and in the course of geological time escape channels were worn through at successively lower levels until the water from the lake flowed out in force carrying with it an immense volume of debris which now forms the delightful terrace walk at Muncaster Castle.[12]

The Mite now meanders through pastoral countryside below Muncaster Fell water-ing fields once covered with several hundreds of metres of ice. It enters these lower reaches by the former bobbin mill whose mill-pond lies close by the ancient trackway between Eskdale and Nether Wasdale. And soon after this it flows under yet another historic route, the drovers' road (now the motor road) along which for 500 years thousands of cattle were driven to markets and fairs at Bootle, Ravenglass, Cockermouth and much further afield to Kendal, Penrith and Appleby. The traffic here must have been intense as this road also served as a major packhorse route and wagon trail. The waters of the Mite no doubt quenched the thirst of many a tired beast. Here is the Bowerhouse, a fine old building once a farm and now a modern inn with a quiet charm much sought after but rarely found.

From this point the Mite seems to lose the character of a Lakeland beck. It now glides sedately like a southern stream through low-lying meadows rich with lush grass and wild flowers. To the south almost hidden in the woods on the craggy flanks of Muncaster Fell runs 'La'al Ratty' or, to

16   *Packhorse bells*

dignify it with its proper name, 'The Ravenglass and Eskdale Light Railway', the narrow gauge line with its endearing miniature locomotives which each year carries thousands of tourists into the heart of Eskdale.[13] Children especially love one of the new engines, 'The River Mite', a name which gives due recognition to the fact that for well over half its length the railway runs beside the Mite rather than the Esk. From Ravenglass the line crosses the flat lands alongside the estuary of the Mite before it enters the woodlands from which it emerges from time to time to give glimpses of wide water-meadows on the one hand and, on the other, the rugged bilberry and heather-clad ramparts of Muncaster Fell.

In the final leisurely miles of its approach to the estuary the Mite passes through a land divided by a pattern of field enclosures and crossed by numerous tiny becks and once important bridleways with a few small coppices and ancient farmsteads – a landscape far removed from the high fells only a short river's-flow away but still worthy of inclusion within the boundary of the National Park. At Murthwaite are the traces of a granite crushing operation with the fast-fading track of a standard gauge railway to transport the crushed stone to the main line by the coast; at Miteside are the fields where, according to Eliza Linton, 'the best wheat in Lancashire' (sic) was grown; and soon after this a mill-race channels the water-power which turns the great water-wheel of Muncaster Mill, a beautifully restored medieval corn mill in an idyllic fairy-tale setting. The present building is about 300 years old but there are records of a mill on this site in 1455 and since this was the manorial corn-mill for Muncaster Manor it is safe to assume that corn has been milled here since the Penningtons first came to Muncaster in the 13th century. The mill ceased to function in 1961 but the machinery was preserved and has been carefully restored by the Eskdale (Cumbria) Trust. The extraordinary skill and ingenuity of the engineers and craftsmen who designed the complex mechanisms are especially impressive in the intricate system of interlinked devices installed here to produce both oatmeal flour and wheat flour, two quite different milling processes. Inside it is possible to visit the ground floor where the array of cogged gear-wheels can be seen.[14]

Beyond the mill the Mite creeps sluggishly towards the coast through the estuarine mud and sand across which passes the ford at Saltcoats, once the route of the Roman road from Ravenglass to the north and later a busy crossing for packhorses, wagons, coaches and travellers of all kinds. All who crossed here had to pay a toll, and in 1703 the tolls paid here equalled all the tolls taken within the town and port of Ravenglass.[15] The name 'Saltcoats', meaning salt-cots or salt-huts, suggests that this was a place where salt-pans were situated and the salt was stored in nearby huts. No record of salt-making specifically on this part of the coast has yet been found but it is known that there were extensive salt-pans further north near Maryport.

Close to the foreshore the Mite joins first the Irt and then the Esk, and all three rivers make their way through an extensive area of mud, shingle and sand banks to end their course in the Irish Sea. This was once the scene of a pearl-fishery: Tacitus refers to the 'ocean pearls' found here and in Tudor times William Camden commented quite confidently on them, although he did not describe them as 'pearls':

> Higher up (i.e. north of Ravenglass) the little river Irt runs into the sea, in which the shell-fish having by a kind of regular motion taken in the dew, which they are extremely fond of, are impregnated, and produce berries, or, to use the poet's phrase, baccae concheae, shell-berries, which the inhabitants, when the tide is out, search for, and our jewellers buy of the poor for a trifle, and sell again at a very great price.[16]

17   *Old cottage, Ravenglass*

The estuarine landscape near Ravenglass is not everyone's idea of natural beauty but to many it has a particular attraction, and especially to the many species of bird which find life here so rewarding and congenial. To the south is the Eskmeals Nature Reserve and to the north the Ravenglass Nature Reserve both of considerable importance and interest for botanists and ornithologists and both now managed and protected, endangered only by the unpredictable consequences of future developments at the nuclear establishment at Sellafield no more than five miles away. Unexpected disaster has already occurred once here: the world-famous gullery where 10,000 pairs of black-headed gulls nested only 25 years ago was suddenly deserted, the entire gull population vanished in a mystery which still remains unresolved.[17]

The little town of Ravenglass – Glannaventa to the Romans – has a long history as a flourishing port and centre of ship-building but as the 19th century drew to a close the *Mannex Directory* pronounced that 'whatever importance formerly attached to this place as a port, it is now deserted'. Since then it has had a quiet and uneventful history but it has preserved the charm of an old fishing village, a unique and unspoiled corner of Lakeland.[18]

Yet there are many purists who would not include Ravenglass – or Muncaster mill or the picturesque journey on Ratty's Railway – in any description of Miterdale. For them Miterdale means only the lonely upland reaches beyond the motor road where any trace of tourism is entirely absent and where the only sounds are those of a wayward lamb, the singing of the birds, the gentle soughing of the wind in the trees and the purl of the Mite as it runs its course between, over and under the granite boulders it has pounded and caressed for countless years. Here, indeed, is the true tranquillity of solitude.

Tawny Owl

8

ESKDALE

The 'green Vale of Esk – deep and green, with its glittering serpent stream', its glowing pastures, its granite farms, barns and drystone walls, and its scattered woodlands of oak, beech and larch, is often acclaimed as the pearl of all the Lakeland valleys. It was, indeed, sanctified as 'holy ground ... the most perfect part of that perfect place', the Lake District of England, in evidence given by Sir William Beveridge opposing the Forestry Commission's plans to cover 8,000 acres of Upper Eskdale and the Duddon Valley with a blanket of conifers. Sir William was pleading a special cause and we may forgive his hyperbole for it was largely through his advocacy that the Forestry Commission was thwarted in its threat to do unto Eskdale as it had done unto Ennerdale, namely to submerge the farms, fells, crags, becks and waterfalls of the higher reaches of the Esk under a sea of plantations.[1] Long before this, the lower reaches of the valley had seen the arrival and profitless departure of many a commercial enterprise: mining prospectors seeking to exploit the copper deposits on Harter Fell or the iron in the fells near Boot and elsewhere; quarrymen blasting out the splendid pink granite near Beckfoot; iron-masters setting up their furnaces and forges fired by charcoal made from acres of coppiced woodlands; even railway engineers driving their iron road through the valley as far as Boot; all have left their mark but none has inflicted on Eskdale the disfiguring scars on the landscape which so often accompany industrial exploitation.

All this is recent history. Eskdale's western seclusion had been disturbed before only by the arrival of the Norsemen in the 10th century and by the Roman Army of Occupation in the first. These, too, were hard, practical men with little time to spare for the natural beauty around them but surely there must have been some among the tough Roman soldiery who stood to marvel at the glory of the sunset over the western sea as they gazed out over Eskdale from the ramparts of their hill-top fort at Mediobogdum, better known today as Hardknott.

Perched high on a spur of rock 700 feet above Eskdale, Hardknott Fort is one of the most impressive sites of the Roman Occupation to be found in the whole of Britain. It commands a memorable view of the head of Eskdale and of the valley below, with a distant prospect of the sea, and on a day of driving storm and mists it is the epitome of desolation in the wilderness, demanding little imagination to experience the feelings of the men from sunny Mediterranean lands whose military duties had brought them to garrison this bleak and lonely mountain fastness. It seems unlikely that on such a day they would have shared the sentiments of some modern visitors who have been drawn into flights of fancy rarely bestowed upon ancient monuments: to the Reverend R.S. Ferguson Hardknott was 'an enchanted fortress in the air, the work of superhuman power rather than mere men'; Wordsworth conjured up Jove and Mars, and Hugh Walpole felt the place was 'so beautiful because all around it are the greatest mountains of Cumberland', a hallowed place where he could 'hear the old proud Romans moving'. One suspects these same proud Romans would have had some difficulty in comprehending Sir Mortimer Wheeler's conviction that he felt 'closer to the Grandeur of Rome at Hardknott than in the Roman Forum'. To the 500 auxiliaries who found themselves posted to Hardknott their time here was probably no more than one of the less congenial stages on their 25-year stretch to retirement and the privileges of Roman citizenship.

Like all Roman forts Hardknott was built foursquare with rounded corners, angle towers, four portals, one on each side, and main streets leading from them. The overall measurements were approximately 350ft. by 360ft. (approx. 107m by 110m) and the outer wall was five feet thick (approx. 1.5m) with a massive earth rampart behind it. Inside the defensive wall were the barrack blocks on the southern side nearest to the road, and in the centre was the headquarters building with a courtyard, an inner colonnade, a large hall extending the whole length of the building, and behind that rooms for various offices. This was flanked on the left by the commandant's house and on the right by a pair of granaries. The ruins of all these are still visible as are the remains of the bath-houses which were constructed a short distance outside the south-west wall. Excavation has identified here the usual features of Roman baths – a frigidarium or cold bath, a tepidarium or warm bath and a caldarium or hot bath, arranged side by side, with at opposite ends of the complex, the furnace and the cold plunge. Near by stood the laconicum, a circular building which contained an extra-hot bath which induced perspiration similar to that experienced in a Turkish bath. 'The whole establishment is an object lesson in military hygiene and a striking testimony to the care of the Roman army for the health of its troops everywhere, even on the remotest frontiers.'[2]

Hardknott Fort has retained a feature of Roman military establishments which has survived only rarely elsewhere. A short distance away from the fort, higher up the fellside, is an artificially levelled area somewhat larger than that covered by the fort itself. This was the parade ground where daily parades, drill, training and military ceremonies took place. On the north side is a raised platform which was the tribunal or dais from which the commandant or officer in charge would address the cohort or supervise their exercises.

18 *Hardknott: The Roman Fort*

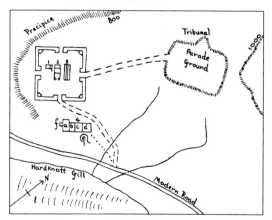

1. Commander's House. 2. Headquarters. 3. Granary. 4. Bath House. a. Caldarium; b. Tepidarium; c. Frigidarium; d. Cold plunge; e. Laconicum; f. Furnace.

Hardknott had a fairly short life as an active military station. It was probably built towards the end of the first century A.D. and appears to have been destroyed and abandoned towards the end of the second. Precise details of its history have yet to be established but to the many hundreds of visitors who come here each year this is of no great moment although there can be few who leave unimpressed by the grandeur of its setting or without some sharpening of the curiosity which brought them here.

The Roman sentries doing their tour of duty on the lonely ramparts of Hardknott must at times have envied their colleagues in the garrison 10 miles or so away down by the sea at the fort of Glannaventa (or Ravenglass as we know it). For here there was not only all the bustle of a busy port but a civilian 'town' or 'vicus' had grown up in the neighbourhood of the fort, with all the attractions and distractions that went with it. Here were markets and shops and entertainments and girls – all benefits notably absent at Hardknott. Furthermore the baths at Glannaventa had more to offer than hot and cold water: these were more like the 'thermae' in Italy or at Aquae Sulis (Bath) in Britain; they were places of relaxation, recreation and social intercourse. Here one met friends to talk or conduct business while proceeding through the succession of baths at a leisurely pace, preceded perhaps by an energetic session in the gymnasium and followed by a visit to the massage room. After this, full of renewed vigour and *joie de vivre*, our off-duty soldiery could then indulge the Roman passion for gambling, at tables set out for a variety of dice games, or play chess, draughts or their version of backgammon. Meanwhile food and wine would be plentifully available; the rooms would be comfortable and warm; the company lively and congenial; and outside under the porticos hovered a group of prostitutes and good-time girls whose charms would be greatly enhanced by the effects of the physical and mental exuberance induced by a few hours' relaxation and stimulation in the bath-house. 'Baths, wine and women corrupt our bodies', wrote one Roman cynic, adding with cheerful nonchalance, 'But these things make life itself.'

At Walls Castle, close by the site of the Roman fort at Ravenglass, there stand the remains of the bath house where the local garrison and the men from Hardknott foregathered to forget for a while the discipline and boredom of military life. It has been described as 'the best preserved Roman building in the North of England' with walls still standing in parts to their full original height. Its size misled archaeologists into the belief that it was a Roman villa – and it was, in fact, lived in as a family residence by the

19 *Walls Castle, Ravenglass*

Penningtons in the 12th century – but its purpose as a baths complex now seems indisputable.[3]

At Park House on the route of the Roman road under Muncaster Fell a pottery and tilery were discovered which probably supplied most of the requirements of the various Roman buildings in Eskdale, making use of the local clay. Those who first read Collingwood's description of this as being 'of immense and expensive construction' and then proceed to search for the site on the ground will be profoundly disappointed. There is very little to see other than a few grassy mounds and only the expert studies which have been made shed significant light on an important piece of Roman archaeology.[4]

Walls Castle, Park House and Hardknott are all on or close by the route of the Roman road from Ambleside to Ravenglass, the Tenth Iter in the Imperial System of highways. The line of this road through Little Langdale is discussed in the chapter on the Langdales (see page 158/159). Its course over Wrynose and Hardknott was traced and described in 1949 by Professor I.A. Richmond with such success that, with his detailed map as guide, it is possible to enjoy a day's walk tramping in the footsteps of the Roman cohorts while modern traffic grinds its way laboriously through the zig-zags and far tougher gradients of the modern roadway. As far as the ancient 'herdwick' farm at Brotherilket the route into Eskdale is fairly certain but from there along the valley to Ravenglass 'the only material evidence for the road ... is confined to a well-attested length immediately east of Ravenglass fort, the river terrace sector south of the Parkhouse tile kilns, the possible causeway west of Wha House Bridge and the oral tradition of the removal of the road in the meadow east of Wha House Bridge'.[5] It does seem apparent, however, that the Roman engineers would have followed the flat valley bottom which was still cluttered with the debris left by the glacier which had once covered much of Eskdale.[6] R.G. Collingwood described Eskdale when the Romans arrived as a harsh and unattractive place:

> The sides and bottom of the valley [were] uninhabited and covered with scrub; the bottom marshy as well; people were living a rough and poor kind of life on the uplands, tilling their little fields and eking out their produce by keeping a few cattle and sheep, and hunting on the mountains and in the forests.[7]

No pre-Roman tools, pottery, weapons or other artefacts have been discovered in Eskdale but, as Collingwood indicated, there is plentiful evidence of Bronze-Age settlements on the higher ground above the valley. Several stone circles, burial cairns and hut circles may be seen near Burnmoor Tarn while at Barnscar, on the uplands near Devoke Water, over 400 cairns, enclosures and hut circles (some 5m to 8m in diameter), remind us that some 3,000 years ago this was a well-populated village whose inhabitants were supported by the fertile and well-stocked woodlands which clothed these now desolate moorlands and by cereals grown in the small field-enclosures nearby. Known for centuries as the 'City of Barnscar', this was clearly a major Bronze-Age settlement, admirably sited high above Eskdale with a wide vista out to the sea and a commanding view of Great Gable and the fells around it.[8] Historical tradition has long maintained that Barnscar was looted and destroyed by Viking raiders: but this seems improbable, for the Norsemen who began to arrive on the west coast of Cumbria in the 10th century had no wish to take over this upland. They were more interested in the fertile and more congenial valley below and in order to create their farmsteads here they began the arduous task of clearing the scrub and glacial debris and draining the marshes. It was they who gave names to so many of the farms, fields, becks, woodlands, crags and fells in Eskdale, although other place-names in Eskdale suggest that there was also some Anglian settlement but these are very few in comparison to names of Norse origin.[9]

The discovery of early medieval shielings on the high ground at Scale Gill would seem to confirm that these Norse settlers in Eskdale practised the system of summer transhumance farming here as in other Lakeland areas, thus making the maximum use of the lower pastures in the winter months.[10]

Recorded history reappears with the grants of land in Cumberland to the conquering Norman barons and with the subsequent founding of religious houses in the area. Roger of Poitou, Randolf de Briquessart, William Meschines and John de Hudleston now held power over these wild and disputed northern lands bringing their unfamiliar foreign names to a countryside where even in the late 12th century the 'sworn men' who served on local commissions still bore names such as Svein, Ulf, Orm and Ravenkell.[11] To the Norman yoke imposed by these secular lords was soon added the exacting authority of the Church. The 'mild monastic faces in quiet collegiate cloisters' would prove to be hard taskmasters, efficient farmers, businessmen and administrators who brought to an end the tax-free, tithe-free, independent existence of the small farmers in the valleys they controlled.

The great Cistercian Abbey at Furness, founded in 1127, held extensive properties throughout the Furness district and also in Borrowdale. In 1242 the Abbot negotiated a remarkable transaction whereby in exchange for a coastal property at Monkfoss, near Black Combe, the Abbey acquired 14,000 acres of Upper Eskdale including the already long-established sheep farm or 'herdwick' of Brotherilket. They thus obtained not only a valuable economic asset but also control of the communications routes, via Hardknott, to their other possessions in High Furness and, via Esk Hause, to their farms and granges in Borrowdale. They also secured access, via Lingcove (where their bridge still stands) and Ore Gap, to the iron furnaces in Langstrath for the smelting of the ore they mined in Eskdale. The earliest date for iron production in Eskdale itself appears in the Cartulary of St Bees in 1354 and it is known that there were bloomeries at Eskdale Green, Dalegarth, Beckfoot and Muncaster Head.[12]

Eskdale's iron ore was mined for close on 2,000 years from Roman times until the last venture ended in 1913. The haematite outcrops may best be seen on the fellsides near Boot.

Late in the 13th century the Abbot of Furness and John de Hudleston settled a long dispute over hunting rights. As Lord of Millom Hudleston claimed the right to hunt and hawk throughout Upper Eskdale as the forest laws allowed. This clearly proved to be incompatible with the Abbot's view of his rights as the new landowner and especially with the interests of sheep-farming, and the Abbey Coucher Book tersely records the tension which prevailed. Eventually the monks were given permission to enclose 'the pasture of Brotherilkeld and Lincove ... with a dyke wall or paling... but such, nevertheless, as harts and does and their fauns could leap'. Remains of this enclosure can still be seen near Throstle Garth Bridge.

The small Benedictine house at St Bees, founded a few years before the Abbey of Furness, controlled four chapelries in the western dales – at Loweswater, in Wasdale, Ennerdale and Eskdale. Only the last still retains its dedication together with its Holy Well, a 14th-century window and font, a 15th-century bell and a silver chalice from the 1630s. St Catherine's Church stands close by the River Esk which is here crossed by a line of stepping stones (not easily negotiated) leading directly on to the route of the old Roman road and also to Stanley Ghyll, a beautiful and impressive waterfall set in a woodland scene of great charm. Stately conifers mix comfortably with more familiar deciduous trees, and from the early spring rhododendrons blaze a trail of colour up to the very lip of the fall which drops some 60ft. into a deep pool enclosed by mossy rocks, an enchanting spot.

In the churchyard by St Catherine's is an interesting reminder that hunting remained a strong tradition in Eskdale long after the Lords of Millom had vanished from the scene and flourishes there still. The gravestone of Tommy Dobson is as fascinating a piece of tombstone sculpture as will be found anywhere. Carved from a massive rock the central scroll records the details of Dobson's life and that the monument 'was erected by nearly 300 friends from all parts of the country'. On either side of this are lively sculptures of the heads of a Lakeland hound and a fox, with a brush, a whip and a hunting horn below. Above it all is the genial face of Tommy himself, delightfully portrayed and set in a fine oval niche. Dobson's life spanned 83 years and when he died in 1910 he had been Master of the Eskdale and Ennerdale Foxhounds for 53 years. Dobson founded this pack in 1857 as one of the first regularly organised Lakeland Foxhounds and it was he, together with his famous contemporaries, Joe Bowman of the Ullswater pack and John Crozier of the Blencathra, who created the modern tradition of fox-hunting in the Lake District.

There are no useful accounts of the sport before the 18th century but parish registers of that time give some detail and James Clarke in his *Survey of the Lakes* (1787) relates a number of hunting anecdotes and tells us that, as well as the fox, huntsmen then also regarded as fair quarry wild cats, pole cats, badgers, foulmarts, pine martens, eagles, ravens and gleads (kites). It is, in many ways, regrettable that the popular hero of Lakeland fox-hunting should be John Peel of Caldbeck who is immortalised in the well-known (and largely erroneous) folk song, for there is some doubt about the veracity of his alleged hunting exploits and he was certainly as notable for his feats in the local taverns as for his deeds of derring-do against the fox. The achievements of Tommy Dobson were more genuine and long-lasting than anything ever accomplished by Peel.

In Dobson's day it was customary for the hunt meets to be announced after Matins on Sundays when 'the parish priest mounted a tombstone in the churchyard and announced to the assembled crowd the dates and places for meets and sales by auction during the ensuing week'.[13] Since Dobson's death in the early years of this century attitudes towards 'blood sports' have changed but fox-hunting in the Lake District is far removed from that social pageant condemned by Oscar Wilde as 'the unspeakable in pursuit of the uneatable'.

The concerns of sheep farming have been the primary pre-occupation of the inhabitants of Eskdale for many hundreds of years but from the mid-17th to the mid-20th centuries the valley was the scene of a much wider industrial activity. Once more, 1,500 years after the Romans had departed, their road along the riverside became a busy trading route. Strings of pack horses wended their way towards the then flourishing port of Ravenglass, laden with panniers of slate, iron, wool, Borrowdale wad, charcoal, tanned leather, turned tools and implements of oak, ash and holly, and even hazel nuts,[14] all local products, and on their return they brought cargoes of rum, brandy, sugar, molasses, tea, lace, salt and tobacco — all dutiable but not all known to the excisemen. Drovers from Galloway and the plains of west Cumberland herded thousands of cattle on their long journey to the markets of the Lune valley and the Midlands. And this was only one of the many trails which converged on Eskdale. The rounded hillock at Randle How, by Eskdale Green, appears to have been a veritable Piccadilly in these days, for this was the meeting point of six main routes.[15]

Other reminders of these busy days are to be seen in the lovely packhorse bridges along the valley – Throstle Garth Bridge by the waterfall on the route to Ore Gap, Doctor's Bridge at Penny Hill where an inn once catered for passing drovers, packhorsemen and travellers, as did the *Woolpack Inn* on the opposite side of the river, and the small bridge at Boot by the old corn mill on Whillan Beck. This mill is first recorded in 1578 but it has been estimated that the number of used millstones here could indicate some 700 years of milling before it all came to an end in the 1920s.[16]

20   *Eskdale Mill, Boot*

Eskdale's contribution to all this traffic lay in its woodland industries, its iron mines and its quarries. The extensive woodlands of Lakeland have played an important part in its economy for many centuries and, even in the late 18th century when the first guide-book writers found abundant tree cover in all the valleys and as high as 1,500 feet, it seemed that the supply of timber for all purposes could never be exhausted. The Report of the Commission on the Dissolution of Furness Abbey in 1537 noted that the Cistercian monks there received a goodly revenue from the proceeds of 'Grenehew, Bastyng, Bleckyng, byndyng, making of Sadeltrees, Cartwheles, Cuppes, dishes and many other thyngs wrought by Cowpers and Turners, with the making of Coles and pannage of Hogges'; that is to say the rent paid by their tenant farmers for the privilege to cut ash and holly branches for winter-feed, the manufacture of baskets, swills and mats, the drying of bark for use in the tanning industry, the making of hoops and barrels, the construction of carrying frames for the backs of horses, the shaping of waggon wheels, the carving or turning of innumerable farm implements and household tools and utensils, the burning of charcoal and the payment made for the right to allow pigs to browse and root in the forests. All these demands on the woodlands continued uninterrupted by the changes in ownership after the disappearance of the monastic foundations without any significant destruction of the woods but the industrial developments of the 18th and 19th centuries were to transform this, not only by increasing the demand from the ancient industries but, more important and more catastrophically, by the emergence of new industries with even greater appetites.

The magic touchstone of success in the first stages of the Industrial Revolution was iron. The iron horse, the iron road, iron ships, iron bridges, iron machines, iron tools, iron implements and utensils of every kind, iron buildings, all created a rapid crescendo of demand. By the end of the 19th century 10 million tons a year were not enough. Wherever iron ore was to be found there were those who strove to mine it. The Romans and the Furness monks had known all about the iron ore in Eskdale and spasmodic mining took place from time to time in later centuries but it was not until the 19th century, that more determined prospectors began to arrive. Undeterred by the failure of earlier veins near Boot, and perhaps spurred on by the success of the new venture at Millom, the Whitehaven Iron Mines Company set to work at the Blea Tarn, Nab Ghyll and King of Prussia mines.[17] It soon became clear that the cost of transporting the ore by horse and cart the nine miles to Drigg Station was prohibitive and as a promising 8,000 tons of ore were being mined each year a momentous decision was taken. This was to construct a 3-foot gauge railway along the valley from Ravenglass to Boot.

This enterprising gamble encouraged another group of prospectors to investigate Eskdale's other valuable mineral deposit, granite. The beautiful pink Eskdale granite, described by Nikolaus Pevsner as 'visually perhaps the most attractive granite in England', is seen in the massive pink-tinted crags, in the huge boulders of the drystone field-walls and in the farmhouses of the valley and the surrounding area. The soft, warm colour of this lovely stone gives Eskdale a unique quality among the valleys of the Lakeland, providing a pleasant contrast to the dark lavas and sombre slates found elsewhere. Unlike the Shap granite which has a similar appearance, the Eskdale granite is no longer worked, all efforts to quarry it profitably having been defeated by the difficulty of transporting the stone from so remote a site and, more recently, by the restrictions necessarily imposed on quarrying within the National Park. Eskdale has been fortunate to escape the scars suffered by more accessible places but in 1875 the opening of the Ravenglass and Eskdale Railway could so easily have decreed otherwise.

Within a year of the inauguration of the line the iron company had every reason to rejoice. Ten thousand tons of ore had been successfully transported and the future seemed assured. A gala day was held to celebrate the introduction of a passenger service to increase the revenues further but the flags had hardly been taken down when it was revealed that the company owed the contractor some £17,000 which it was not able to pay. Less than two years after its opening 'La'al Ratty' as the line was affectionately called was put into the hands of the Receiver and remained in Chancery for the next 30 years. In the 1880s the ore mines were abandoned as the veins became too difficult to work; the little railway fell into a state of neglect and was only sustained at all by the arrival of tourists. Twenty-thousand passengers were carried every year and one wonders just how many of them realised the risks they ran, for during these years the railway was 'more like one of the fancier Emmett creations than a working transport system' with a history of 'make-do-and-mend against a background of local intrigue'.[18] New attempts were made to mine iron at Christcliff and Gill Force and quarrying for granite was revived at Beckfoot and Fisherground. None of these came to anything but, for a short time, they provided a few pounds of extra revenue to enable the 'engineers' to patch up the locomotives, to put a few more nails into the disintegrating rolling stock, and to keep the track in a more or less workable condition. Tales of the line are legion, some no doubt losing nothing in the telling, but most well within the bounds of credibility when one considers the recorded improbabilities in this most eccentric of railways.

Passengers were called upon fairly frequently to push the ailing locomotives up inclines and local athletes taunted desperate engine drivers by pacing and then beating them to the next stations. It is said that the station building at Irton Road was mistakenly appropriated as a chicken coop and another consisted of an up-turned boat; that dalesmen turned down offers of a lift because they were in a hurry; that timetables went sadly awry on the many occasions when sheep, lambs or cows had to be persuaded to leave the track. There was no adequate overhaul of any part of the system for more than 30 years and the locomotives and rolling stock survived only by ingenious cannibalism as broken parts put first one and then another out of action, but as Miss Mary Fair wrote in 1903, as the speed 'never exceeded five miles per hour nervous passengers need not be deterred for it is quite within the bounds of safety to alight while the train is going at full speed'. There did appear to be a limit to the liberties permitted, however, for when a visitor to the valley stopped the struggling engine to ask the time of day, he was politely requested not to do it again as this was 'felt to be encroaching too much on the conveniences of the line'.[19]

Shortly before the First World War an adventurous but entirely misguided project was launched to revive yet again the ore mines at Nab Ghyll and the granite quarries at Beckfoot. Within weeks the Inspector of Railways declared the line unfit to be operated. Mines, quarries and railway had all ceased to function by 1913.

There followed a sequence of events as important for the future of Eskdale as they were fraught with fantasy. An enterprise known as Narrow Gauge Railways Limited, which had interests in 15-inch gauge pleasure and exhibition railways at English seaside resorts and a number of European holiday centres, acquired the Eskdale Railway from a former chairman of the company who had no legal authority to carry out such a transaction and who, it was alleged, quietly pocketed the proceeds. In great 'secrecy' and amid local rumours that it was to be extended along the valley and over Hardknott to Langdale, the track was relaid and re-equipped with the entire stock of the Narrow Gauge Company's Exhibition Line installed in Oslo and with parts of the Duke of Westminster's private model railway at Eaton Hall. Similarity to the more bizarre products of Emmett's fertile imagination now became more apparent. For in spite of the personal enthusiasm and capital of Sir Aubrey Brocklebank, chief of the Cunard Line, who did inject a little business reality by breathing new life into the granite quarries, there is a strong suspicion that from 1915 until 1948 'La'al Ratty' was little more than an opportunity for model engineers to play at running a railway. Brocklebank's successors did not share his boyish delight in this activity and, no doubt with relief, they sold the whole embarrassing liability for £12,888 and nine pence to the Keswick Granite Company.

The superior quality of the Beckfoot granite was indisputable and, either as a last desperate throw to make their acquisition worthwhile or under the illusion that they had bought the goose that laid the golden egg, the new owners planned to quarry on a gargantuan scale. On an August day in 1949 the valley echoed and re-echoed as an unprecedented blast dislodged 50,000 tons of granite. But the languishing and dispirited railway could not turn even this heroic effort into a profit and, when in 1953 the Finance Act made it no longer legal for losses of subsidiary companies to be set against the profits of the parent company, the Keswick Granite Company decided smartly to rid itself of this dubious asset. The line was put up for sale and the scrap merchants gathered for the final humiliation.

After a tense campaign to save the line it was finally rescued for the sum of £12,000 and passed into the hands of the Ravenglass and Eskdale Railway Preservation Society whose members, by virtue of Herculean efforts and a great deal of private money, were able to undertake a full-scale programme of renovation and modernisation. By 1964 the first profit for 70 years was shown as 'Ratty' became one of the Lake District's most popular tourist attractions. This popularity has steadily increased since then and the 45-minute journey gives passengers the opportunity to experience something of the delights of Eskdale without contributing to the traffic on the valley roads: as the 'biographer' of the Eskdale Railway wrote many years ago – 'It is an asset to one of Britain's finest National Parks especially at a time when motor cars threaten to choke the Lake District unless alternative transport is available.'[20] As the tiny trains thread their way from the coast through the woods and up towards the hills, it seems appropriate to reflect that an enterprise originally intended to facilitate the industrial exploitation of Eskdale should have been so successfully developed to enable many thousands of visitors to enjoy the unspoit beauty of the valley in so pleasurable a manner.

Modern travellers on the line include Rowf and Snitter, the two Plague Dogs in Richard Adams's book, who made their escape from the soldiers hunting them by stowing away on one of the trains on its journey down to the coast.

'La'al Ratty' gives to Eskdale a distinction unique among the valleys of Lakeland but even without it there is a wealth of interest in the variety of the landscape and in the history of the generations of men and women who have lived, worked and died there. No reminder of these people could be more poignant than the ruins of the many tiny stone huts scattered on the moors between Blea Tarn and Burnmoor. Some are built like miniature bank barns, others are plain, low structures with simple gables; all are of the local Eskdale granite and, when new, must have made a welcome splash of colour on these drab uplands. They have been identified as peat storage huts, or peat scales, where local folk left their cut peat to dry, later to be taken down along sledways some of which can still be traced. The depletion of the woodlands had by the mid-19th century made it necessary for them to seek out the deep peat deposits on the moors as an alternative source of fuel for cooking and to heat their cottages. It is easy to forget in an age of electricity and central-heated comfort that such basic necessities of life had to be won by so much constant effort and hard labour.[21]

Hazel nut cluster

9

THE DUDDON VALLEY

A few quaggy steps away from the Three-shire Stone on Wrynose summit the River Duddon oozes from a green and mossy hollow.[1] It is an unimpressive source in a landscape which to many may seem a bleak and inhospitable terrain: even Wordsworth commiserated with the new-born stream – 'Desolation is thy Patron Saint' – but this is more truly a scene of wild, unspoiled and invigorating grandeur, an appropriate birthplace for a river whose course was seen by Eliza Lynn Linton as 'a pathway up into a world of beauty and strength unusual and supreme'.[2] The Duddon Valley was much admired by Wordsworth and his wife, Mary, and it proved to be the inspiration for his sequence of 'Duddon Sonnets' in which he follows the river from its source to the sea. Little of importance has changed in the natural beauty of the valley since then and there are few who would dissent from the poet's view that this is, indeed, 'the most romantic of our vales'.

The Duddon gathers strength briskly as the steep fellsides above Wrynose Bottom pour down their abundant waters and within a very short distance the river presents an interesting hazard for walkers wishing to cross. Few have to make the attempt as even today this is not a popular route; and a century ago only the most intrepid of tourists chose to abandon their carriages at Cockley Beck and venture into a place which John Murray's *Handbook* warned them was no more than 'a scene of almost unmitigated desolation' where 'the river is merely a brawling mountain stream'.[3] The tourist of today, likewise, shrinks from the wilderness here and hurries on to more gentle scenes; both they and Murray might heed the words of William Green's 1818 *Guide to the Lakes*: 'What enjoyment can be experienced by those who, lolling in their chariots, confine themselves to the glimpses to be obtained from their windows'.[4]

The Roman legionary had no choice. As he pounded out the miles of Highway Ten between Ambleside and Ravenglass his route from Wrynose summit to Hardknott Fort ran alongside or within sight of the infant Duddon, a spectacular but arduous stretch of this short and hazardous road. Along Wrynose Bottom we may follow in his footsteps on the north bank of the river. We cross the river where he crossed it – first about a mile or so from the Three-shire Stone, a second time just beyond Gaitscale Close, and finally at Cockley Beck Bridge. Here the Roman road parts company with the Duddon as it swings in its steep zig-zags up to Hardknott Pass. Except for short distances where it coincides with the line of the modern road, the Roman highway is now only a somewhat boggy footpath. On it we may savour the freedom of the wilderness or deplore its desolation, enjoy the dashing vitality of the tumbling waters or think only of shelter from the driving rain; and we may be sure that our thoughts will not be far removed from those of the Roman soldier on the same spot 1,800 years ago, dreaming of his home in Dalmatia or looking forward to the hot baths less than half an hour's march away in Hardknott Fort.[5]

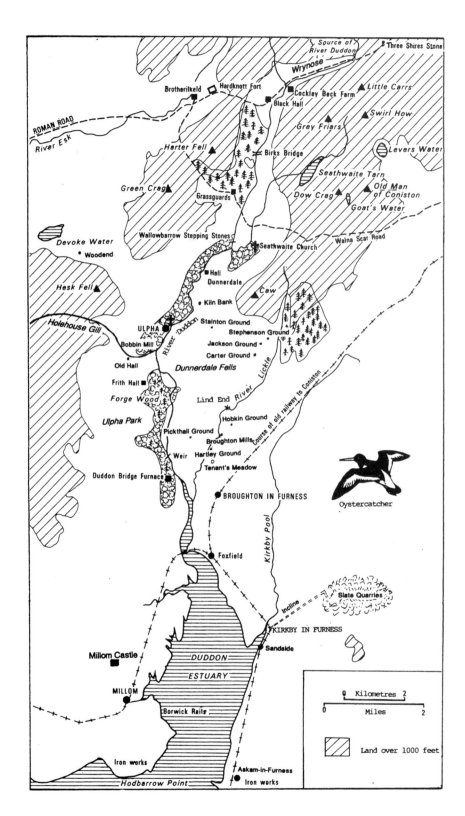

Source of River Duddon

Three Shires Stone

Wrynose

Brotherilkeld

Hardknott Fort

Cockley Beck Farm

Little Carrs

Black Hall

ROMAN ROAD

Swirl How

River Esk

Grey Friars

Harter Fell

Birks Bridge

Levers Water

Green Crag

Seathwaite Tarn

Old Man of Coniston

Grassguards

Dow Crag

Goat's Water

Devoke Water

Wallowbarrow Stepping Stones

Walna Scar Road

Woodend

Seathwaite Church

Hesk Fell

Hall Dunnerdale

Caw

Kiln Bank

Holehouse Gill

Stainton Ground

ULPHA

Stephenson Ground

Bobbin Mill

Jackson Ground

Old Hall

Carter Ground

Dunnerdale Fells

Frith Hall

Forge Wood

Lind End

Ulpha Park

Hobkin Ground

Pickthall Ground

Broughton Mills

Weir Hartley Ground

Duddon Bridge Furnace

Tenant's Meadow

BROUGHTON IN FURNESS

Oystercatcher

Foxfield

Kirkby Pool

Slate Quarries

Incline

KIRKBY IN FURNESS

Millom Castle

Sandside

MILLOM

DUDDON ESTUARY

Borwick Rails

Kilometres

Miles

Iron works

Land over 1000 feet

Askam-in-Furness

Iron works

Hodbarrow Point

DUDDON VALLEY

The upper reaches of the Duddon Valley were in battle array much more recently than this. Sixty years ago the quiet farmsteads of Black Hall and Cockley Beck were at the centre of a bitter controversy, with the Government on the one hand and the National Trust, the Friends of the Lake District and an influential section of public opinion on the other. In 1935 the Forestry Commission, already unpopular following the insensitive plantations in Thornthwaite and Ennerdale, acquired over seven thousand acres of the Muncaster Estate in the upper valleys of the Duddon and the Esk and proposed to establish there the Hardknott Forest Park. This nefarious plan to submerge these wild uplands under a sea of conifers led to a public outcry notable for its energy, eloquence and polemic and for its total condemnation of the scheme. A petition against any further State Forests in the Lake District was signed by 13,000 people; Sir William Beveridge proclaimed that 'This is holy ground'; and the Reverend H.H. Symonds, founder of the Friends of the Lake District, demanded to know if this was truly an appropriate place for the State to grow trees for profit. Forestry Commission officials were received in the district with the same chilly contempt as the excisemen of earlier times, and eventually the forces of bureaucracy bowed before the storm. An Agreement in 1936 ended all further proposals for afforestation of any kind in 300 square miles of central Lakeland. The battle resumed, however, when plantations threatened to engulf the farms of Black Hall by the Duddon and Butterilket in Upper Eskdale. Once more the Commission gave way, selling to the National Trust some six thousand acres of the disputed land. This, and the creation of the new Forest of Dunnerdale, began a happier period of more fruitful co-operation between the foresters and the public. Dunnerdale Forest is now an accepted feature of the landscape enjoyed by naturalists, geologists, horse riders and walkers, with waymarked paths to guide them and a delightful picnic site at Froth Pot. The Lakeland landscape is no longer under threat from massive regiments of conifers but enriched by a diversity of tree species and a more sensitive approach to forest plantations.

Emotional prejudice and aesthetic controversy have often obscured certain important facts of the Lakeland ecology. The science of pollen analysis has established that in pre-historic times, perhaps 4,000 years ago, most of the land up to about 2,000ft. was covered with extensive broad-leaved forest which renewed and protected the soil at these high levels. Subsequent clearances of these woodlands for the purposes of industry and agriculture resulted in severe impoverishment and devastating erosion of the soil making regeneration of the forest impossible. The only known way in which such de-graded soil can be restored to stability and fertility is by planting coniferous trees, preferably spruce, larch and pine. The native English oak, hazel, ash, birch and willow flourish only in deeper, richer soils; for the foreseeable future their variety and colour will not adorn the uplands. Not that the 'alien conifers' are lacking in either variety or colour: the springtime loganberry-red flowers and the autumn gold of the European larch, the silvery sheen of the Sitka spruce and the long, pendulous brown cones of the Norway spruce, the blue-green needles and orange twigs of the Japanese larch, and the warm russet stems and deep green foliage of the Scots pine, all lend enhancement to the landscape when planted sympathetically. Nor should we forget that these new forests quickly become the home of many birds, mammals and insects. Dunnerdale Forest itself provides shelter and food for roe deer and red deer, for buzzards, sparrowhawks, crossbills, and three species of owl, for weasels, stoats and the rare pine marten. The scene above Birks Bridge has changed a great deal since Eliza Lynn Linton was here but she would still find within the unfamiliar forest that 'the fellside and river meadows are covered in sweet gale and the loveliest bog plants are to be found here'. Indeed there is a strange irony in the tale she tells of the stranger she met in the inn near Pen Hill who, when asked where in the valley he had visited, replied 'As far as it is finished': perhaps Dunnerdale Forest has 'finished' it![6]

The stretch of the Duddon below Birks Bridge has inspired poets, guidebook writers and generations of appreciative visitors. Wordsworth's 'Duddon Sonnets' were inspired by these few miles of scenic beauty which, remote, unspoilt and scarcely touched by the works of urban man, are still considered by many to be the most idyllic part of Lakeland, 'a reach of the Duddon', as John Murray put it, which 'once seen can never be effaced from the memory', exhorting his readers to leave their carriages the better to enjoy this 'continuous series of pictures, a combination of rock, wood and water seldom equalled'.[7]

And, now as then, when the elements blot out this enchanting scene, when the rain drives and the bleak winds roar, there can be no more congenial place than the cosy *Newfield Inn*

> to seek the warm hearth, exalt the mantling ale, and
> Laugh with generous household heartily
> At all the merry pranks of Donnerdale.

Now, as then, we may wonder at the magic symbol engraved on the Seathwaite Footbridge or share the delight of youthful spirits dallying on the Seathwaite Stepping Stones: 'To stop ashamed, too timid to advance'.[8] The Duddon flows close by the church at Seathwaite and the inn at Newfield where in 1804 William and Dorothy Wordsworth stayed and were delighted to discover that their supper of char caught in Seathwaite Tarn, their overnight lodging, their breakfast, ale and horse fodder amounted to only four shillings and sixpence. The inn still offers hospitality to visitors to the valley but the church there is no longer the old chapel known to the Wordsworths; this, much to Ruskin's displeasure, was replaced in 1874 by zealous rebuilders. The original chapel may have been an Elizabethan foundation built by one of the Earls of Derby. This was a secluded living in the outermost limits of the County of Lancaster, with a minimal stipend and unlikely to bring promotion in the Church or to provide many of the material comforts of life. Nor would its priest find much opportunity for scholarly or gentlemanly company. It was, therefore, a parish where one would be most likely to find 'a pastor such as Chaucer's verse portrays':[9]

> riche he was of hooly thoght and werk.
> He was also a lerned man, a clerk
> That Christe's gospel trewely wolde preche;
> His parisshens devoutly wolde he teche.[10]

Such a man was the Reverend Robert Walker, curate of Seathwaite for more than sixty-six years. He died on 25 June 1802, in his 93rd year, just a few months after his wife, Anne (also in her 93rd year), a local girl, mother of their 10 children and devoted companion in his ministry. The parish register records that Robert Walker was a man notable for his temperance, industry and integrity – qualities regrettably not widely reported among the clergy of the 18th century, many of whom were better known for their aspirations to the rank and life-style of the country gentry. Walker was no well-endowed Parson Woodforde; his Seathwaite stipend amounted to no more than £5 per annum and on this it was clearly impossible for him 'to feast his people on sirloin of beef roasted and leg of mutton boiled and plumb puddings in plenty ... and as much liquor as they would drink'.[11] But if he could not dispense largesse such as this to his flock, 'Wonderful Walker' had much of more practical value to offer: he 'was schoolmaster and doctor of the district; he made Wills and prepared and engrossed Deeds, was the amanuensis of his uneducated parishioners, sold home-brewed beer, cultivated his glebe with his own hands, spun wool, made his own clothing, and worked for wages at haymaking and sheepshearing'.[12] He was a skilled shepherd and craftsman, a well-known Hebrew scholar, and, above all, a conscientious parish priest devoted especially to the children and to his own family. The *Annual Register* for 1760 describes how a visitor to the parsonage found Walker 'with a child upon his knee, eating his breakfast; his wife and the remainder of his children were some of them employed in waiting upon each other, the rest in teazing and spinning wool, at which trade he is very proficient; and, moreover, when it is ready for sale, will lay it, by 16 or 32 pounds weight, upon his back, and on foot, seven or eight miles, will carry it to the market (at Broughton) even in the depth of winter'. Several generations of Seathwaite children were taught to read, to understand the Christian faith and to appreciate the wonders of nature by this remark- able man who loved to share with his pupils his love of learning and his enthusiasm for fossils, plants, flowers, animals and insects. Like the later and more famous educationist, Robert Dawes, Walker's aim was 'to instruct them in the school of surrounding nature, and to bring their minds to bear upon the everyday work of life'.[13] There can be few more appealing pictures of a teacher than that of Wonderful Walker seated with his charges in his chapel 'within the rails of the altar; the communion table was his desk ... and he employed himself at the spinning wheel while the children repeated their lessons by his side'.[14] Walker's grave is in the churchyard of Seathwaite Church and by the porch is the 'clipping stone' on which he used to shear the sheep at lonely Gatescale Farm high above the Duddon on Wrynose Pass.

A life of hard work and thrift enabled Walker to leave in his will the small fortune of £2,000 and it was this, it would seem, which led the high-principled Mrs Lynn Linton to voice her dissent from the customary adulation. Wonderful Walker, she wrote, was 'not so wonderful after all, but simply a shrewd and thrifty "stateman-priest" who knew how to turn an honest penny with the best of them ... (he was) in no wise superior to many others of the ancient parson class in the mountain district, save in the ability to make money by a variety of means, even including that of unlicensed beer-selling'.[15] There speaks a true daughter of the Victorian cathedral close!

A few miles beyond Seathwaite Church, at the junction of the valley road and the steep moorland road to Eskdale, is a house which was once an inn known as *The Travellers' Rest*. This features in Hugh Walpole's novel *The Bright Pavilions* as the starting point for Philip Irvine's plot to settle his account with Nicholas Herries, a dramatic journey which led to the murder of the farmer and his wife at Crosbythwaite and to Irvine's own death at the hands of local avengers by the shore of Devoke Water. Coleridge stayed at the inn, too, and, rather patronisingly perhaps, declared the landlord to be 'a very intelligent man'. This might well have been the same landlord who, according to the anecdote related by Harriet Martineau, gave a group of arrogant students their well-deserved come-uppance: they planned to enjoy themselves at the landlord's expense by demanding that he should present their account in Latin – he sent it to them in faultless Greek and the crestfallen jokers were compelled to ask for an English translation.[16]

A short distance downstream, standing high above the Duddon, is 'the Kirk at Ulpha', first recorded on Saxton's map of 1577 and probably of late medieval founda- tion, although much restored. St John's Church is an unpretentious dales chapel with its thick walls, exposed beams and tiny bellcote. Inside are some good examples of local craftsmanship: a churchwarden made the altar from a huge cherry tree; a local carpenter made the pulpit; the brass metalwork and woodcarving were the work of the parish priest; an enterprising parishioner created the pitch-pipe to ensure that the services should not be without music whenever the fiddler could not attend. A number of 17th- and 18th-century wall-paintings were discovered in 1934. It is a peaceful, idyllic spot as William and Mary Wordsworth found when they spent two hours here over their lunch sitting in the church porch, 'soothed by the unseen river's gentle roar'.

Not every dalesman in the Vale of Duddon worshipped at Ulpha Church. The stronghold of Quakerism at Swarthmoor Hall was but a short distance away and it is no surprise to find that the Quakers were well established in the area near the Duddon. There was a Quaker Meeting House — still known as the Quakers' House — high on Birker Moor at Woodend and a Quaker Burial Ground down in the valley not far from the river. The latter is now a rather neglected walled enclosure containing a few pine trees near the old track between Ulpha Bridge and Kiln Bank: it is known as The Sepulchre and was last used in 1755.

Methodists and Baptists arrived in the 19th century but their chapels failed to survive. The public path from The Low, the former Baptist Chapel, goes across the meadows to the river and marks the route taken for the ritual baptism by immersion performed in the waters of the Duddon.

Ulpha once possessed an important treasure from an age long before any of these post-Reformation forms of religion appeared on the scene. This was a fine ivory carved diptych depicting a well-known biblical story in exquisite detail. The craftsmanship of this work led those who were fortunate enough to see it to believe that it could have come only from the abbey at Furness. A similar diptych was also seen in Eskdale.[17]

Standing dark and jagged against the skyline above Ulpha the ruins of Frith Hall have caught the eye of many visitors to Dunnerdale but to most of them these gaunt, ivy-covered fingers of ancient stone have remained a mystery. Frith Hall, was, in fact, built, probably in the 16th century, as a hunting lodge for the Hudleston family who had established an enclosed deer park in the area as early as the 13th century. It seems likely that Frith Hall replaced Ulpha Old Hall when the latter became too old and austere for comfort. The ruins of the Old Hall may be seen about one kilometre to the north-west of Frith Hall strategically sited above the ravine of Holehouse Gill, and it is believed that it was built as a defensive fortified house — possibly a pele tower with a farmhouse attached — a theory supported by the evidence of the boulder-built walls some of which are six feet thick.[18]

The wide and unchallenged power of the Hudlestons as Lords of Millom and masters of Ulpha Park came to an end with the victory of the Roundheads in the English Civil War. The Royalist sympathies of the Hudlestons cost them dear and resulted in a sudden and severe decline in their fortunes. Frith Hall was abandoned and eventually became an inn of somewhat dubious reputation. Its wild and romantic situation, with its dramatic and exhilarating view over the Duddon towards the distant, dark-blue ramparts of the highest fells, made it an ideal refuge for eloping couples whose runaway marriages were often performed here. In 1730 no fewer than 17 such ceremonies were celebrated in these rooms now obscured by fallen rubble and open to the sky. These clandestine romances, and doubtless other questionable activities, were facilitated by Frith Hall's convenient position on the minor coach road which led over Corney Fell.[19] Such a place must, inevitably, have its ghost and here one may come across the spirit of William Marshall, described as a 'sojourner', who was murdered on this spot on 10 October 1736. After this, little is known of the history of Frith Hall except that by the early 19th century it had become a farm.

Ulpha Park, the deer enclosure established by the medieval Hudlestons, was part of the great Forest of Millom which covered the whole Duddon valley and, even though the process of disafforestation was well advanced by the 18th century, the remaining wood-lands were still extensive and provided the raw materials for a number of important industries. It is not difficult to trace the remains of these earlier industries in Duddondale. Not far from Ulpha Bridge stands the old bobbin mill which produced wooden bobbins for the Lancashire textile mills until 1910. Each bobbin maker turned out an average of 13,000 bobbins each week and the demands made on the resources of the coppiced woodlands were enormous and continuous. The remains of the great mill chimney still stand to remind us that this was once a busy industrial site where workers toiled long hours in deafening noise and swirling dust, slaves to endlessly repetitive work at danger-ous and fast-moving machinery. Nor, apparently, did the apprentices at the Ulpha mill find any comfort in the food provided for them: they insisted on a clause in their contract of work which stipulated that they should not be given salmon on more than three days each week! Today's luxury was clearly yesterday's surfeit!

Other ancient industries of these Duddon woodlands included the making of 'swills' or all-purpose baskets, bark-peeling for the tanning industry, the manufacture of barrels, casks and kegs (the cooper's trade) and of hoops to go with them, the turning of handles for farm and household implements, the brush-making industry and the cutting of timber for fuel. Nor should one forget that many women, and often children too, were busy producing thousands of birch-twig besoms.[20]

But by far the most important woodland industry was charcoal burning. The round 'platforms' or pitsteads can be found in many places in the Duddon woods but the charcoal-burners' little round huts have long disappeared. The great demand for char-coal here was for iron smelting and, although there were also copper mines on land above the bobbin mill, it was the iron industry which dominated this stretch of the Duddon from the 16th to the late 19th centuries, from Ulpha Park to the river estuary. In the name 'Forge Wood' we make our first acquaint-ance with the small 'bloomeries' or smelt-ing hearths of the early years of this indus-try. Ulpha Forge was worked in the late

21   *Charcoal burning: a reconstruction in Grisedale Forest*

16th and early 17th centuries by the Hudleston family who appear to have become quite prosperous on the proceeds, for in 1625 Sir William Hudleston received no less than £300 per annum in rent from his son, Ferdinando, for this forge alone, a clear indication of its value and importance. Another such bloomery may be seen at Stonestar but of far greater significance was the massive furnace at Duddon Bridge, a few miles downstream, the most famous charcoal-burning furnace in the north.[21]

Iron came to Duddon Bridge in 1736.[22] The Cunsey Iron Company saw that this site had the important advantages of an abundant supply of coppice woods for charcoal, plentiful water power, and ready access to water transport as the ore could be brought to and the processed iron sent out from small quays along the Duddon.[23] Coastal ship-ping could reach the tiny estuary harbour at Borwick Rails to bring in ore by sea from John Curwen's mines at Harrington and to carry the finished iron to various ports as far afield as Chepstow. Duddon iron was ranked with the best quality Swedish iron and was in great demand. Ore was also transported more laboriously by road from Lindal Moor.

Among the notable design features of the Duddon Furnace were the huge iron bellows and the mechanism which operated them. These were the invention of the great 18th-century iron-masters, Isaac and John Wilkinson, and were unquestionably master-pieces of skill and ingenuity. Water-power was used throughout the working life of this furnace and a half-mile watercourse had to be cut from a weir on the Duddon up-stream.[24]

When the final blast was blown in 1867 Duddon Bridge furnace was one of the last charcoal furnaces in the country – only Newland and Backbarrow survived longer – and with its demise a unique episode in the history of the Duddon Valley came to an end. After 230 years silence descended on the woodlands which had surrounded this scene of industry and would soon almost engulf it as nature reclaimed its own. The furnace was stripped during the First World War and for many years afterwards steadily fell into ruin. Only the efforts of conservation groups in the late 1980s rescued it from eventual obliteration and it is now an interesting and informative place to visit, one of our most important sites of industrial archaeology.[25]

Vastly more conspicuous but infinitely less attractive is the Duddon's other industrial relic – the extensive scars of the former iron mines on either side of the smooth flat sands of the river estuary. For over a century this was the scene of a mining enterprise involving all the skill and inventiveness, all the triumphs and failures and all the sweat and perseverance of a great capitalist venture in the heyday of British industrial supremacy, and also in the disillusion of its 20th-century decline.

22   *Duddon Bridge: Iron Furnace*

In 1850 H.W. Schneider discovered the second largest deposit of haematite ore in Britain on the east bank of the Duddon estuary near the village of Askam-in-Furness.[26] This was a continuous mass of ore calculated at between eight and nine million tons and, most important of all, it was a non-phosporic ore, then urgently needed in the manufacture of steel. For many years these mines supplied almost all the requirements of the Bessemer Convertor process and by 1856 over 120,000 tons of ore were mined annually. Forty years of prosperity were succeeded by a rapid decline as the costs of mining became uncompetitive and by 1916 the operation had virtually ceased.[27]

Soon after Schneider's discovery at Askam, Nathaniel Caine, a Liverpool businessman, and John Barratt, a mining engineer who had already breathed new life into the copper mines at Coniston, founded the Hodbarrow Mining Company on the opposite shore of the estuary near the hamlet of Millom and lonely Hodbarrow Point. Caine and Barratt were the successors of a line of prospectors who since the 17th century had sought their fortune from mining ore on this site, and at first, as Caine's *Journal* reveals, it seemed that they, too, would retire defeated:

> We spent upwards of £3000 in our first operations without getting any ore and did not divide any profits till over £57,000 had been expended during a period of about 10 years.

But at the end of these 10 years he was able to write: 'So far ... we have discovered one Million Tons of Ore' and with the discovery of yet more massive deposits annual output was by 1880 well over 340,000 tons. Much of the ore was in such close proximity to the shoreline that on two occasions – in 1885 and in 1900 – barriers or sea-walls had to be constructed to enable mining to continue. These barriers were remarkable achievements of civil engineering, the Inner Barrier being a concrete wall and a bank of puddled clay well over one thousand yards in length, the Outer Barrier a mile-long semi-circle of concrete blocks weighing 25 tons each with quantities of limestone rubble and a water-tight heart of clay re-inforced with steel and timber piles. These measures and an enterprising management ensured continued prosperity: production steadily increased reaching an average of about 500,000 tons a year in the later years of the century and a peak of 545,736 tons in 1907. At the same time profits remained healthy and the average wage rose from about £1.28 to £2.04 a week. It was 'a period of prosperity so great that in retrospect these years assumed an almost mythical quality'.[28]

The few farms and cottages of Millom were swallowed up in a sprawling mining district as the whole area became a landscape of craters, engine houses, pumping sheds, chimneys, furnaces, storage buildings, tramways, railways, workshops and offices, all surrounded by spoilheaps and muddy pools. The air was full of noise and the sound of unfamiliar accents from Ireland, Scotland, Cornwall, Yorkshire and other mining regions. The diminutive harbour at Borwick Rails developed into a port handling over a thousand ships each week. The scenic contrast with the higher reaches of the Duddon could not be more manifest.

The Hodbarrow Mine came under Government control during the First World War and this did nothing to ensure its long-term efficiency and there occurred a dangerous and extensive robbing of safety pillars. In the 1920s and '30s the company was beset by labour troubles, by an adverse change in the iron trade, by increasing costs and falling profits, and in 1932 by yet another invasion by the sea. Early closure seemed inevitable but the urgent need for ore of the high quality mined at Hodbarrow during the Second World War, whatever the cost, provided a reprieve. But these were abnormal conditions and with the return of an international competitive market the problems of the mine were fully exposed. The last manager summed up the position concisely: 'The mine closed as the getting of ore was uneconomical due to the shape of the deposits, the method of working and the increasing cost of materials and pumping.'[29] 1968 marked the end of an era in the history of Millom and of the Duddon Estuary.

The Victorian streets of Millom bear eloquent witness to the impact of the Hodbarrow mining operation: 'For more than a century the mine was instrumental in changing not only the appearance but also the prospects of the district, and such a legacy will not soon be forgotten.'[30]

Long forgotten are the days when Millom was the 'capital' not only of the Forest of Millom but also of the Manor of Hougun which in medieval times embraced the whole of the Duddon Valley and most of Eskdale. Once the property of the Danish Earls of Northumbria, this mysterious manor passed in 1092 to Roger of Poitou, the great Norman baron whose lands included much of the old county of Lancashire and Furness. Millom remained as the administrative centre of a powerful and extensive barony under the Normans and in the 12th century a strong and imposing castle arose to re-affirm that the new Lords of Millom were here to stay. For 500 years from the mid-13th century the castle and its lands were in the hands of the Hudleston family who retained control until the great estate was broken up in the 18th century. The castle has long been in ruins and it is one of the most neglected of all our Norman castles, receiving little attention from historians and rarely mentioned in guidebooks. Yet, as Dr. Angus Winchester has shown, there are important surviving records which 'provide a rare glimpse of life on a northern English manor house in the early 16th century', giving a comprehensive picture not only of the farming and industrial management of the estate but details of the domestic economy of the household. So we learn that they ate mainly wheaten bread while the vast quantities of oats they grew went to make ale, dog bran and fodder for the stables; that their fish diet included turbot, salmon, herrings, eels and 'salted porpas'; that they had a special taste for butter, eggs, beef and 'crokes' (old Herdwick sheep which produced tasty mutton). We read, too, of their clothing – linen shirts and smocks, sheepskin gloves and jackets, fine doublets and coarse working clothes, and, touchingly, an insight into the wardrobe of 'Little Anne'.[31] This once formidable fortress overlooking the Duddon sands

23   *Millom Castle*

may be no more than a ghost of its former self but it may still have much to tell us about the lives of all those who lived in its shadow throughout the Duddon Valley and Upper Eskdale, on the sheepfarms of Black Combe and in the woodlands of Furness.

The Duddon Channel was a highway not only for iron from Duddon Bridge, Askam and Hodbarrow but also for the highly-prized 'Westmorland Dark Blue Slate' from the still active quarries at Kirkby-in-Furness. It is uncertain when these quarries were first worked – possibly as early as the 17th century – but by the beginning of the 19th century contemporary writers refer to slate being loaded on to vessels from the Duddon sands nearby and from the tiny port of Sandside (or Angerton as the shipping records prefer to name it) 'conveyed in small four-wheeled wagons on an iron rail-way'.[31] After the opening of the Furness Railway in 1846 an inclined-plane railway carried the slate from the quarries to the station at Sandside. Much of the embankment of this line is still in place, now a public footpath leading to the Duddon sands.

Today the Duddon Estuary is no longer an industrial highway but an internationally famous Nature Reserve. In 1675 Edmund Sandford described the Duddon here as 'a brave river where the famousest cockles of all England is gathered in the sands, scraped out with hooks like sickles, and brave salmons and flookes, the bravest in England, hung up and dried like bacon', and 200 years later Mrs. Lynn Linton maintained that the Duddon cockles were still 'the best and finest in the North country', gathered at the rate of 8,553,600 cockles a month, there being 90 cockles to the quart![33] Cockles are no longer a fashionable or popular dish and it is doubtful whether Duddon cockles would now have a wide appeal, bred as they are in mud and sand polluted by industry and nuclear waste. Today it is not cockles but birdlife, rare flora and a colony of natterjack toads which give the Duddon Estuary a special place in European nature conservation. It is a 'Wetland of International Importance' as defined by the Ramsar Convention; it is protected by the Bern Convention on the Conservation of European Wildlife and Natural Habitats; it is a Special Protection Area under the European Directive for the Conservation of Wild Birds; and it is a National Nature Reserve. This extensive area of saltmarshes, sand dunes, mud flats, slacks and wetlands provides habitats for a significant proportion of the British and European population of curlew, dunlin, merganser, oyster-catcher, pintail, ringed plover, sanderling and shelduck, together with large numbers of Arctic and little terns and other migratory birds; and it is the breeding ground of more than 20 per cent of the national population of natterjack toads. As we stand on the high dunes of Sandscale Haws to watch the Duddon finally lose itself in the sea, we may find below us a colourful tapestry woven from the silvery sheen of the sea purslane, the yellows and purples of the sea lavender and the sea aster, the delicate pink of the creeping rest harrow, the soft blue-green of the sea holly, the creamy-yellow of the Isle of Man cabbage, and the elusive pinks and purples of several rare and precious orchids.

From this vantage point, too, we may enjoy a surprising and spectacular view into the Lakeland fells and over the landscape through which the Duddon has run its course. And with Wordsworth we may reflect on the life-story of the Duddon from its birth as a sparkling spring in the mosses of Wrynose Summit to its death in the silent vastness of the sea.

Wordsworth had a particular affection for the Duddon – he spoke of it as his 'favourite river', and in his valedictory sonnet he expressed this in four lines of his most memorable poetry:

> For backward, Duddon! as I cast my eyes,
> I see what was, and is, and will abide;
> Still glides the stream, and shall for ever glide;
> The Form remains, the Function never dies.[34]

As the Duddon flows into its estuarine marshes it is joined by a tiny tributary, the River Lickle, which in its short course of six miles has steadily converged on the course of the Duddon through its own special and little-known valley hidden on the eastern border of the Dunnerdale Fells. From its source among the pikes on the north-west flanks of Caw the Lickle has cut a channel along the narrow band of Coniston limestone which separates the rocky terrain and craggy peaks of the Borrowdale volcanics of Dunnerdale from the gentler landscape of the Silurian shale country of South Lakeland. Until its waters reach the flatlands near the estuary the Lickle is a secluded river which has to be sought out in damp, rocky ravines and silent woods where tiny ancient bridges and the crumbling remains of human habitation remind one that once this was the home of a simple farming community. Above and by the Lickle are farms or the ruins of farms which have a special significance in the history of High Furness. This land was part of the vast estates of Furness Abbey and in the early 16th century the Abbot signed a series of agreements with its tenants here which permitted the enclosure of the unimproved grazing in order to create new farms. These farmsteads were called 'grounds' and usually bore the name of the family with whom the agreement was made. Of 36 'grounds' in Furness seven are in or near the Lickle Valley, some now abandoned, others still working farms. So between Duddon and Lickle we find Carter Ground, Hartley Ground, Hobkin Ground, Jackson Ground, Pickthall Ground, Stainton Ground and Stephenson Ground, all of which made a contribution to a change in the Lakeland landscape almost five hundred years ago. Paradoxically the Lickle Valley retained into the 20th century an example of the open-field system of agriculture. Just to the south of Hartley Ground is Tenants Meadow, a common field which until the First World War was still managed, mown and grazed by seven farmers whose strips were marked off by 'meir stones' which, it was decreed at a meeting in 1900, each farm must keep in repair so that they 'stand up well out of the grass that they may be seen in cutting'. A study of Tenants Meadow made in the 1920s described the details of the system of agricultural management as it was operated in this remarkable survival from a long-vanished age.[35]

Few visitors walk the paths by the River Lickle: those who do will come across the remains of past industry – a potash kiln, a charcoal pitstead, an abandoned quarry; or, if botany is their pleasure, they will find rare plants of the mountain bogs on the Lickle's infant reaches and by the lovely Dunnerdale tarns, a colourful tapestry of flowers in the meadowlands and the shady woodlands and, as the river merges with the Duddon among the wetlands of the estuary, a springtime blaze of kingcups and the muted colours of the strange plantlife which thrives at the edge of the tide.

Natterjack toad

I *Borrowdale*

II *Newlands Valley: view towards the head of the valley*

III *Buttermere Valley: Buttermere Lake with Fleetwith Pike*

IV *Vale of Lorton: view across the valley to Whiteside and Grasmoor*

V   *Ennerdale Water with Pillar and Steeple*

VI   *Wasdale: Wastwater and the Screes*

VII   *Miterdale: the River Mite with Scafell*

VIII   *Throstle Garth Bridge and Lingcove Beck*

IX   *Duddon Valley: the Stepping Stones, Wallowbarrow Crag*

X   *Winster Valley: Undermillbeck Common*

XI   *Lyth Valley: Damson blossom*

XII   *Kentdale: the head of the valley*

XIII   *Long Sleddale: Sadgill*

XIV *Patterdale: Hartsop Dodd and Brothers Water*

XV *Martindale Common and St Martin's Church*

XVI   *Vale of St John: Castlerigg Stone Circle*

XVII   *Blea Tarn and the Langdale Pikes*

10

THE WINSTER VALLEY

Two rivers rise only a short distance apart in the quiet uplands just south of Windermere Town. In their infancy they flow on almost parallel courses through a landscape formed by glacial debris but now lovely in its confusion and variety. Eventually the River Gilpin turns away toward the flat and fertile Lyth Valley to the east of Whitbarrow Scar while the Winster continues on its direct southerly course, winding its way through rocky hillocks, craggy woodlands and undulating pastures: it passes under ancient bridges on shady lanes leading to scattered white-washed farms, flowing finally along strict and channelled courses among the meadows and marshes of Meathop and so into the sandy estuary of the Kent.

The Winster Valley is gentle unspoilt country. For walkers who do not seek the high fells this is bliss: the rambling lanes have little traffic, the noises heard are only those of the countryside, and the many footpaths and bridleways are undemanding and well-marked. This is no place to hurry or measure time and distance, for here there is an infinite variety of scenic gems, a wealth of bird-and plant-life, a succession of woods and hedgerows, tiny streams and glimpses of small tarns, tempting grassy knolls to sit and admire the scene, with neat cottages and farms lying discreetly in sheltered hollows, their white walls shining bright against the many shades of green. Here it is easy to share the thoughts of the poet John Clare, when he wrote:

> How pleasant it is thus to think and roam
> The many paths scarce knowing which to choose
> All full of pleasant scenes – then wander home
> And o'er the beauties we have met to muse.[1]

These beauties are not entirely nature's handiwork. For nature left only chaos and disorder in the wake of the glacier which spilt over the col at the head of the valley and ground its way slowly down to the sea. On the way the rocks and debris it carried were deposited as the ice melted leaving a scene of unappealing disarray which time and man transformed into the fortuitous harmony we see today.

When man first arrived in this valley we do not know but there is no trace of human settlement before the appearance of the Anglian and Norse colonisation in the 9th and 10th centuries. A few names of Anglian origin are found near the coast – Helton, Newton and Meathop – but most of the Winster valley place-names are Norse.[2]

In later years some of these early farmsteads became the sites of 'manor houses' which are still a feature of the Winster landscape. The surviving records of Cowmire Hall and Burblethwaite Hall make it quite clear that these were substantial holdings: the owners of Cowmire aspired to emulate the Stricklands of Sizergh by building a pele-tower house in the 16th century, when the need for such fortress homes had passed, and adding a six-bay residence in the following century; the Burblethwaite estate had its own corn mill, iron forge and drying kilns, with 64 acres of orchards and arable land and pasture on the fells.[3] No powerful aristocratic family ever established a base here (other

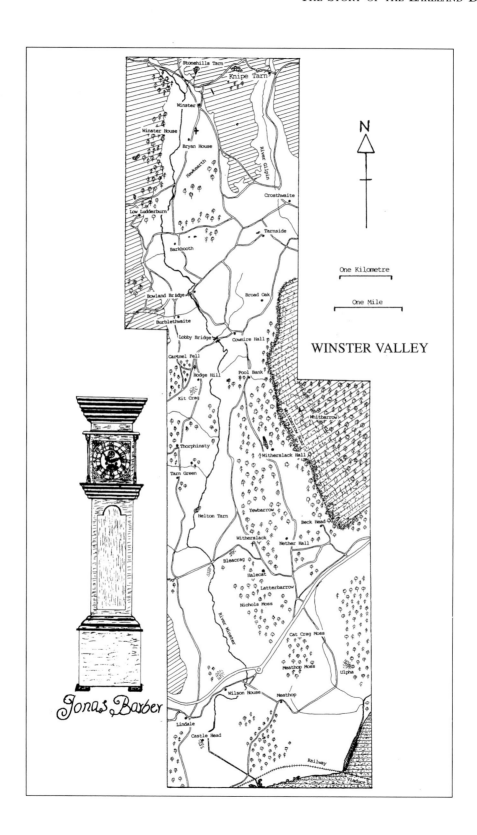

WINSTER VALLEY

One Kilometre

One Mile

N

Jonas Barber

than a brief tenure of Witherslack Hall by the Earl of Derby) and only two families were ever given the title of 'Esquire'. Even so, the history of such homesteads as Burblethwaite, Ludderburn, Cowmire, Hodge Hill, Thorphinsty and Nether Hall indicates an unusual number of prosperous yeomen none of whom were socially pre-eminent or possessed of significant estate. The 43 extant wills from the valley between 1536 and 1727[4] reveal that by far the wealthiest inhabitant was Brian Philipson of Hodge Hill who left estate to the value of £471 10s., a modest fortune in those times. Yet these moderately wealthy northerners showed the same sense of social responsibility as their more affluent southern counterparts in the bequests they made to charitable and educational causes. Susannah Briggs bequeathed £12, the interest on which was to provide one dozen loaves of bread to be distributed to the poor at Cartmel Fell Chapel on the first Sunday of every month; Lawrence Newton gave the house at The Height for use as a Quaker Meeting House and Miles Birkett left 10

24   *Cowmire Hall*

shillings to assist the Friends there; Benjamin Fletcher provided £200, the interest on which was to be used to maintain four teachers at schools in Staveley, Lindale, Flookburgh and Cartmell Fell; and John Barwick, a famous native of the valley, founded the school and church at Witherslack.[5] Bequests for the relief of the poor were customary as was the financial assistance given by the parish to pay for apprentices to serve their time: in 1748 John Philipson was paid 15 shillings to put his son as an apprentice to Jonas Barber, the famous Winster clocksmith.

Three generations of the Barber family brought national fame to the Vale of Winster. All were clockmakers of high repute but it was Jonas Barber the second who showed the unique touch of creative genius which has made Barber clocks renowned for distinguished and original craftsmanship. Born in Skipton in 1688, Jonas was the son of John Barber, clockmaker in that town. In 1717 he married Elizabeth Garnett of High Mill, half a mile north of Winster village, and for 10 years he carried on his craft at Bowland Bridge. He then moved to Bryan House, just south of Winster, and for the next 37 years until his death in 1764 this secluded spot in a remote northern valley became the centre of design, expertise and craftsmanship for some of the finest clocks ever produced by an English clocksmith. As Barber's recent biographer comments: 'If this had happened in the midst of a centre of clockmaking and clocksmiths it would not seem so remarkable. But ... in Winster [it] is really astonishing.' Jonas's work was continued, with rather less creative flair, by his son in the later years of the 18th century. Fine examples of Barber clocks and an unusual watch may be seen in the Abbot Hall Art Gallery in Kendal.[6]

At the time when the Barbers were engaged in their fine engineering the rest of the valley folk were occupied in the more conventional and traditional activities of a farming community. Sheep farming had long been the main agricultural concern and from this had developed naturally a local textile industry which provided employment and income for spinners, weavers, fullers, carders and all the other skills needed in the processes of wool manufacture. In addition, the woodlands here, as in other Lakeland valleys, created their own industries: timber for building, bark for tanning, staves for the cooper, oak and hazel strips for the hooper and the makers of spelks and corves, coppice poles for the bobbin mills, birch twigs for besoms, and withies for the Winster basket weavers. The smoke of charcoal burning drifted through these woods, too, for Burblethwaite could boast an iron forge and at Wilson House, near Lindale, was the smelting furnace where John and Isaac Wilkinson carried out their first experiments in 1749.

Developing industrial activity was accompanied by a steady but modest increase in the valley's population. In 1537, at the time of the Dissolution of Cartmel Priory when these lands came into the hands of the Duchy of Lancaster, there were probably about 250 inhabitants. By the time of the 1821 Census this figure had risen to 371, a total which did not change significantly in the next 100 years. All the apparatus of parish government had now arrived – overseers of the poor supervised the weekly pension distributed to the old and infirm, the constable apprehended wrong-doers, the chapel wardens kept a close eye on the wider aspects of parish discipline, a surveyor of the highways reported on the state of such roads as existed, the most notable being the busy pack-horse route between the thriving towns of Kendal and Ulverston which crossed the river near its source by a now rarely seen pack-horse bridge with an 8ft. span and no parapets.

The spiritual needs of the valley folk were also receiving better attention than in the

25   *Packhorse Bridge, River Winster*

days of the monks of Cartmel. In 1504 a local yeoman, Robert Briggs of Cowmire Hall, left a bequest which led to the foundation of the chapel at Cartmel Fell, dedicated to St Anthony, the patron saint of charcoal burners and basket weavers, and one of the gems among the pre-Reformation churches of northern England. Its simple unadorned stone-work, its rustic oak-beamed roof, its three-decker pulpit and its fine east window (probably from Cartmel Priory and a splendid example of English medieval stained glass), make this a place of beauty still very much as it was 400 years ago.[7]

Three miles away on the other side of the valley John Barwick built his church at Witherslack in the early years of the reign of Charles II. With his brother, Peter, who was the King's Physician, he designed a church in a traditional Elizabethan style which had gone out of fashion in the 1660s but which seems now, and almost certainly seemed then, to be entirely appropriate to the architectural harmony of the valley's many new manor house buildings. Nikolaus Pevsner described St Paul's, Witherslack as 'an almost perfect example of a plain Gothic church of that date, honest and unpretentious', praise indeed from one not notably effusive in his enthusiasm for Cumbrian churches. Only minor alterations have been made to this church since it was built and it still retains its 17th-century pulpit, lectern and heraldic glass.

Like so many other churches, St Paul's at Witherslack had its holy well, discovered, according to Thomas Short, in 1656 just a few years before the church itself was built. The story goes that children playing on a hot summer's day were tempted to quench their thirst at a nearby spring with unexpected and drastic results: they were, it is said, 'purged severely'. This attracted attention to the water and it was not long before the medicinal properties of this slightly sulphurous spring acquired a reputation for 'miracle cures'. Thomas Machell, Chaplain to King Charles II, writing of his travels in this part of the world in 1692, records that the well 'has done divers cures and thus has received the name as having something of sanctity in it'.[8] His list of local folk who had been 'cured' of various ailments in the years immediately preceding his visit included Kathleen Barwick of Halecat who had been relieved of jaundice, Robert Warton of Sedgwick who was successfully purged of worms, John Watheman of Carnforth cured of leprosy, and an un-named woman of Gressingham who had suffered from a painful swelling in the abdomen. The popularity of the well at Witherslack into the 18th century is attested by Thomas Short in his 'Essay towards a Natural and Medicinal History of the Principle Mineral Waters' (1740) where he states that the waters had proved 'good for Stone, Gravel, Worms, Inappetency, Cachexy, Corpulency, Jaundice, Dropsy etc.' Indeed, Short seems to have been quite overwhelmed by the charms of Witherslack: 'The ground is all charmingly beautiful with shrubs and plants, with the largest and fruitfullest field of junipers I ever found ... Sure England has scarce another such Romantic place, exceeding dry and warm, facing the hot sun and well-fenced from the cold blasts.'[9]

At a time when the spa-cult was rapidly becoming the height of fashion among the wealthy classes and 'taking the waters' was believed to be the answer to almost every real

26 *St Anthony's Church, Cartmel Fell*

or imagined ailment, every village and hamlet with a mineral spring at hand seemed to have aspirations to the status of a 'Spa'. There were clearly those who envisaged a prosperous future for Witherslack and, for a while, 'Witherslack Spa' enjoyed a modest local fame but its geographical remoteness, the absence of substantial landed gentry in the area to invest capital in all the facilities expected at a spa-resort, and the lack of a wealthy clientèle, all ensured that, however attractive the setting, Witherslack could never hope to succeed. By 1829 it was recorded that the spa had entirely disappeared and today Spa Lane is its only memorial.[10]

The hamlet of Winster had no such pretensions and did not acquire its own church until 1875 but it is a good example of the best in restrained Victorian architecture with some fine craftsmanship and some fine glass, and built in a style which blends well into the landscape.

The chapel at Cartmel Fell served for many years as the local school, founded, as we have seen, under the will of Benjamin Fletcher in the late 17th century. Few records of this school survive and one must hope that those that do tell us of only the least favourable episodes in its history. Here are references to the 'just causes of complaint' that the schoolmasters there were less than diligent either in their teaching or in their attendance; in 1833 there were 15 boys and five girls on the register but in 1877 an inspector reported that 'no school existed as the managers had failed to provide a schoolmaster'. Dean Barwick's school at Witherslack proved to be a much more successful enterprise and has happily survived all the hazards and upheavals of the 20th century.

Thousands of children who have never heard of Winster, Witherslack or Cartmel enjoy many hours of blissful reading enthralled by adventure stories created here in this quiet Lakeland valley. For it was here that Arthur Ransome penned his famous tales of the Swallows and Amazons, the Coot Club, Winter Holiday and Pigeon Post, all written in Ransome's home at Low Ludderburn, a house whose many inconveniences and discomforts he found well compensated for by the fine views he enjoyed over the valley and to the sea and to the hills beyond. Blake Holme, the small island in the lake not far from Ludderburn, was said by Ransome to have been the inspiration for Wild Cat Island (with its harbour borrowed from Peel Island in Coniston Water).[11] Sailors of another kind are commemorated at Storrs Temple, a few miles to the north, where a stone-built structure with wonderful views along the lake was erected to honour four British admirals of the 18th century: Admirals Duncan, Howe, Nelson and St Vincent, a unique monument in the English Lake District.[12]

On its 12-mile journey to the sea the River Winster flows past many homesteads with unusual and fascinating names: Ludderburn itself, the pure, clear stream; Barkbooth, the hut where bark was stored for tanning; Burblethwaite, the clearing where the butterbur grows; Thorphinsty, the path by Thorfin's farm; Cowmire, the marshy land where cows graze; Witherslack, the damp hollow where withies grow; and Meathop, the middle plot of enclosed marshland. Place-names here also remind us of the wildlife which once haunted the valley – the wild cats of Cat Crag, the harts of Hartbarrow, the sparrowhawks of Hawkearth, the kites of Kit Crag and the wolves of Ulpha.

Near the end of its course the Winster winds its way through low-lying meadows and mosses, a flat and estuarine landscape, once an arm of the sea and only reclaimed for farming by generations of drainage and embankments.

One of the most dramatic effects of this extensive drainage has been the virtual disappearance of the raised bogs of this area together with their special flora and fauna. These bogs consist of a deep layer of peat on a clay base and were originally formed on the beds of lakes or tarns. As the margins of the waters filled with silt and peat the resulting marshland or carr was colonised by such plants as the bog myrtle and the cross-leaved heath which raised the surface above the level of the water thus building up a peat whose natural acidity could not be neutralised by the water. This peat was then readily colonised by sphagnum moss which has a number of empty cells which absorb water like a sponge. These cells enable the moss to carry its own water upwards and outwards as it grows while the decaying leaves at the bottom submerge and kill off the earlier vegetation, all the time forming a deeper and deeper layer of very acid peat and eventually creating a raised bog entirely dependent on nutrient-deficient rainwater and on the absence of extensive peat-cutting or land drainage. The bogs of Lakeland can usually rely on a plentiful renewal of rainwater to sustain them but almost all are under serious threat from agricultural drainage. Many have disappeared entirely; others are suffering rapid and irreversible change. The efforts of the volunteers of the Cumbria Wildlife Trust are helping to preserve these bogs for as long as is possible. Among the many interesting plants which can be seen on Meathop Moss are the insectivorous sundew, the bog asphodel and bog rosemary, cranberry and bilberry, numerous mosses and fungi and the white, silky heads of cotton grass.[13]

The level expanse of Meathop Moss serves to emphasise the contrast between the vale of Winster and most other Lakeland valleys. Winster is the least dramatic of the valleys: here we find none of the scenic spectacle of Wasdale or Borrowdale, none of the legacy of great industrial enterprises as in Newlands or the Duddon Valley, no major highway here has echoed down the years to the march of Roman Legions or the thunder of a thousand herds of driven cattle as in Eskdale or Little Langdale. No rivals can be discovered here for the romantic legends of the Vale of St John or the Maid of Buttermere. Nor is this gentle valley secluded and encompassed by mighty fells like Kentdale, Martindale and Longsleddale. Even Winster's name has been robbed of any exotic or glamorous origin: it is, the linguists would have us believe, no more than the Old Norse 'vinstri', the left-hand (river) – as opposed to the Gilpin on the 'right'. No damsel so lovely could be allowed to suffer so sad a fate and Lo! we find a gallant knight comes riding to her rescue. Sir Ifor Evans firmly pronounces that Winster is no less than the Welsh/Breton 'gwyn-ster', 'The White River,' referred to in the Book of Taliesin as the site of a battle between Urien, king of the ancient Cumbrian kingdom of Rheged, and the Anglo-Saxon invaders from Northumbria. Winster's name is redeemed.[14]

Even so, the high drama of Lakeland has been left behind on this tranquil southern fringe, and the softly murmuring Winster leads us resolutely away from the awesome majesty of the high fells and the breathtaking beauty of the shining lakes, away from the roaring cascades and the mighty tree-clad crags, and takes us gently through Arcadia down to the sands and the sea.

Duke of Burgundy Fritillary

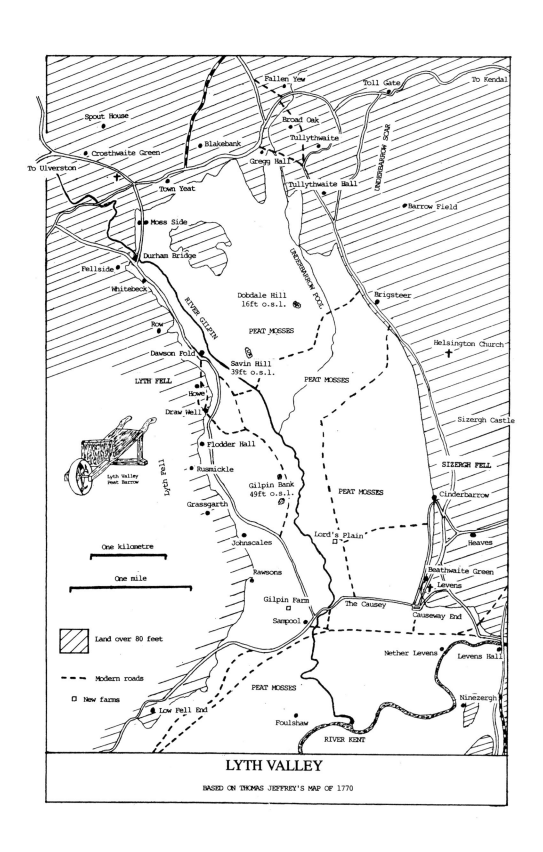

Spout House

To Kendal
Toll Gate
Fallen Yew

Broad Oak
Blakebank
Tullythwaite
Crosthwaite Green

To Ulverston
Gregg Hall
Tullythwaite Hall

Town Yeat

Barrow Field

Moss Side

Durham Bridge
UNDERBARROW SCAR
Fellside

Whitebeck
UNDERBARROW POOL
Brigsteer

Dobdale Hill
16ft o.s.l.
RIVER GILPIN
Row

PEAT MOSSES

Helsington Church
Dawson Fold
Savin Hill
39ft o.s.l.
LYTH FELL
PEAT MOSSES
Howe
Draw Well
Sizergh Castle

Flodder Hall

Lyth Valley
Peat Barrow
Rusmickle
SIZERGH FELL

Gilpin Bank
49ft o.s.l.
PEAT MOSSES
Cinderbarrow
Grassgarth

Lord's Plain
Heaves
Johnscales
One kilometre

Beathwaite Green
Rawsons
Levens
One mile

Gilpin Farm
The Causey
Causeway End
Sampool

Land over 80 feet
Nether Levens
Levens Hall

Modern roads

New farms
Ninezergh

PEAT MOSSES

Low Fell End
Foulshaw
RIVER KENT

LYTH VALLEY

BASED ON THOMAS JEFFREY'S MAP OF 1770

11

LYTH VALLEY

From the precipitous limestone edge of Underbarrow Scar the landscape of the Lyth Valley appears to be a vast medieval tapestry woven with intricate detail and set in a scene of romantic improbability. The blue silhouette of the high fells of Lakeland draws the eye inexorably to a dramatic skyline beyond the valley head; on the far horizon to the west mist and light play with the rolling tides as the sea sweeps in to cover the great bay of treacherous golden sands; and across the chequer-board of the valley itself looms the massive bulk of Whitbarrow whose mighty cliffs were once washed by this defeated sea. Green pastures divided by hedges and dykes cover the valley floor: a herd of well-fed cows amble their way towards milking time, sheep graze with indifferent ease, their fleeces whiter than white in the summer sun; a few roe deer feed alertly on the lush grass at the edge of a wood; a dark shadow strokes across the plantations and slowly passes by; the river, now channelled and confined, seems to be halted in its course, no more than a dull metal ribbon unwinding across the levels towards the estuarine sands. The only sounds are the mewing of buzzards and the hollow bark of a distant farmyard dog. Where the flatlands end, where the rising land marks the former limits of the tidal flow, rocky outcrops and an undulating landscape with rushing becks and wooded gills, drystone walls and ancient farmsteads, are a reminder that Lyth is, unmistakably, a Lakeland valley. Along the sharply rising slopes above the level of the reclaimed land is an array of little hamlets, farms, barns and whitewashed cottages, shyly hidden in the spring behind a lace curtain of damson blossom but at other times standing in light relief against the dark background of the Whitbarrow woods. It is this western slope which gave Lyth its name: the Norsemen who gave names to so many of the features of the Lakeland landscape called this the 'hlith' or 'sloping hillside', at that time the only dry and fertile land above the fenland morass just a few feet below, a boggy watery waste, beloved by wildlife of many kinds, which less than two hundred years ago was transformed by the ingenuity and economic needs of man.

The great glaciers of the last Ice Age and the almost unimaginable floods which followed their melting scoured away the deep sedimentary limestone rock which covered much of the Lake District thus carving out the valleys and lake-beds. Ice and meltwater sweeping south left unscathed the limestone escarpments of Whitbarrow and Underbarrow Scars but gouged out between them a valley which may at one time have been a lake but which had more the character of an estuary or an arm of the sea. There is no cartographical depiction of the Lyth Valley earlier than the 1770 map of Thomas Jeffreys, but it is believed that most of the lower lands were frequently flooded by the tidal flow which extended some five miles 'inland' from the present confluence of the Rivers Kent and Gilpin to the five-metre contour near to Gregg Hall in Underbarrow. Even as recently as 1852 when much of the reclamation had been completed the sea swept over the new embankments, flooding the low-lying land near Levens several feet deep 'driving the inhabitants to the upper rooms for several hours, drowning the cattle in considerable numbers and otherwise inflicting serious damage'. Similar flooding occurred in 1860, 1902, 1907 and 1915 by which time Brigsteer had acquired its droll sobriquet 'Brigsteer by the Sea'. It seems not unreasonable then to imagine that before the process of serious drainage began in the early 19th century the Lyth mosses were largely very wet fenland with large shallow pools of open water, extensive areas of swamp and bogland, and small islands such as Savin Hill, Dobdale Hill, Low Heads and High Heads. Much silting up had occurred over the years and, while the frequent tidal flooding and periods of prolonged rainfall must have resulted in a generally high water level, conditions in 1800 would have been markedly different from those existing in the 11th century when the name Levens is first recorded as 'Lefuenes' or Leofa's headland, a promontory above the sea which washed its foot as it did the cliffs of Whitbarrow on the further shore.

The first viking settlers here would have found the deposits of peat already well advanced as the impermeable underlying clay had from the earliest times prevented natural drainage and peat would have been forming for hundreds, perhaps thousands of years, gradually reducing the area of deeper open water and creating a vast fen or moss, utterly useless for agriculture but a bountiful source of food in the form of wildfowl and fish and as an apparently bottomless supply of peat for fuel. William Pearson's *Notes on the Natural History of Lyth* compiled in 1844 recall that in the years before the great reclamation began it was possible to find within the confines of these mosses 'almost every variety of bird common to the North of England', and among his extensive list he includes not only those still familiar in Lakeland – curlew, heron, water ouzel, lapwing, snipe, pheasant and wild duck – but also others which are now more rarely seen – kingfisher, bittern, corn crake, crossbill, red grouse and sandpiper. Pearson's *Journal* describes how the local diet was frequently supplemented by roast woodcock apparently present in large numbers on the Lyth mosses and caught by 'springing' or 'sprenting' – Shakespeare's 'springes to catch woodcocks'. A line of stones was laid in the areas where the birds fed at night which they would not cross; a snare was placed in a gap in the line and the woodcock were duly trapped. Fish, too, were plentiful in the many open pools and many a farmhouse table would be able to offer a feast of fresh salmon, trout, carp, eel or pike. Also at home in this fenny landscape were wildcats, polecats (or foulmarts), otters, badgers, weasels and both the red and the larger grey fox, while overhead the kite soared surveying it all. This was nature's kingdom: man ventured there only to seek the food he needed for himself and his family and to dig peat for fuel to keep a fire in the cottage hearth.[1]

Peat cutting or graving took place in the early summer and each farmstead or cottage had its own 'peat-pots' which were jealously guarded against encroachment. These were scattered about the mosses and even after the reclamation some were retained as part of a traditional inheritance, for the peat was not only essential as domestic fuel, it also made an important contribution to the domestic economy by generating income from regular sale to the households of Kendal and Milnthorpe. A daily procession of peat carts along the road to Kendal was a customary sight until the early years of the 20th century but by then the impact of first the canals and then the railways had become fully apparent: cheap coal brought commercial digging to an end by about 1915 and almost all private digging had ceased some 10 years later. The observant eye of Captain James Budworth in the course of his *Fortnight's Ramble to the Lakes* in 1792 has provided us with an interesting glimpse of the enterprising verve of the country-folk of Lyth whom he commends for their 'meritorious spirit of industry ...

both men and women [who] were knitting stockings as they drove their peat carts into the town',[2] where the market apparently had no difficulty in handling the 2,000 pairs of knitted socks brought in each week. Kendal market was also the outlet for the other products of the mosses: an article in the *Lonsdale Magazine* in 1822 comments that 'poor people in the neighbourhood of the mosses make a tolerable living by peeling rushes for candles and making besoms and bears [i.e. mats] of the peelings',[3] and F.W. Garnett described how others took apples and damsons to market on horseback 'in panniers lashed together two or three on each side with the driver, man or woman, seated on top'.[4]

But it was the peat which was at the heart of this primitive economy. The six feet deep deposits had been dug for a thousand years and seemed inexhaustible. The growth of the population, especially in the town of Kendal, in the 18th and 19th centuries created an expanding market and peat digging became a commercial enterprise with dealers operating as small-scale capitalists both in Kendal and close at hand near the moss. The cottages at Causeway End housed mainly peat dealers at one time and the decline of this trade is starkly shown in *Bulmer's Directory* which in 1906 lists only one remaining peat dealer in the Levens area, Henry Cross of Causeway End.

A peat pot produced at least two distinct types of peat: a layer of fibrous peat often more than two feet in depth which when dried was used as kindling while the fine dusty material was collected for the special purpose of baking bread as it generated great heat; and below this lay several feet of black peat which lasted longer in burning and was used for general fuel creating a steady glowing heat. The tools used in 'graving' were the flaying spade to strip off the upper layer of peat rather in the manner of a push-plough, and the peat spade, a flanged implement with a section of flat shaft to cut the peat cleanly along the whole length of the piece, the size of which obviously depended on the dimensions of the flange and the spade shaft. The cut peats were placed in windrows and stacked in circular ricks for several weeks to allow the wind to dry them out. They were then carried to the farm or cottage on peat barrows, which were long wheelbarrows without sides and with an iron wheel several inches wide to prevent it sinking into the soft peaty ground.[5]

After the Enclosure Acts of 1803 and 1838 and the reclamation of almost all the moss land for agriculture, peat-pots were allocated to a number of individuals who continued digging until the peat was exhausted or, more usually, until there was no longer a market for it.

The roads to Kendal must have been very lively, indeed, as the procession of laden horses and carts bumped and jostled on its way, noisy with the loud chatter and shouting of the farmers, peat-cutters and housewives of the Lyth Valley hoping to earn a few pence with the products of their labour – orchard fruit, eggs, poultry, candles and rushlights, mats, besoms, swill baskets, butter, cheese, oak bark for the Kendal tanning yards, charcoal for the iron-masters, perhaps a little woven cloth or a few skeins of newly-spun flax, and, of course, many creaking cartloads of good black peat for the domestic hearths and bakers' ovens. They were a rough, uncultivated folk, uneducated and still firm believers in the ancient superstitions and country lore passed down through many generations. William Pearson tells us that they considered it unlucky to begin a new task of work on a Friday, to see a single magpie, or to meet a woman on setting out for the market; but they placed great store on the sight of a black cat or a five-leaf clover. Belief in the existence of household dobbies, who were benevolent, and ghosts, which were not, was as strong as their belief in 'wisemen' such as Isaac Atkinson of Beathwaite Green who knew how to identify thieves and how to make butter turn in

27   *Peat stacks*

the churn, or in 'charmers' who could say the right incantations to remedy warts and burns or to cure cattle of the sickness. They firmly retained the old faith in the power of a rowan twig to turn cream into good butter or to ward off evil, and of the needfire to cure cattle of the 'murrain'.[6]

Yet these were rugged independent folk who had successfully resisted all attempts by the two principal landowners in Crosthwaite and Lyth – the Crown and the family of Bellingham – to undermine customary tenure and to change the legal status of tenants from tenant-right to tenant-at-will. Following an agreement between the Crown and the tenants in 1579 it could be said that 'in general, the holder by tenant-right in Crosthwaite and Lyth enjoyed no small degree of independence, with a title to his land that did not depend on the Lord of the Manor and with a right to let his land on lease and even to dispose of it by will'. He had the right to fell and use timber on his land and 'to stub and grub all old dead wood' to improve his arable land and to extend his meadows,[7] Enclosure and reclamation would change all this but until that time this was very much a community of husbandmen, minor yeomen, leasehold farmers, artisans, craftsmen, and the labourers who assisted them.

These families did not, of course, make their homes on the moss. With only two exceptions all the settlements shown on Jeffreys' map of 1770 are above the five-metre contour, on the slopes of Whitbarrow, at Beathwaite Green and Brigsteer, and on the higher ground at Underbarrow and Crosthwaite Green. Only 'Foulsha' and 'Sampha' are situated on the moss; it is probable that these were protected by an embankment but both must have become accustomed to frequent floods. Life there must have been hard, hazardous and an unremitting struggle against poverty.

The map indicates the existence of a single road on either side of the mosses, linking the settlements with the main highways (pack-horse routes) between Kendal and Furness and between Kendal and Lancaster. The former passed from Kendal over Underbarrow Scar, and then by the *Punchbowl Inn* to Gregg Hall, Town Yeat, Cartmel Fold and on to Crosthwaite Green where it turned south to cross the River Winster at Bowland Bridge before heading for Cartmel, Newby Bridge and Ulverston. John Fell's 1782 *Guide over the Kent and Levens Sands* seems to suggest that anyone travelling into Furness, even from Lancaster and the south, would proceed northwards to this highway as the only safe way to circumvent the barrier of the Lyth Mosses.

There was an ancient route across the morass known as the 'Causey' or Causeway, a corduroy road constructed by placing birch logs over a firm peat base and binding them in position by timbers driven deep into the underlying clay.[8] There is nothing to suggest that this road was ever regarded as an acceptable alternative to the longer route even though it offered a tempting 'short-cut', providing a direct line from Newby Bridge via High Newton, Towtop Hill, Bleacrag Bridge and Witherslack, and then straight across the moss via Sampool Bridge and, briefly following the meanders of the Gilpin (straightened out in the 19th century), direct to higher ground at Causeway End where it joined a track ascending a short, steep hill before turning north through what is now the village of Levens to the main north-south Kendal-Lancaster highway. The hazards of this causeway and perhaps a fear of the mosses were enough to persuade travellers with valuable merchandise to keep to the familiar and established route which was safely punctuated with well-known farms, cottages and hostelries.

The age of the causeway has never been determined and the constant repair and renewal it must have demanded make it almost impossible to arrive at a date for the original construction. It may be medieval but the first written reference occurs in the records of the Barony of Kendal which in 1654 have a note on 'Sampull Cawsey'. Almost 40 years later Thomas Machell on his journey through Westmorland relates that from Levens he 'passed by a long causeway over the moss', a passage apparently noteworthy only for the strange aromatic shrubs (probably bog-myrtle) along the way.[9] The King's Chaplain must have chosen a propitious time to make his crossing for it would seem that the normal state of the moss road was such as to deter all but local folk from using it. Throughout the 18th century this and the other roads in Lyth are constantly referred to as 'ruinous', 'in decay' and 'greatly out of repair', and the *Levens Highway Book* in 1817 declared that 'the moss roads are at present impassable'.[10]

It would be misleading to assume that the flat, lush meadows which have now replaced the former mosslands are all there is to see in the Lyth Valley.

On the eastern escarpment, the tract of land between the Rivers Kent and Gilpin, stand two great houses which have played an important part in the history of the life and economy of the local community. Less than two miles to the north of the 'new' village of Levens is Sizergh Castle, now a property of the National Trust but the home of the Strickland family since 1239; and less than a mile to the south is Levens Hall, a truly enchanting, mainly Elizabethan mansion, the home of the Bagots and the venue for many events in the local calendar. Each of these stately homes deserves a chapter

NETHER LEVENS HALL.

28   *Nether Levens Hall*

to itself for both are among the most handsome houses in the country, with impressive medieval pele-towers skilfully conjoined to Elizabethan, Jacobean and Georgian residential wings, with interiors rich in contemporary furnishings and a wealth of beautiful oak panelling and plasterwork. No other house in England has such a display of Elizabethan woodcarving as that at Sizergh; no other great house has achieved such an atmosphere of warmth and intimacy as that at Levens. Both are much visited in the summer months but few of those who pause here for a while on their way to the scenic delights of the nearby Lakes give more than a passing glance to the quiet pastoral Vale of Lyth and fewer still ever see the great elliptical chimneys of the 16th-century farmhouse at Nether Levens perched on a slight eminence, 20ft. above sea-level, on the bank of the Kent.[11]

The large village, known today as Levens, is mainly a modern development which has comprehensively absorbed the original settlement of Beathwaite, a hamlet with a Norse name built on the rising ground on the eastern edge of the watery moss. A number of well-preserved houses dating from the 17th and 18th centuries distinguish the older parts of

Levens from the new, and at Causeway End are cottages which were probably the homes, workshops and storehouses of peat-cutters and peat-dealers.

The four-mile-long escarpment of Whitbarrow Scar soars like a fortress wall above the flat lands of the valley below. Its almost inaccessible rocks and ledges provide safe nesting sites for ravens, buzzards and peregrine falcons while the rough screes and damp crevices are bright with a variety of mosses and ferns; the exposed limestone on the summit is rich in heather, juniper and all the flowers of a natural rock garden; the woodlands of the lower slopes have a wealth of wild flowers, plants and trees enhanced by many fine specimens of ancient yew. Plantations of conifer now cover areas which were once open pasture lands until, as William Pearson lamented, bare stone walls like giant chains were thrown across the bosom of the fells as if to hold them down: the relics of these now lie broken and derelict among the enveloping trees.

An enduring mystery of Whitbarrow and Lyth is referred to in Nicolson and Burn's *History* where they recount the popular belief in the existence of underground water-ways beneath the limestone mass:

> In a meadow near here are three pits of unknown depth which overflow when there is much rain about Whitbarrow or Cartmel Fell; when salmon smelts abound in the Kent, they are plentiful in these pits, which argues that they come to them through subterranean passages.[12]

The waters which emerge from beneath Whitbarrow at Beck Head – 'situate where the Beck springs romantickly out of the Rock' as an 18th-century record put it – appear to lend support to the idea of underground water-courses but the mystery remains.

The parish of Crosthwaite and Lyth embraces not only the flatlands of the moss and the great limestone ridge of Whitbarrow but also hamlets and farmsteads set among plantations and woodlands which conceal small green pastures and the old damson orchards which famously clothe the valley in the early springtime; and, in the upper reaches of the River Gilpin, a countryside rich with all the diversity of the Lakeland scene: well-nourished and startlingly green fields enclosed by drystone walls and fruitful hedges, rocky knolls adorned with thyme, craggy outcrops ablaze with gorse, hazel coppices and beech woods interspersed with plantations of larch, spruce and pine, all threaded by tiny becks and gills fed by a multitude of springs. Here, too, is a network of ancient tracks leading to isolated farms and past the remains of many mills which once worked here – corn mills at Crosthwaite and Bulman Strands, fulling mills at Tarnside, Mirk How and Hollow Clough, paper mills at Starnthwaite[13] – and, at the heart of it all, Crosthwaite, now a prosperous village but only fairly recently acknowledged on the modern Ordnance Survey map. Jeffreys' 1770 map names the hamlet as Crosthwaite Green with the church more than half a mile away at Churchtown, and almost a hundred years later the 1863 map still refers to Crosthwaite Green (with a post office) and to Churchtown (with the church, the school and the vicarage).

The earliest reference to a christian place of worship in Crosthwaite and Lyth is in the field-name, St Aldam Cross, almost certainly derived from St Aldhelm, an influential figure in the early Saxon Church in Britain who died in 709. There is also a reference to a Chapel of St Mary here in the 12th century but until 1556 the whole of Lyth was part of the extensive parish of Heversham. In that year the bishop of Chester acknowledged that the barrier of the mosses had led to the spiritual as well as the geographical isolation of the people of the Crosthwaite area and issued a licence for mass to be said and the sacraments to be administered in the chapel at Churchtown. The vicar of Heversham seemingly resented the loss of part of his parish and relations with the folk of Crosthwaite were less than cordial until an agreement was negotiated in the 1580s by which Crosthwaite was to have its own chaplain 'to be maintained by their own salary and charge and not otherwise'; the parish was to be administered by a body of 12 parishioners and, for administrative purposes, the new parish was to be divided into three parts (called 'quarters') – Church, Lyth and Town End.

The parish officers and the more affluent parishioners appear to have carried out their duties conscientiously but, as elsewhere in the country, the ever-increasing burden of poor relief eventually proved too much for the system to cope with. Wills, trusts and charities made financial provision to assist the poor but, even when added to the general poor rate, these contributions were quite inadequate to contend with the 85 per cent increase in the monies required for poor relief in the last quarter of the 18th century, with a further increase of over 60 per cent between 1801 and 1831.[14] In his report to the Poor Law Commissioners in 1832 William Pearson declared quite un-equivocally that a family of a labourer, his wife and four children could not even subsist ·on their earnings. The many references to the distribution of such items as bread, clothes and tea, to the payment of doctors' bills and to direct financial aid, suggest that a considerable number of the 700 folk who lived in Lyth in the 19th century were living on the very edge of extreme poverty. Young people were leaving the valley for better conditions and better employment in Kendal and this, too, must have destroyed any hope for the future among those who remained. These labouring folk were to suffer further hardship as the enclosure of the common lands of the mosses proceeded. William Pearson again drew attention to this injustice:

> The lord of the manor, the vicar or rector of the parish, all had their allotted shares, and often very valuable ones, yet there was one party who had a right, a privilege in these commons, often of much service to him, whose claim was entirely forgotten. This was the poor labourer. Is it any wonder that the labourer has become pauperised.[15]

The ministrations of the church and the exactions of a succession of landlords had done little to endear their spiritual and political masters to the people of Lyth at any time since the Norman Conquest. Before that calamitous upheaval in their lives the Norsemen who had so recently established their farmsteads on the slopes above the moss had enjoyed a freedom and independence from any external authority which was never to be recovered. Henceforward they were subject to the governance of powerful landowners, the successors of the Norman Baron Yvo Taillebois, most of whom were notable for their ruthless impositions on a populace whom they looked upon as no more than a source of revenue and exploitation. The Church established by the Normans also curtailed this independence – as an agent of a Crown blessed by the Papacy it held spiritual authority over everyone, with the power to enforce fearsome punishment on those who defied its laws, its creed and its moral code and, perhaps above all else, the right to demand payment of tithes, an annual levy of one-tenth of all the produce and stock of each farmstead, a deeply resented imposition which the vicars of Heversham rarely failed to exact. Was the 'careless workman' who caused Heversham Church to burn down in 1601 guilty of negligence, or expressing, in the only way he knew, a bitter animosity towards the Established Church?

Certainly, when George Fox came this way in 1652 on his journey to Swarthmoor Hall, he found a ready response to his teachings, and during his stay at Tullithwaite Hall, Underbarrow, and at Pool Bank, Crosthwaite, he discovered a keenly-interested group of 'Seekers', some of whom were later to make great sacrifices and suffer constant persecution. As in so many other parts of Westmorland and North Lancashire, the newly formed Society of Friends – the Quakers – soon had an active following in

Crosthwaite and Lyth. More than a dozen of the 'Valiant Sixty', those chosen by Fox to take his message to all parts of the country, came from this area including four from Underbarrow and six from Kendal. The centre of Quakerism in Lyth was at Pool Bank, the home of Thomas and John Pearson who, together with Thomas Pearson the Elder of Witherslack and Richard Simpson, stood firm in their faith in the face of steady persecution by the vicar of Heversham and the local magistrates. Joseph Besse in his book *The Sufferings of the People called Quakers* relates that the Pearsons were in 1664 arraigned by the priest before a Commission of Rebellion for their refusal to pay tithes and were committed to prison, only to secure release when they established that the priest had proceeded against them illegally. The family were again in trouble a few years later when they were fined and had their property seized for holding and attending a Meeting at Witherslack: 'they were levied by Distress and great Spoil and Havock made of their Goods'. Richard Simpson and others were also fined 'for praying there'. In 1678 further heavy fines were incurred by the Pearsons who were also 'distressed of £1 13s. 4d. and two heifers worth £2 6s.8d.', a severe loss and indicative of the sacrifices demanded of those who, at that time, defied the authority and beliefs of the Church.[16]

In contrast to the apparent enthusiasm for the Quaker Movement there is little evidence that Nonconformist ideas had any significant following in the valley. In 1692 the house of James Garnett at Moss Side was licensed for preaching by Richard Frankland, the leading Presbyterian rebel against the Church in the time of Charles II and James II, enjoying the new religious tolerance shown by William III. Some years before this a Nonconformist Academy had been set up at Dawson Fold, a remarkable enterprise in so remote a place but, it would seem, not blessed with the success which attended so many other similar foundations.

Support for these new religious beliefs, with their dangerous intellectual challenge to the established social order, would have been most evident among the more educated folk, the yeomen farmers, the craftsmen – carpenters, wheelwrights, blacksmiths, millers, stonemasons, shoemakers and shopkeepers, all of whom appear in the early censuses – and perhaps those who held their land by tenant right. But these constituted only a very small percentage of the population of 500 counted in the first census of 1801.

Lyth was essentially an agricultural community of small farms and cottages and it is agriculture which is at the very heart of its history. And that history was about to undergo a change so fundamental that it would transform not only the lives of many of the inhabitants but also the entire appearance of the landscape in which they lived. Land which for thousands of years had been covered by the sea, then frequently inundated by high tidal flows, and in more recent times a vast fen or marsh, was about to be reclaimed for agriculture – drained, embanked, channelled, partitioned and fenced, marled, fertilised, ploughed and sown with crops of oats, corn, potatoes, turnips, mangolds, ryegrass and clover. Within the lifetime of one man the moss was 'divided into fruitful fields teeming with luxuriant crops'[17] and 'instead of a wide expanse of marsh and bog often supporting little but snipes and wild ducks, there now appeared wide fields of golden grain and glistening green crops'.[18] There had been no such dramatic, man-made transformation of a Lakeland landscape since the clearance of the primeval forests.

The driving force behind this stupendous and costly enterprise was the urgent national need to produce food to feed a population which had doubled during the 18th century from five and a half million to 11 million and was set to double again within 50 years. New systems of agriculture had shown how this could be done but their

introduction on the scale which was required involved a revolution in traditional farming methods and in the use of the land; and, as in all revolutions, there were gains and
losses, winners and losers, many suffered and some rejoiced.

The key to the success of this revolution was enclosure and this meant not only the
consolidation of scattered landholdings into a single area of land appropriately fenced
or hedged but also the legal expropriation for enclosure of common pastures, wasteland, woodlands and marshlands in which local people had enjoyed valuable rights for
countless generations. The threat to these ancient rights met with determined opposition
in many parts of the country and the wealthy landowners who initiated almost all the
enclosure proposals resorted to Acts of Parliament, at first private but later general, to
secure their objectives. There is no evidence to indicate that there was any notable
opposition to the draining and enclosure of the mosses of Lyth nor was there any
depopulation of the valley as a result of the changes. In fact the 1801 population of 509
increased to 606 ten years later and to 781 in 1821 and changed little thereafter in the
19th century. The General Enclosure Act of 1801 had made the whole process of
enclosure less complex and soon pressure to exploit the economic potential of agricultural land in South Westmorland came from local gentry and others who saw the
prospect of a substantial enhancement of their rents and income. These included Viscount
Lowther, Trinity College, Cambridge, Richard Howard, and a dozen others, one of
whom was the vicar of Heversham.[19]

The culmination of this political pressure came in 1803 with an Enclosure Act which
covered land in Heversham, Crosthwaite, Lyth, Levens, Milnthorpe, Hincaster, Stainton,
Sedgwick and Preston Patrick; subsequent Acts extended the areas to be enclosed and
the Underbarrow Act of 1843 completed the process. Change was rapid once these
legal processes were completed and already in 1844 William Pearson could write in his
Journals that 'no event has produced a greater change in the appearance of our district
than the enclosure of the commons'.

The Enclosure Awards were very specific in every detail:[20] the location and acreage
of each award were, of course, precisely defined but equally precise were the instruc-
tions for the drainage procedure including the size and construction of the ditches,
channels and embankments, the planting of thorn hedges along the boundaries, the
allocation of rights to dig peat, the restriction of land on Whitbarrow Scar for use as
pasture and for quarrying limestone, 'the profits or produce, if any, arising therefrom,
to be disposed of in ease of the public rates'. Attention was given to the necessity for
new roads across these newly reclaimed lands: bridleways 24ft. wide were to be made
at specified routes, the cost to fall on the owners of the land; a new public highway was
to be built, 30ft. wide and with appropriate bridges, from Levens Bridge to Sampool
Bridge to provide direct communication with Ulverston and Furness, the meanders of
the River Gilpin were to be straightened out, stone for the road surface was to be
obtained from a quarry at the foot of Whitbarrow Scar. The foundations of this road
were to be floated on the moss and to consist of birch and heather faggots reinforced
with water-resistant juniper branches; cross timbers were to be laid on three lines of
supporting logs staked every three feet; the old causeway was to be realigned near
Sampool Bridge to follow the new course of the Gilpin. Lyth Lane, the old track which
ran along the eastern slopes of Whitbarrow (above the modern A5074), was widened
at the expense of the tenant farmers and its hedges replaced by drystone walls – an
undertaking which clearly displeased William Pearson who believed this was done
merely 'to facilitate tourist carriages'. He lamented the loss of the valley scene familiar
to him since his youth and exclaimed against the many changes which were taking

place before his very eyes: 'Lyth Lane! thou art changed − metamorphosed − vanished − extinguished!'.[21]

These changes proceeded with remarkable rapidity in the first decades of the 19th century. Work on the drainage trenches and channels was quickly set in train, field boundaries were marked out, new farms established at Lords Plain, Gilpin Bank, Foulshaw and Sampool, and the map of 1824 shows that an enterprising publican had already seen the possibilities of an inn at Gilpin Bridge. Before long the land was sufficiently drained to allow agriculture to be contemplated but the Bagots of Levens Hall had soon discovered on their new farm at Lords Plain that the drained areas were peaty and acid and would require extensive liming and marling before crops could be successfully grown. The 200 acres of oats and turnips grown as the first harvest on the farm had involved the carting of 40,000 cartloads of marl and the spreading of 120,000 bushels of lime.[22] Others soon became familiar with this labour as well as with the need for constant maintenance of the drainage ditches: F.W. Garnett states that 250 cartloads of marl were required for every acre reclaimed plus another 300 cartloads five or six years later, and this together with clearing, draining, fencing, gating, fertilising, repairs to drains and other expenses made the cost of reclaiming the mosslands about £13 4s. 10d. an acre, an outlay offset not only by the crops produced but by a fourfold increase in the value of the land within a very short period of time. Indeed, Garnett claims that 'the whole of the outlay [was] often returned in two or three years' and 'large profits were made'.[23]

Such gains would be enjoyed only by those such as John Wakefield who had acquired the largest award of 1,400 acres and perhaps James Burrow, James Adam, John Robinson and Sir Daniel Fleming who obtained between 75 and 200 acres. Of the remaining awards more than half were under 10 acres in extent and three-quarters were less than 25 acres: the size of these holdings would offer little incentive to embark on the costly improvements demanded by the newly reclaimed land, even if the capital had been available, and most of these became pasture for sheep and cattle or feeding grounds for vast flocks of geese − 'never was there pasture so incessantly nibbled as this';[24] some became orchard closes, planted with apple and damson trees the fruit of which sold well in Kendal Market and whose springtime blossom was to bring the valley tourist fame. A few could have been no more than peat diggings for those who still made a living by supplying fuel to the surrounding district, a market which steadily declined when first the canal and then the railway brought cheap coal into the area. The construction of the railway viaduct across the Kent estuary was in itself a major engineering triumph of the time but its effect on the tidal flow and the waters of the Kent created a problem for the drainage system and sluice gates which became choked with sand. After several serious floods it became necessary to install new drains in tunnels, an expensive operation which has had to be repeated at intervals in the 20th century as engineering technology has advanced. Ambitious estimates were made of the extent of land reclamation which would follow the building of the railway crossing, one putting the figure at 46,000 acres or more than seventy square miles. The reality was some 500-600 acres of the Castlehead and Meathop marshes which became 'luxuriant pastures' filled with a great many sheep,[25] and more drainage problems for the Lyth valley.

The railway was opened in 1857 by which date the reclaimed fields in Lyth were producing profitable crops, mainly oats and roots, which were unaffected by the collapse of wheat prices in the 1860s and '70s. A Land Use Survey Map of 1858 shows that a large proportion of the reclaimed land was still under arable farming and the lime kilns which had been built in many places nearby were still flourishing as the soil demanded constant fertilising. The Kendal Agricultural Society inaugurated ploughing matches which were held on the lands of Sizergh Castle and Levens Hall and local plough makers introduced improved ploughs to increase efficiency on these fruitful fields. Even so there were already signs that the future of these Lyth Moss fields would be as pastures for sheep and cattle rather than as arable land. It was not only that the railways could now bring in cheaper grain and vegetables from more favoured areas but it was becoming increasingly evident that the land itself was very well suited to the rearing of stock. After 1918 there was very little arable left in Lyth and almost all the valley was eventually given over to pasture with farmers placing their future on the still steady market for British beef and lamb and on the rising consumption of milk.

With the disappearance of the mosses and the steady migration of younger people to Kendal there also disappeared many of the customs and traditions and ancient superstitions which had been a feature of life in the valley for many generations. Wisemen and charmers had few clients in the 20th century and fewer still believed that ghosts could be banished to permanent exile under Hawes Bridge or that dobbie-stones would protect household, stable and byre from the machinations of evil spirits. The 'need-fire' was last used in the valley in 1840, and the traditional, genuine English mince-pie at Christmas made from minced mutton, fruit, eggs, spices and sugar, almost forgotten in most of England but still made in Lyth in 1830, was unknown less than a century later. One custom of more recent origin was the annual meeting held in the local inn to determine who should have the right to graze his beasts on the wide grass verges of the gated roads and tracks across the former moss. This was decided by a ritual which had all the elements of high drama ending in an agonising climax and at its centre was a single domestic candle, ceremonially lit as the proceedings began.

The participants gathered round a table, no doubt well-fortified with food and drink as the long evening progressed, all well-aware of the rules of the game and all keen to secure the valuable extra grazing which was at stake. At first bids would be casually and lightly made in the intervals of farmers' talk of the weather, the condition of the stock after the long winter, prices at the mart, perhaps the latest outbreak of disease among the cattle or foot rot among the sheep. A slash of wind-driven rain on the window would recall the high spring-tides which had flooded the fields and blocked the drains with sand. The new tiles from Lupton would improve drain construction but heads would shake at the heavy cost this would involve and the talk would lead easily to the iniquities of landlords and ever-increasing rents. The merits of the new iron plough recently introduced to the area by Dudgeon of Lawrence House Farm would be discussed and a lengthy debate would ensue on the various mechanical inventions which were then set to revolutionise farming practice. Where was the advantage in paying out to hire new-fangled threshing machines when you had cheap labourers to use the flail which had done the job for centuries? Candles take a while to burn and everyone there knew that the grazing would go to the man who made the last bid before the candle guttered out. As this time drew near the talk and banter would fade away, pies and pints would be set aside, eyes would become tense and watchful, concentrated on the slowly dying flame, as the bidding grew fast and furious until a final shout rang out as the light was suddenly quenched in the black and sizzling fat. Subsequent wrangling was probably less than amiable; but the proceeds of the auction went to the parish funds.[26]

Just as at the end of the 19th century time seemed to have run out for a way of country life which had survived the vicissitudes of countless generations, so at the end of the 20th century time seems to be running out for a pattern of farming which has been characteristic of Lakeland for 200 years and for the moss farmers of Lyth since arable gave way to pasture. The whole future of upland farming is in the balance and fraught with uncertainty: serious problems are already widespread; many farms are abandoned with each year that passes; farmhouses and barns are sold for conversion to 'luxury residences' for 'off-comers'; flocks and herds are sold off and dispersed, those remaining are severely reduced; some upland pastures have already been left to encroaching bracken and scrub. Indeed, there are those who envisage changes in the landscape such as few, at present, would wish or dare to contemplate.[27] The Lyth Valley will not be exempt from these changes.

The Moss

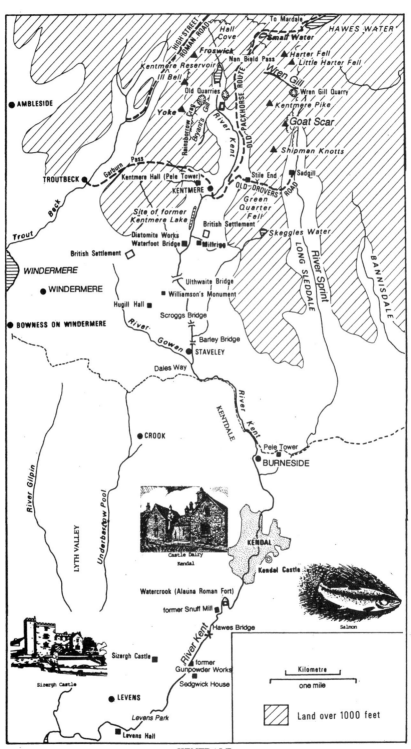

To Mardale

HAWES WATER

Hall Cove

HIGH STREET ROMAN ROAD

Small Water

Froswick

Kentmere Reservoir

Nan Bield Pass

Harter Fell

Little Harter Fell

Ill Bell

Wren Gill

Old Quarries

Wren Gill Quarry

Yoke

Kentmere Pike

Rainsborrow Crag

Bryant's Gill

River Kent

Goat Scar

OLD PACKHORSE ROUTE

Shipman Knotts

AMBLESIDE

Garburn Pass

Kentmere Hall (Pele Tower)

Stile End

Sadgill

TROUTBECK

KENTMERE

OLD DROVERS ROAD

Trout Beck

Site of former Kentmere Lake

Green Quarter Fell

British Settlement

Skeggles Water

Trout

Diatomite Works

Waterfoot Bridge

Millriggs

British Settlement

River Sprint

WINDERMERE

LONG SLEDDALE

BANNISDALE

WINDERMERE

Ulthwaite Bridge

Williamson's Monument

Hugill Hall

River Gowan

Scroggs Bridge

BOWNESS ON WINDERMERE

Barley Bridge

STAVELEY

Dales Way

CROOK

River Kent

KENTDALE

Pele Tower

BURNESIDE

River Gilpin

LYTH VALLEY

Underbarrow Pool

Castle Dairy
Kendal

KENDAL

Kendal Castle

Watercrook (Alauna Roman Fort)

former Snuff Mill

Salmon

Hawes Bridge

Sizergh Castle

River Kent

Sizergh Castle

former Gunpowder Works

Sedgwick House

LEVENS

Levens Park

Kilometre

one mile

Levens Hall

Land over 1000 feet

KENTDALE

12

KENTDALE

The river Kent has its source in a lonely and unfrequented cove among some of the wildest and most picturesque mountain scenery in the whole of Lakeland. Hall cove, birthplace of England's fastest flowing river and guarded by the dark bastions of Gavel and Bleathwaite Crags, lies in a marshy hollow 2,300 feet above sea-level only a short stride from the mighty uplands of High Street and Thornthwaite Crag. Nearby are the sweeping precipices of Ill Bell, Froswick and Rainsborough Crag and the imposing grassy heights of the Knowe, Kentmere Pike and Harter Fell. Along the fellside winds the ancient trackway to the Nan Bield Pass, now a fell-walker's favourite route to the high fells but once busy with packhorse trains and travellers laden with the products of the industries of Kentdale and South Westmorland. High in the hidden recesses of the mountains which enclose the valley head, the river which turned so many mill-wheels, watered so many pastures and gave its name to the town of Kendal, has its shadowy origins. It is a wild, beautiful and awesome spot; for some it is a place of pilgrimage.

Rejoicing in the discovery of life, the new-born river, like a young lamb, gambols irresponsibly over a precipitous waterfall, cascading steeply down before proceeding rather more sedately to enter Kentmere Reservoir. This was constructed in the late 1840s to ensure a supply of water to the many mills along the river in times of drought, a project made necessary – with expressive irony – by the deliberate draining of a large natural lake only a few years earlier to create land for cultivation, a scheme which proved to be only marginally successful. Another sign of recent human activity here is the scars of the long-abandoned slate quarries, man-made gashes in the fellsides.

There is little human settlement now in the valley of the Upper Kent but, slowly and painstakingly, archaeologists are revealing evidence that there were once farmsteads and field-systems here whose slight remains will one day enable us to reconstruct a convincing portrait of an ancient way of life. Work has scarcely begun on a study of these sites but settlements dating from the early centuries A.D. to the 14th century have already been identified: at Tongue House, Bryant's Gill, Overend, Stile End, Kentmere Hall and Millrigg. Writing of the excavations at Bryant's Gill in the 1980s, the leader of the archaeological SEARCH group comments that

> The Bryant's Gill site is just part of a fossil landscape extending over at least 125,000 square metres under the mountain wall of Rainsbarrow Crag. Such landscapes are rare in Britain and are unique for the amount of information they contain, frozen as it were out of time, about a cluster of peoples.

Old field walls and enclosures, cultivation terraces, hut circles, house platforms have already been uncovered and many hundreds of artefacts have been identified, including whetstones, spindle whorls, stone arrowheads, a cornelian bead and a great deal of pottery, iron and glass. It now seems possible that as more evidence is accumulated these studies may provide positive identification of prehistoric field systems, Romano-British farmsteads, Norse shielings and medieval homesteads.[1] Two discoveries aroused particular interest as they seemed to point conclusively to a Norse presence in Kentmere. Both were uncovered during the digging operations at the diatomite works in the bed of the former lake: the first was a Viking spearhead found in 1942 with a head 13½ inches long (34.3cm) and a socket over four inches long (10.7cm) and engraved with the herring-bone pattern common on many spearheads found in Norway; the second was a dug-out canoe, made of oak and 14ft. long (4.25m), which expert examination also provisionally dated from the Viking period.[2]

Archaeology and place-name evidence combine to indicate that the Norsemen were strongly represented among early settlers in Kentdale but they were clearly not the first, and, in this valley at least, they had to contend with a more positive Anglian colonisation than in many other valleys.

One mile from its source the Kent flows through Kentmere Reservoir, a half-mile long stretch of water which, although it is a man-made lake, does enhance the wild and craggy scenery around it. Beyond this lies a narrow belt of pastures overshadowed by steep crags beneath which are small farmsteads bearing names both Norse and English in origin: Hartrigg, Overend, Scales, Hallow Bank, Brockstones and Stile End. Through a narrowing gap the Kent approaches the tiny hamlet of Kentmere which until 200 years ago stood at the head of the lake. This is one of the most attractive parts of Upper Kentdale. In a moment of joyous impatience with its placid course through the pastureland the river surges through a rock-strewn gorge in a sparkling cascade among the sun-dappled woods before resuming an unruffled glide through the water-meadows beyond.

Kentmere's Church of St Cuthbert is thought to stand on the site of a much older Saxon or Early Norman Church but no records have survived. Most of the stone-work and the roof beams of the present church date from the 16th century but there is an unusual arrangement of Norman windows set in groups of three. Bernard Gilpin, perhaps the best-known of the talented Gilpin family who lived at Kentmere Hall, is commemorated here by a bronze tablet of intricate design created by the Keswick School of Industrial Arts.

The Gilpins acquired lands here in the reign of King John and lost them again during the Civil Wars of the 17th century as a result of their royalist sympathies. Famous Gilpins include Richard who impressed King John by his feats in battle and became a hero in Kentmere when he

29   *Kentmere Church*

despatched a wild boar which had been wreaking havoc amongst the crops. The Gilpin coat-of-arms incorporates a boar's head in reference to this accomplishment. William Gilpin was killed in 1485 at Bosworth Field; George Gilpin was Queen Elizabeth's agent in the Netherlands; Sawrey Gilpin, famous for his paintings of horses, became President of the Society of Artists and a Royal Academician in 1787; his brother, William, was a leading educational reformer, biographer of the principal Protestant churchmen of the Reformation and author of an outstanding guidebook to which he gave the resounding title *Observations relative chiefly to Picturesque Beauty made in the year 1772 on several parts of England; particularly the Mountains and Lakes of Cumberland and Westmorland.* His nephew, William Sawrey Gilpin, had a distinguished career as a water-colour painter and landscape gardener during the Regency period.

The most famous of them all was Bernard, the Apostle of the North, an outspoken cleric who survived the hazards of the religious and political upheavals of the 16th century to serve the post-Reformation Church of England in the diocese of Durham during the volatile reigns of Edward VI, Mary Tudor and Elizabeth I. His attacks on the condition of the Church, the quality of the clergy and the doctrines of the Roman Catholic faith almost brought him to the stake in 1558 but on his way to London to face charges of heresy he broke a leg and by the time he had recovered the Catholic Queen had died. Her successor, Elizabeth I, restored him to his parish of Houghton-le-Spring and to his position as Archdeacon of Durham; and for the next 25 years he laboured to secure the Queen's Church in an area largely loyal to the old faith. Bernard died in 1583 following an encounter with an errant bull in Durham Market Place.

The Gilpin home, Kentmere Hall, is a 14th-century pele-tower – now ruinous – with a 16th-century farmhouse attached to it. The tower has four storeys and a staircase in one corner and with its tunnel-vaulted ground floor is typical of the house-fortresses built in the area to withstand attacks by marauding Scottish raiding parties: others locally may be seen at Levens Hall, Sizergh Castle, Burneside, Beetham and Longsleddale.[3]

The farmhouse was built in the mid-Tudor period and its 30ft. long main beam is said to have been lifted into place, single-handed, by Hugh Hird, a local giant and the son of a former nun of Furness Abbey. He entertained visitors by uprooting trees with his bare hands and, not surprisingly, was a Champion at Cumberland Wrestling. He attributed his great strength to a diet of 'poddish [porridge] that thick that a mouse could walk dry-shod on, in t'mornin', and t'sunny side of a wether for t'dinner'. Hugh's story is still one of the unverified legends of Lakeland but a farm at Troutbeck Park where he later lived with his mother was known as Hird's Holding and his feats of strength earned him the name by which he is now usually known, The Troutbeck Giant.

30 *Kentmere Hall: The pele-tower.*

The Kentmere township was divided into four 'quarters', each subdivided into individual holdings each of which had to provide a man to do Border Service for the
Crown, the land being held under what was known as 'Border Tenure', a reminder of
more turbulent days in Lakeland. These four quarters still appear on the map of Kentmere
– Crag Quarter, Hollowbank Quarter, Green Quarter and Wray Quarter.

After the Union of the English and Scottish Crowns in 1603 James I attempted to
impose general military service on these tenants and to dispossess them of their holdings. Their case went to the Court of Star Chamber which allowed their petition in
respect of the land but rejected their pleas concerning military service.

As the threat from Border raids gradually eased in late medieval times the farming
economy of the Kentmere Quarters became quite prosperous. Surviving records and
maps indicate a high degree of regulation and organisation in the seasonal schedule of
work and in the equitable allocation of upland pasture. Cattle and sheep were kept in
significant numbers and useful crops of oats, barley and rye were grown, with sufficient
'home' pasture to ensure an adequate hay harvest and a supply of Spring grass. A recent
study of this period of Kentmere agriculture concluded that:

> The medieval land-use of Kentmere suggests that Kentmere may have made not only a significant
> contribution to the leather and woollen industries of medieval Kendal but perhaps also to the
> droving trade which was re-establishing itself after the disruption of the Scottish Wars.[4]

Kentmere Hall once enjoyed a fine view over Kentmere Lake which stretched
southwards for well over a mile, a glacial lake which must have played an important
part in the economy of the settlements on its shores and added much to the natural
beauty of the valley. The British village at Millrigg occupied an enviable position on a
shelf above the lake with an open aspect towards the south and west: the fertile soil and
the waters of the lake must have been a plentiful food source, and, as excavation has
shown, its defences were formidable. The site covers about three-quarters of an acre
(approximately three thousand square metres) and has an enclosing wall between seven
and ten feet thick. An internal enclosure contained at least seven hut circles and various
other structures. It is almost certainly an Iron-Age village and probably survived during
the Roman Occupation and possibly for some time after.[5]

All that remains of Kentmere Lake today is a narrow strip of water known as
Kentmere Tarn, privately owned and beloved of anglers, but perhaps best-known for
its deposits of diatomite, a substance which in its natural state is not unlike soft, dried
clay, and has a remarkable variety of uses. It is made up of the skeletons of millions
of minute single-cell organisms belonging to the algae family which extract silica and
similar elements from the water to build up an external shell. When they die they sink
to the bed of the lake, decompose and leave their silica skeletons in massive deposits.
Each diatom is of such microscopic size that between 50 and 60 million are contained
in each cubic inch of deposit. Under the microscope the silica shell appears as a
delicate pattern of perforations and it is this extremely porous property, together with
its light weight, light colour, chemical inertia and thermal conductivity, which has made
diatomite one of the most valuable natural materials mined in recent times. It was
extensively used in many heat insulation products as it is the most efficient natural
material for this purpose; it is an important 'filler' in the manufacture of plastics, paper,
paints, fertilisers and soap powders; it is a highly efficient absorbent for gases, toxic
liquids, fungicides and disinfectants; it is probably the best filter-aid in water-treatment
and in the manufacture of air-conditioning units, pharmaceuticals, sugar, soap, petroleum

and in the production processes of wines and beer. It was also at one time used as an ingredient of cosmetics, face creams and dental powders.

Diatomite is found in many countries and world production is about one million tons a year. England's only known deposits are in the bed of the old lake in Kentmere and in Skeggles Water, a remote tarn on the moors above Kentmere. The Kentmere deposits vary in depth from five to 35 feet and are too impure for use as filter-aids but have been in demand for the manufacture of insulation materials and resin wool filter pads for air-conditioning units. Work has now ceased in Kentmere but during the 50 years of dredging some 10,000 tons of the lake-bed deposits were removed each year with the result that a new lake was created, about half a mile in length, less than 200 yards in width, and so gracefully adorned with a pleasant fringe of trees that it could easily be taken for an elongated tarn placed there by nature.

In common with most other Lakeland valleys Kentmere's geological history has left a legacy of mineral deposits which man has inevitably tried to exploit. Slate quarrying and lead mining on a small scale supplemented the modest income of many a hill farmer and, certainly from the early 18th century, there is documentary evidence to show that the farmers of Upper Kentmere owned quarrying tools. These were put to use in the vein of high quality slate which runs across Kentmere under Ill Bell and Kentmere Pike and over to the Wren Gill Quarry in Long Sleddale. The quarries of Kentmere did not enjoy the advantages of those in the neighbouring valley which were backed by the wealth and trading expertise of the thrusting Howards of Levens Hall and it was not until the railway came to Staveley that Kentmere slate was able to secure easier access to a wider market. Between 1847 and 1914 the output of slate steadily increased from the seven main quarries reaching a peak production of 725 tons in 1911. Despite its superior quality as endurable roofing slate this fine Westmorland slate could not compete with the inferior and cheaper slate from Wales and the whole enterprise rapidly declined into extinction in the mid-20th century.

Just before it thunders over the weir at Barley Bridge the river Kent passes close by the tumbled relics of two lead-smelting mills, one near Scroggs Bridge, the other in Haw Wood, remnants of a Kentmere industry of which few records have survived. The first speculative venture in lead-mining began in the 1750s by the river near Sawmill Cottage but repeated flooding forced an early move to higher ground on the fell above Millrigg. A second shaft was sunk very shortly afterwards close to the summit of Staveley Head Fell and this proved to be Kentmere's most productive mine employing up to 20 miners from Cornwall and Derbyshire in its heyday. An interesting feature of this mine was the use of a horse-gin to hoist the kibbles of ore from the workings 200ft. (60m) below. The outline of the circle of the horse's 'treadmill' may still be seen and the raised rim round the mouth of the shaft forms a distinct 'polo-mint' feature in the landscape. A third exploration for lead was begun on the slopes of Potter Fell between Side House and Frost Hole but although the samples of ore yielded 8½ ozs. of silver per ton of ore, a main vein was never struck and the operation ceased. Kentdale is fortunate to have one of the best preserved of the chopwood kilns which are found in the lead-mining areas. These were oval-shaped kilns in which green timbers were slowly dried out to produce the special chopwood – pieces roughly 6ins. x 2ins. – used in the process of smelting the lead ore. The kilns were conveniently sited in close proximity to the smelting mills.[6]

The Kentmere mines created no great fortunes for those who risked money in the venture and they exacted a high cost in injuries to those who toiled in them. The well-known hazards of mining in the fells of the Lake District may, perhaps, account for the muted reaction to the discovery in 1968 of gold in shingle dredged from the bed of the

31   *Horse-whin used to raise water or ore from lead mines*

Kent near Barley Bridge. There are those who achieve extremely modest and hard won gains from a search for gold in Lakeland but this is an eccentric's hobby rather than a capitalist's enterprise.[7]

The Kent now flows through verdant pastures and woodlands, as quiet and peaceful a rural scene as any poet would wish to find, past ancient farms and elegant houses, past the important British settlement on Hugill Fell, past the fine 17th-century bridge at Ullthwaite, foaming under Scroggs Bridge, thundering in a graceful curve over the weir at Barley Bridge and so to the 'mill town' of Staveley. In these two miles the Kent and its tributary becks have in former days provided water-power for at least ten mills but from this point onwards the waters were harnessed to drive the wheels of at least fifty more.[8]

In its journey of 25 miles the Kent falls more than two thousand feet, a descent which ensures an unusually fast flowing stream, and the high fells surrounding its source provide a volume of water sufficient to maintain a steady and forceful current. It is, therefore, not surprising that the Kent and its tributaries were favoured by the engineers of water-mills for at least a thousand years. Cornmills and fulling mills are recorded in the early Middle Ages and the former almost certainly existed before the Norman Conquest. By the late 18th century such mills were well outnumbered by the mills of the early Industrial Revolution which for its first century relied almost entirely on water-power. It has been suggested that for a time the great concentration of water mills in the Kent valley generated almost as much power as the City of Birmingham, often regarded as the true power-house of the Industrial Revolution. The mills of Kentdale produced woollen cloth of many varieties, cottons, linens, tweeds, carpets, snuff, bobbins, rope, paper, gunpowder, combs, polished marble, flax, dyes and hats; and to these may be added the brewing mills, fulling mills, saw mills, and the vital corn mills.[9]

The dominance of steam-power after the middle of the 19th century put an end to the growth of Westmorland's water-powered industries and by 1950 only a very small number of mills were still working, powered no longer by water but by electricity. By 1975 most of these had closed. It is salutary to recall that 150 years ago the dark, satanic mills of industrial Britain were just as much in evidence in the pleasant countryside of the valley of the River Kent as they were in the Pennine towns of Lancashire. The beauty of nature and the pure air of the fells were of little consequence to those who were slaves at the mill from 6 a.m. to 6 p.m. from the age of 11 onwards. It mattered not one jot whether your chains were in Stockport or in Staveley.[10]

For about one hundred and fifty years from the late 18th century to the early 20th century Staveley was a busy industrial village, the centre of the Lakeland bobbin industry. There were five bobbin mills in the village (as well as corn and woollen mills) and together they produced tens of millions of bobbins each year for the Yorkshire woollen mills, the Lancashire cotton mills, lace mills in Leicester, silk mills in Derbyshire and Huddersfield, and for many other textile mills as far apart as Shrewsbury and Glasgow. Foreign competition and the development of the plastic bobbin put an end to this trade but Staveley has developed a number of other manufacturing enterprises which still give the village the air of a place of industry. It has, however, lost its once thriving agricultural market, with a charter dating from 1329, and its famous sheep fair which survived until 1914.

From Staveley to Burneside the Kent winds a fairly tranquil course through a landscape of lush meadows and woodlands bright with primroses, bluebells and wild daffodils in the springtime, and herons fish throughout the year. Here the Dales Way hugs the river-bank and passes close by the picturesque millpond at Cowan Head and the thunderous fall of water over the sweeping curve of the weir at Bowston. The industrial village of Burneside is dominated by the internationally known paper mills of James Cropper which have prospered here for over one hundred and fifty years, manufacturing a range of high-quality specialist products.

A stone's throw away from this still expanding factory stand the ruins of Burneside Hall, a 13th/14th-century fortified house or pele-tower still impressive with its fine gateway and ivy-covered crenellations. The earliest reference to the Hall is in 1290 when it was owned by Gilbert de Burneshead who was, in fact, the last of the family to live there. Later tenants included Thomas Machell, the 17th-century 'Antiquary on Horseback', whose recorded travels tell us so much about the topography of Westmorland at that time, and Richard Braithwaite (1588-1673), the poet and satirist, who was born at the Hall and was the epitome of the cultured Royalist country gentleman. The Hall in his day seems to have been an elegant estate with pleasant gardens and well-appointed rooms; the Great Chamber was 50ft. long and 25ft. wide and has been compared to the Halls of the Colleges of Oxford and Cambridge:

> The roof was exposed to view, of massive timbers, ingeniously constructed, beautifully enriched with elaborate mouldings and carvings, and of high pitch; in the centre of which rose a little graceful spirelet, called the louvre, open to the air, as a means of escape for the smoke from the fire which burnt on a hearth in the middle of the floor, the fuel being large logs supported by andirons or fire-dogs.

Thomas Machell tells us that in 1692 the Hall was approached by 'a court, with lodge and battlements, through which was the ascent to the Hall. Before the court was

32   *Burneside Hall*

a large pond stored with tench, trout and eels ... and on either side is a little island with plane trees planted on it'.[11]

Braithwaite wrote prolifically producing plays and verse of varying merit, some of it achieving a certain poetic elegance, much of it no more than popular doggerel. It was, perhaps inevitably, one of the latter which gained him most fame: this was *Barnaby's Journal*, a saga of the travels of a drunken horse-trader, published in 1638. A brief extract may suffice to give a taste of its style and flavour:

> To Banbery came I, O profane one!
> Where I saw a Puritane-one
> Hanging of his cat on Monday,
> For killing of a mouse on Sunday.

Braithwaite wrote a more polished poesy in *The Fatall Nuptiall*, an elegy mourning the death of 47 people drowned when the Windermere Ferry sank in 1635 while carrying guests returning from a wedding at Hawkshead.[12]

Braithwaite has been described as 'the first of the Lake poets and probably the earliest [writer] to notice descriptively the characteristics of scenery'.[13]

The green luxuriance of the fields around Burneside owes much to the abundant rainfall borne on the south-westerly winds to which the valley is exposed. On the high fells where the River Kent has its source annual rainfall often exceeds 100 inches (250cm) but in the lowland area towards the coast it is less than half this amount – no more than in some parts of Devon and with the generally mild humidity of the south-western counties. Harriet Martineau in her *Complete Guide to the English Lakes* tells of a reply she received to her enquiry concerning the local weather: 'It donks and it dozzles; and while's it's a bit siftering; but it don't make no girt pel.' – a pronouncement which Miss Martineau is thoughtful enough to translate for her readers as: 'It is misty and it drizzles and it can be a bit showery but there is rarely any great downpour.' Her informant might have added that in hours of sunshine and in levels of temperature the lower Kent valley compares very favourably with the seaside resorts of Lancashire.

Its waters re-inforced by those of the Sprint and the Mint, the Kent now leaves behind green fields and woods and grazing sheep and cattle to enter the busy town of Kendal which in former days it was wont

33   Helsington Snuff Mill

to harass with mighty floods. Kendal still retains much of the character of an old market town and its story has been well chronicled by a succession of local historians.[14]

Soon after leaving Kendal the Kent passes by a small stone building which until 1991 played a key rôle in the Kendal snuff industry. This was Helsington snuff mill, the only water-mill still in use in the 20th century for the grinding and blending of snuff, the source of such famous names as 'Kendal Brown' and 'Camphorated Menthol', just two of the many blends which emerged from this Aladdin's Cave of aromatic snuffs before the demands of modern economy forced its closure after more than a century of activity. Before its wheel turned to grind snuff in 1887 Helsington Mill had already been grinding corn for perhaps a thousand years. The first historical reference to it is in 1297 but, as with many other ancient mills, this could be merely an indication that a Norman landowner had taken possession from a Saxon or Norse predecessor. Its disappearance was a sad commentary on the late 20th century and made all the more apposite the comment by A. Wainwright on this very mill:

> Here at Helsington Mill is a simple device that never fails, that uses only river water and returns it unpolluted, that costs next to nothing to operate, that produces no fumes or other noxious substance, that generates no heat that would impair the flavour of the finished product, that leaves no litter, makes no noise and always works perfectly. It could have a lesson for the 20th century.[15]

On the opposite bank of the river to Helsington Mill, largely hidden under the meadow grass on which sheep and cattle graze, are the remains of the Roman fort of Alauna, known today as Watercrook. Archaeological excavations have over the years brought to light a good deal of pottery, numerous coins, many miscellaneous artefacts and a fairly clear outline of the foundations of the fort. Today, in this green and pleasant meander of the Kent it is not easy to conjure up the sights and sounds of a Roman military camp of almost two thousand years ago, with all the noisy bustle of preparations for arrival and departure and the routine activity of a garrison of 500 men.[16]

The Kent now enters limestone country. Under the high arch of Hawes Bridge – where local ghosts were banished – the waters surge through a deep cutting before purling widely on to a lovely stretch where its banks are fringed with a variety of trees and the water-edge is alive with herons, kingfishers, ducks and dippers. At Sedgwick near the site of the old gunpowder works the river has carved for itself an impressive channel down into the limestone where the rocks are adorned with dripping mosses and ferns and glitter with a sparkling cascade of icicles in the winter frosts. In a final display of drama, as if to remind us of its mountain origin, the Kent plunges spectacularly over Force Falls before gliding placidly onwards through the serene parkland of Levens Hall and so on to its meeting with the measureless sands of Morecambe Bay and finally the sea.

The gunpowder works at Sedgwick were opened in 1764 and eventually stretched along the bank of the Kent for about a kilometre downstream from the suspension bridge. Almost all trace of this industry has been erased and the main area is now occupied by houses and by the National Trust caravan park. The river and the local woodlands readily supplied the water, the power and the charcoal, while saltpetre and sulphur which had to be imported were transported from the nearby port of Milnthorpe through which the barrels of powder were shipped out to Liverpool and elsewhere. With the coming of the railway in the mid-19th century and the silting up of the Milnthorpe channel use was made of a special siding at Hincaster which had strongly-built storage facilities for the needs of this dangerous enterprise. The Wakefield family who initiated the manufacture of gunpowder here had by the late 19th century taken over control of all the Westmorland Gunpowder Mills except that at Elterwater and were producing about half of all the gunpowder manufactured in the United kingdom.[17]

John Wakefield had laid the foundations of the family fortunes by a successful business career in Kendal based on banking, brewing and woollen textiles. It was an astute judgment on his part to see that in South Westmorland were all the resources necessary to take advantage of the increasing demand for gunpowder, particularly in quarrying, mining and in the armaments of war. By the 1850s the original works at Old Sedgwick had expanded to give the family control of the mills at New Sedgwick, Basingill, and Gatebeck. Success in business was followed, as was customary in Victorian times, by the construction of an imposing country residence, and in 1868 there arose on a small eminence a few hundred yards from the Kent and the first gunpowder works, a mansion furnished with all the luxury that Victorian inventiveness could devise but so uninspired in its architecture that the new partnership of Paley and Austin must surely have lived to regret it. From this country seat William Wakefield played a leading part in the public life of the Kendal area and was awarded the most fulsome obituaries on his death in 1869.

His daughter, Mary, was a remarkable woman who achieved not merely local but national and international renown as a lively and spirited personality and as a talented singer and musician. Her lecture-recitals in London and elsewhere were regarded as outstanding musical occasions and her interpretations of the songs of Grieg, with Grieg himself as pianist, were rapturously received. It was she who created the tradition of musical excellence of which Kendal is justly proud. Her memorial is the annual Mary Wakefield Music Festival.[18]

And so the Kent proceeds to the comfortable lowlands. Here the river flows through prosperous farmlands and adds grace and dignity to the estates surrounding the stately homes of the heirs of the powerful families of Norman England. Ivo de Taillebois' great Barony of Kendal controlled all the land between the river Lune and Lake Windermere with its centre in the valley of the Kent. This created a secure medieval power base for the Redmans of Levens and the Stricklands of Sizergh.

Levens Hall was the home of the Redman family for over three hundred years, a family which typified that solid phalanx of country gentry on whom England relied for political stability and who often balanced the dangers inherent in the intrigues of an ambitious feudal nobility. The Redmans maintained a high position among the families of England by virtue of their great possessions and the distinguished service they rendered to their country as soldiers, statesmen, diplomatists and churchmen. At the heart of Levens Hall is a pele-tower probably from the early 14th century but it is the later medieval and Elizabethan additions which give the house its special distinction, although, for many, the main attraction here is the famous topiary garden. Others find equal pleasure in the walk through the park which adjoins the Hall with its magnificent trees, its herd of rare Bagot deer and flock of Bagot goats, its birdlife and the swans cruising gracefully on the broad sweep of the river Kent.[19]

Less than a mile from Levens is Sizergh Castle, home of the Strickland family for 750 years during which they, too, have maintained a tradition of distinguished public service. Stricklands went from Sizergh to the Scottish Wars of Edward I, to Agincourt with Henry V, to the Yorkist cause in the Wars of the Roses and to the Royalist cause in the Great Civil War. A Strickland sat in almost every Parliament from 1258 to 1688 and frequently thereafter until 1928. Sir Gerald Strickland, 1st and last Baron Strickland of Sizergh, was Prime Minister of Malta and Dominion Governor and also a member of both Houses of Parliament. The massive pele-tower at Sizergh dates from the early 14th century and the Great Hall is a Tudor development. Extensive additions were made in the reign of Elizabeth I when most of the fine panelling and wood-carving were created. There were substantial alterations in the 18th century in order to conform to the prevailing fashion for elegant drawing-rooms with exquisite objets d'art, beautiful furniture and specially commissioned family portraits to adorn the walls. In 1950 the Castle became the property of the National Trust and it is visited by more than fifty thousand people each year.[20]

Before it comes to the end of its 25-mile course the Kent passes by two farmsteads, placed no more than a few feet above sea-level, whose pastures it has watered for many generations: Nether Levens with its solid 16th-century masonry, its Elizabethan mullioned windows and its massive elliptical chimneys; and Ninezergh, the pastureland of the Norseman, Hnigandr, a reminder that from the mountain to the sea we have found everywhere in Kentdale indelible traces of the ubiquitous Norsemen.

The Kent now flows into the sands through a landscape of flat mosses and saltmarsh, an estuarine scene beloved by botanists and ornithologists, and rewarding to all who enjoy a wide seascape and the colours of the purple sea aster, pink thrift, blue sea lavender and white scurvy grass. Here, too, may be heard the poignant cry of the curlew, the lapwing and the oyster-catcher, or the long, low radiant horizon may be crossed by a flight of tern, sandpiper or greylag goose. In the background the soaring escarpment of Whitbarrow Scar overlooks the farmlands and woodland copses of the Kent's final reach – a gentle pastoral country, almost reminiscent of England's southern shires, and yet within sight of the rugged hills which surround the gathering grounds of Kentdale's swift and sacred river.[21]

Badger

13

LONG SLEDDALE

In 1867 John Murray published his *Handbook for Westmorland, Cumberland and the English Lakes*, a guidebook which was to become as essential a companion for the Victorian tourist as Wainwright's *Pictorial Guide to the Lakeland Fells* is to many modern fell-walkers. But whereas Wainwright sought out the tracks and footpaths to the high fells, Murray aimed to lead his readers to a discovery of the secluded valleys. So it was that the 19th-century tourists were introduced to the remote eastern valley of Long Sleddale, a valley, as Murray describes it, 'thoroughly free from the intentions of art. There is nothing to mar its harmony; and while passing along the narrow lanes enclosed by thickly-lichened walls, tufted with wild flowers, the eye rests on the brilliant green of the meadows, the sparkling purity of the stream or the autumnal tints of the copses, we acknowledge it to be a genuine and lovely specimen of natural scenery.'[1] By good fortune Long Sleddale has changed very little since then; the visitor today may see here, as perhaps nowhere else in the district, the Lakeland countryside as Wordsworth knew it: no 'deforming' plantations of alien conifers but a succession of natural woods and native trees; no overgrown intrusions of 'foreign shrubs' but a natural scattering of 'holly, broom, wild-rose, elder, dogberry, white and blackthorn etc.'; no discordantly ostentatious 'residences', only modest farmsteads 'gently incorporated into the scenery'; in brief, a valley almost 'unsullied by the works of Man'.[2] Wordsworth idealised the life of the folk who inhabited these valleys and his views on the changes which were taking place, even in his time, in the economy and landscape of the Lake District were often no more than prejudices fraught with snobbery, conservatism and inconsistency, but we should be grateful for his poet's insight into a world we have now almost lost and that in Long Sleddale we have been left a small corner of that world almost as he described it.

John Murray was far more down-to-earth, not to say downright uncomplimentary, in his opinion of the valley folk in his day: 'The simple, but rough manners of the Westmorland and Cumberland peasantry have not undergone any material change from their increased intercourse with the world; and education has hitherto had but little effect in refining their tastes, elevating their character and improving their morals.'[3]

Perhaps more reliable was the description he gave of the typical farmhouse of the time, a scene as familiar in Long Sleddale as in any other Lakeland valley:

> The farmhouses are generally very ancient and the interior economy has been but little changed with time. They are generally built of stone with very thick walls, and are either thatched or covered with coarse blue slate. The floor of slate is kept scrupulously clean and is ornamented by scroll-work done with red and yellow ochre or chalk, according to the taste of the inmates. The great oaken beams are generally polished and bright brass and mahogany often decorate the kitchen. The furniture generally consists of a long oaken table with a bench on each side where the whole family, master, children and servants, take their meals together. At the side of the fireplace is the 'sconce', a sort of fixed bench, under which one night's elden, or fuel, is deposited each evening. The clothing of the family was formerly made from wool spun from native fleece,

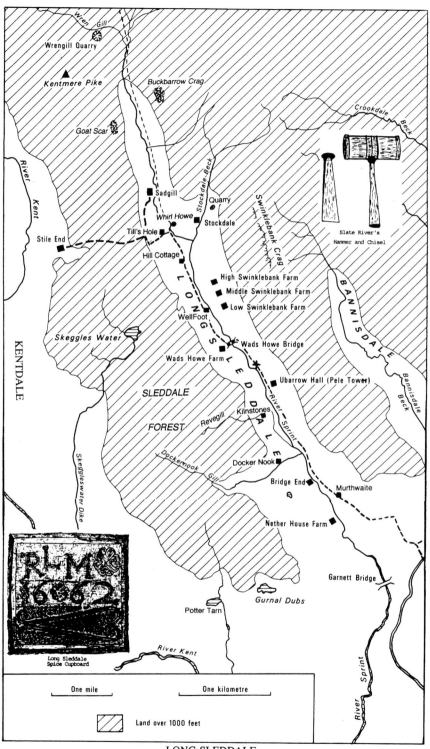

LONG SLEDDALE

and of linen made from the flax which was grown almost on every farm; the hemp ridge in fields still bears its name. Clogs and wooden-soled shoes, well adapted to a mountainous and rainy country, continue in common use.[4]

The next century would bring changes undreamt of in Murray's generation but Long Sleddale had already seen far more of the world's commerce than these late Victorian visitors could ever envisage.

For more than five centuries – until the coming of the railways – Long Sleddale had been a major highway, part of the network of packhorse routes and drove roads along which hundreds of laden pack-ponies and thousands of sheep, cattle and geese were driven each year on their way to markets and fairs in all parts of the country. It is easy to forget that before the mid-19th century most of the wealth of the kingdom was transported on the hoof and that through Cumberland and Westmorland there ran a complex system of highways carrying a constant tide of traffic on its way to satisfy the enormous appetite for food and material goods which a growing population and an expanding economy demanded. From Scotland and from the lush coastal plain of Cumberland, from the farms, mines, mills and quarries of Westmorland, animals and goods poured along these ancient routes, several of which converged to join the main highway through Long Sleddale. From Kentmere and the Garburn Road the well-worn track came to Sadgill at the head of Long Sleddale where a bridge had been built early in the 18th century in response to a petition from a wide area complaining that there was 'great prejudice of trade' when the river was in flood:

> The inhabitants of Long Sleddale, Langdale, Grasmere, Rydal and Loughrigg, Ambleside, Troutbeck, Kentmere and several other townships in the Barony of Kendal, show that the great road and public highway between Hawksyde, Ambleside, Shap, Penrith and Appleby, very much used by travellers, drovers and others having occasion frequently to pass and repass to and from the said markets with cattle and other goods, on which public highway there is a water or rivulet called Sadgill which by violent and sudden rain there, is often roused and overflows its banks so that no passenger dare venture to cross the same, and many travellers are forced to stay two or three days before they dare venture to cross ... to the great prejudice of trade, and pray that a bridge may be erected over the same'.[5]

Before this bridge was built the road followed the west side of the valley, where it may still be clearly traced, and crossed the Sprint at Wadshow Bridge which was the subject of another petition in 1750 complaining that this important link 'on the high road from Ambleside to Appleby was entirely destroyed'. From Wadshow the pack-horse trains and the hustling beasts went on by Ubarrow, and Murthwaite to Selside, Grayrigg and beyond.[6]

It is doubtful whether John Murray would have invited his well-brought-up tourists to experience the delights of Long Sleddale if this traffic had survived. The mud, mire and odours of the churned up road and the appalling cacophony of animal noise would have totally ruined the pastoral and scenic idyll he portrayed but by 1867 an unaccustomed silence had fallen over the valley. The iron horse now bestrode the land; the railway had, in the course of a few years, transformed the transport system and made these ancient roads, for a time, redundant. Indeed, the highway through Long Sleddale was itself almost transformed into a railway, no less than the main line from London to Scotland. By the 1840s plans were well advanced to construct this line over the fells to Carlisle; only one major problem remained to be solved – how to negotiate the steep gradients of the Shap Fells. The chief engineer Joseph Locke, had accepted the probability that the power of the early locomotives would be insufficient to cope with such a long and arduous climb, and he had accordingly conducted a survey of a less demanding route via Long Sleddale with a tunnel cut through the high ground at the head of the valley. In the end new locomotive technology came to the rescue and Locke was able to take his preferred route over Shap. We can only imagine what the effect would have been if Locke's decision had gone otherwise but, as Wordsworth realistically proclaimed, 'the railway power, we know well, will not admit of being materially counteracted by sentiment', an axiom only too familiar to modern conservationists in their battle with 'motorway power'.

Today Long Sleddale acts as a highway of quite a different kind. In 1941 the then Manchester Corporation Waterworks completed the first stage of their aqueduct to convey water from the reservoir recently constructed at Haweswater. This was a nine-mile section through the Mardale Tunnel and then along the length of Long Sleddale to a primary treatment plant near Garnett Bridge. Under the quiet pastures and un-known to most visitors a seven-foot aqueduct carries an unceasing flow of many millions of gallons of water every day into the homes, farms and industries of Cumbria, Lancashire, Manchester and Merseyside.

For the visitor who demands that his Lakeland scene should include an expanse of water Long Sleddale may well be a little disappointing. There is no lake here now to reflect the mountain scene, only the sparkling waters of the River Sprint which, after a spectacular birth among the cascades and waterfalls of Wren Gill, threads its way through flower meadows and rocky gorges, adding its own glittering charm to the valley scene. Thousands of years ago, following the melting of the glaciers, Long Sleddale may have had no less than four lakes whose limits are clearly defined by rock barriers today: at Sadgill, at Wads How Farm, at Bridge End and at Garnett Bridge. The church stands on a massive moraine which reaches almost right across the floor of the valley while at Bridge End there is a distinct bench indicating the 'shore-line' of a former lake. It is unlikely that men ever lived here to see these long-lost lakes: it is certain that there would have been little scope for men to farm here if they had remained.

The names of the farmsteads scattered along the valley tell us that these former lake beds have been cultivated for at least a thousand years. Most are of Norse origin and have a recorded history from the 13th or 14th centuries. The name of the valley itself is a tautological compound of the Old English 'slaed' and the Old Norse 'dalr', both of which mean 'a valley', but the medieval name was properly 'Sleddale Brunolf', referring to the local Norseman, Brynjolfr, who also gave his name to Burneside. He would certainly have known Sadgill, Murthwaite, Stockdale, Swinklebank and Ubarrow, and he would have known, more precisely than we do today, the true origins of Goatscar, Ancrow Brow and the mysterious mound at Whirl Howe.[7]

One place-name at the head of Long Sleddale, familiar enough to modern ears, would have puzzled these medieval valley folk. Above Sadgill and the interesting geological divide between the Silurian Slates and the Borrowdale Volcanics is an impressive 500ft. rock step which conceals the intricate ravine known today as Wren Gill. This was, origi-nally and appropriately, named Wrangdale – the twisting valley – and acquired its modern name only in the 19th century when it achieved a modest fame as a quarry for very high-quality slate. Hodgson's *History of Westmorland* records that in 1816 'Wrangle Head' was 'famous for its large and excellent quarries of the finest blue slates which are conveyed on the backs of ponies', but by 1851 the Mannex *Directory of Westmorland* stated that the quarry 'was not wrought for several years'.

The quarry was opened in 1728 and recent studies have shown that the exceptional quality of the slate soon became well-known among the aristocratic families who through-out the 18th century were busy building their country mansions in all parts of the country.

34 *Whirl Howe*

In 1792 the Honourable Richard Howard was urged to use Long Sleddale slate because it was 'deemed the best, allowed by all to be inferior to none'; the Earl of Suffolk's London house and Lord Andover's house in Bath were also roofed in Wren Gill slate and other records refer to orders from gentry in Surrey and Berkshire.

William Green's *Tourists' Guide to the Lakes* published in 1819 observes that 'Great quantities of the finest blue slate are got at this place and conveyed on horseback to some distance'. Most Lakeland quarries have few surviving records but from the sparse details we have from Long Sleddale we learn that the slate was taken by packhorse from the quarry to the end of the track at Sadgill and thence by cart or wagon to Dix's Wharf at Milnthorpe from where it was shipped onwards to London, Bristol and other ports. Ten packhorse loads made up a ton of slate and the cost of transport to the buyer was 23 shillings per ton to Sadgill and 35 shillings to Milnthorpe: the cost 200 years later of Lakeland blue slate is £600 per ton excluding transport.

Wren Gill quarry was revived at intervals in the late 19th and early 20th centuries and enjoyed a final lease of life during the Second World War when it was worked by Italian prisoners of war. On their departure Wren Gill became a ghost quarry which has steadily decayed and can now be identified only by the skeletal remains of water-races, derelict sheds, tiny railways and a few tumble-down cottages, while the crumbling quarry-face merges slowly into the mountain mass of Harter Fell.

Hidden away in the small side-valley of Stockdale is Long Sleddale's other main quarry. This was worked mainly in the 18th century and produced slate notably inferior in quality to that of Wren Gill: it was described as 'heavier and coarser' and was 'chiefly used about barns and other mean buildings in the neighbouring Hamlets and Villages and not sent away by shipping'.[8]

Stockdale was the centre of another industry almost all trace of which has now vanished and its name no longer appears on the 1:25000 Ordnance Survey map. The *Gazetteer of Westmorland* for 1829 refers to the hamlet of Little London in Stockdale which was not only the home of most quarrymen who worked at Wren Gill but also had a long history of textile manufacture. Two fulling mills here are recorded in the

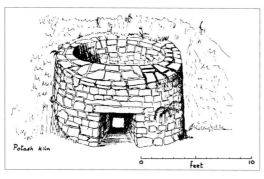

35 A potash kiln

16th century which suggests a population numerous enough to have a flourishing cottage industry and its own corn mill. Stockdale is still a hamlet in its own right, part of and yet separate from the main valley, but its industrial satellite, Little London, is no more than a minor historical footnote.

Also minutiae of history and archaeology are the many other mills and industries of Long Sleddale. Two mills are known to have existed at Docker Nook, and others at High Mill and at Revegill where the canons of Shap Abbey owned the 'convent mill' in 1283. At Garnett Bridge there was once a small industrial site with a corn mill, a bobbin mill and a sawmill.[9]

Long Sleddale's contribution to the important textile industry of South Lakeland may also be traced in its numerous potash kilns and fulling mills. In the former, bracken or birch twigs were burned to a fine ash to which lime was added; water was then percolated through the mass to produce a crude potash. This was boiled with tallow to manufacture a soft soap or lye for use in the fulling mills where the woven cloth was soaked and washed and beaten by trip-hammers to create a thick, felted mass by meshing and shrinking the fibres. At least half a dozen fulling mills have been traced in Long Sleddale, enough to keep the ashburners at the valley's four potash kilns in constant employment. After the fulling process the cloth was stretched on tenter rigs to dry and recover its shape and traces of these tenter grounds may still be seen at various sites along the valley. Long Sleddale clearly played its part in the woollen industry which was the foundation of the economy of the Kendal area for so many years.[10] Lime for this industry and for agriculture was produced in the lime-kiln at Stockdale situated within a few metres of the narrow bed of Coniston Limestone which crosses the upper reaches of the valley.

At the heart of the valley, standing proud on its glacial moraine, is St Mary's Church, the focal point of much of the social life of the dalesfolk, not least the annual summer 'gathering', a true Fête Champêtre. The present church dates from 1863 but there has been a chapel on this site for over six hundred years and from these earlier days have survived a cup and cover-paten from Tudor times and also a pewter dish and flagon. Here, too, is a finely carved oak spice cupboard bearing the date 1662 and the initials RLM.

A glimpse into the time of the older chapel is given in a charming book written by 'A Country Parson' in the later years of the 19th century. In his *Annals of a Quiet Valley* he gently but vividly describes the daily lives of his parishioners, their sorrows and their moments of joy, births and deaths and wedding days, the preparations for feast-days and the humdrum routine in the kitchen and at the spinning wheel. His note on a ritual at the old chapel reminds one of a similar custom in the far-away chapel at Wasdale Head:

> For many years the Church ... was without a door, with the consequences that in rough weather the cattle used to take advantage of it as a 'bield' or shelter, by reason of which it was not infrequently polluted. To prevent this a large thorn bush was dragged into the doorway. After Service it was generally understood that the last who left the Church was to place the thorn in situ.[11]

36 *Lime kiln, Stockdale*

It is not surprising that such a primitive place of worship did not survive the test of Victorian standards and expectations but Long Sleddale does have a rich heritage of houses and other structures from the 17th century and before. The Royal Commission on Historical Monuments lists no less than 10 of Long Sleddale's farmhouses: Low Sadgill, Till's Hole, Hill Cottage, Wellfoot, Nether House, Murthwaite, Bridge End, Kilnstones, Docker Nook and Ubarrow Hall.[12]

Ubarrow is a 15th-century pele-tower with a typical barrel vault and a circular staircase. It was probably somewhat higher than its present two storeys and the windows would be much smaller in keeping with the usual design of these medieval defensive structures. It passed from the Catholic Leyburne family in the reign of Henry VIII to the Harringtons who paid a rent of one shilling to the Parrs of Kendal Castle. During subsequent changes of ownership the tower has been used as a domestic residence, a dairy and a storehouse. In the 1990s restoration work began to create a 20th-century home compatible with its historical dignity.

The defensive capabilities of Ubarrow were never put to the test as the great events of history have, fortunately, passed by this secluded valley. Nor has it suffered greatly from country-house development or from 20th-century tourism. It now lies just within the boundary of the National Park and its conservation should, therefore, be assured. George Eliot's epigram – 'the happiest of women, like the happiest of nations, have no history' – may, with only slight reservations, be applied to Long Sleddale, for although man has lived and worked here for many centuries his impact has been restrained and his influence kind.

Long Sleddale offered just that combination of wild grandeur and romantic solitude beloved by so many Victorian novelists and it was chosen by Mrs. Humphry Ward as the setting for her best novel Robert Elsmere in which she gave the valley the name Long Whindale. Many of the important events in the story take place at the head of the valley at Sadgill and on the path leading to High Street but the book opens with a description of the valley in the Springtime as it was in 1888:

> The narrow road ... was lined with masses of the white heckberry or birdcherry, and ran, an arrow of white, through the greenness of the sloping pastures. The sides of some of the little becks running down into the main river and many of the plantations round the farms were gay with the same tree, so that the farmhouses, gray-roofed and gray-walled, standing in the hollows of the fells, seemed here and there to have been robbed of some of their natural austerity.[13]

One hundred years later Robert Elsmere and Long Whindale have almost sunk into oblivion but Long Sleddale has had another literary reincarnation under the name of Greendale. For it was this gentle valley which inspired John Cunliffe to write his tales of the most famous postman in the world, Postman Pat, stories which reflect so well the minor crises and incidents of daily life familiar to all country folk.

Long Sleddale is a part of the Lake District National Park which embodies the ideal which so many conservationists would like to achieve. It is a living community where families have their homes and earn a livelihood; it is a valley where the interests of natural beauty and practical farming are reconciled, where tradition and progress can be harmonised; it is a place where the world is quiet and where the wild fell ponies can roam at will on the empty moorlands above.

Blackthorn

14

PATTERDALE

In the autumn of 1805 William Wordsworth and his sister, Dorothy, were staying at Side Farm in Patterdale, the home of Captain and Mrs. Luff. It was here, on Saturday, 10 November, a bright and frosty day, that at the breakfast table they heard the news of the naval victory at Trafalgar and of the death of Lord Nelson, events which had taken place just three weeks earlier. It seemed worthy of comment that news could now reach so remote a spot in such a short time:

> In the rebellion of 1745, people fled with their valuables from the open country to Patterdale, as a place of refuge ... At that time, news such as we had heard might have been long in penetrating so far into the recesses of the mountains; but now ... the approach is easy, and the communication, in the summer time, almost hourly.[1]

Wordsworth had a profound suspicion of the development of modern communications. Unlike his friend Thomas de Quincey, he did not at all 'enjoy the velocity of motion' offered by the descent into Patterdale from Kirkstone 'made at 18 miles per hour in horse-drawn coaches and carriages'. Indeed for Wordsworth, long before his famous protest against the coming of the railways, there was already 'far too much hurrying about in these islands', a haste which characterised the new tourists who dashed by the lakes with an exclamation or two, and the 'strangers not linked to the neighbourhood' who flitted 'to and fro between their fancy villas and the homes where their wealth was accumulated'. These were the 'off-comers', the new men of the industrial age, who were to adorn so many parts of Lakeland in the late 19th century with their pretentious mansions set in splendid grounds adorned with elegant lawns, paved walks, conservatories, exotic shrubs, shapely conifers and imposing mounds of brilliant rhododendrons, all now part of the natural beauty of the scene but at that time alien, intrusive and in conflict with all that Wordsworth wished to see in his unsullied idyll of ancient woodlands and gleaming waters in a wild and untamed landscape. In prose of poetic beauty he takes us through the woods of Patterdale where 'the grass on which we trod, and the trees in every thicket were dripping with melted hoar-frost', and where he observed 'the lemon-coloured leaves of the birches, as the breeze turned them to the sun, sparkle, or rather, flash like diamonds, and the leafless purple twigs were tipped with globes of shining crystal'. He notes the wild goats and the wandering deer, the old yew trees, the rich green berries of the hawthorns, the grey trunks of the ancient oaks embellished with mosses and fern, and the smooth silver branches of the ash, the steely brightness of the lake, the drizzling vapour of rain 'never a drop upon our clothes or hair larger than the smallest pearls upon a lady's ring', while Ullswater itself presented 'perhaps, upon the whole, the happiest combination of beauty and grandeur which any of the lakes afford'.[2]

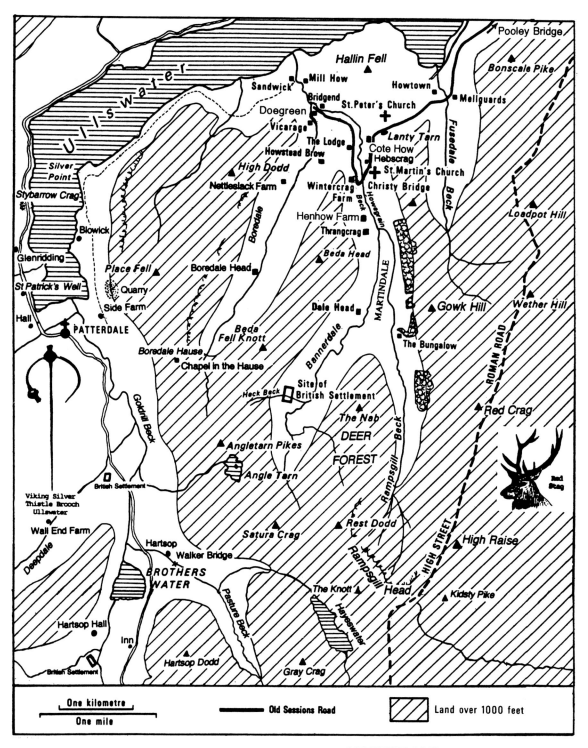

PATTERDALE   and   **MARTINDALE**

37   *Wagon and horses by a cottage*

It was on Ullswater, by Stybarrow Crag, that Wordsworth experienced, perhaps for the first time, that powerful influence of nature's mystery and grandeur which was to permeate so much of his poetry.[3]

Two hundred years later we should consider ourselves fortunate that, despite all that a modern industrial society, mass tourism, commercial pressures and the cult of the car have done, we can still discover in the valley of Patterdale all those delights which Wordsworth's *Guide* describes – the joy of the daffodils in spring, the beauty of the autumn woodlands, the sparkling lake, the view from Blowick and the showers of rain sweeping in over Kirkstone.

What Wordsworth chose not to describe are the squalid cottages in which the poorer folk of his time had to live – 'sad little huts made up of drye walls, only stones piled together' as Celia Fiennes saw them; or the decaying village church, 'the poorest church I ever saw', according to Joseph Budworth; or the tipsy tyranny of the Mounseys, 'the King and Queen of Patterdale'; or the impact on the valley of the Greenside Lead Mine which was already polluting the lake and whose miners were, according to James Clarke, 'the most abandoned, wicked and profligate of mankind' who 'propagate their vices among the innocent and unsuspecting inhabitants' deserting the women they seduced and leaving them 'to all the horrors of poverty and shame'. The poets and the writers of contemporary guidebooks do not dwell on the harsher realities of daily life as experienced by the miners, millworkers, quarrymen, hired farmhands and the womenfolk of Patterdale. Thomas Gray saw in the day-long, year-long struggle to survive only 'peace, rusticity and happy poverty'. It is well that we should always be aware that there is another side to the Lakeland idyll portrayed by the Age of Romanticism.[4]

38 *The Good Shepherd: an embroidery by Ann Macbeth (1875-1948).*

Patterdale has little recorded history before modern times. The name itself first appears in the late 12th century as 'Patrichesdale', thus helping to give birth to the legend that St Patrick came this way in the fifth century, founded the Christian Church here, baptised local converts at 'St Patrick's Well' and so gave his name to the valley. Unfortunately, there is no evidence to support this appealing fable: there is no record or trace of an early Christian chapel here, and the only trace of any church earlier than the 14th century is a medieval font in the present 19th-century structure. Perhaps even more conclusive is the absence of an important medieval parish such as so eminent a missionary as St Patrick would have founded: Patterdale was no more than a chapelry of the church at Barton.

The present church at Patterdale was built in 1853 and, although it was designed by Anthony Salvin, one of the most successful Victorian architects, it is quite undistinguished but its interior walls are greatly enhanced by the widely acclaimed embroideries of Ann Macbeth, a pioneer of craft education who lived and worked in Patterdale in the first half of the 20th century. A panel illustrating *The Good Shepherd* is set against a background of Patterdale village and the local fells with sheep and flowers skilfully included; below this is a small panel embroidered with the score of Parry's music for Blake's *Jerusalem*. Another colourful embroidery by Ann Macbeth, again in a Patterdale setting, and occasionally loaned to the church, shows a scene of the Nativity.

In the churchyard is a large mound on which the 1,000-year-old Patterdale Yews stood until they were destroyed in a violent storm in 1883. These would still have been firmly in place at the time of Patterdale's most celebrated curate, the Reverend Mattinson, who lived from 1676-1766 and whose ministry lasted 60 years during which, on a stipend of £12 a year, he managed to live a life of some comfort and leave £1,000 on his death – all facts which clearly made a great impression on William Gilpin who also noted that:

> he himself read the burial service over his mother; he married his father to a second wife; and afterwards buried him also. He published his own banns of marriage in the church, with a woman whom he had formerly christened; and himself married all his four children.[5]

The 'Patrick' who gave his name to Patterdale was probably a Norse-Irish settler, Patraic, who arrived on the scene in the 10th century to create a farming hamlet in the forest clearing. It is unlikely that his descendants enjoyed the freedom and independence which characterised the Norse farmer for more than a short time. For the Norman Conquest of England established a new society in which the free peasant lost most of his legal and political rights as well as ownership of his land. Patterdale became part of the vast estates of William de Lancaster, Baron of Kendal, who made Hartsop Hall his local manor and enforced all the rigours and restraints of feudal obligation. Throughout the medieval period and beyond Hartsop Hall exercised manorial control over all the lands around it. The present Hall is the oldest building in Patterdale with some features which appear to date from the 15th century.[6]

Medieval Patterdale was remote and almost isolated from the world outside. Its few inhabitants lived in damp, wretched cottages and with little spiritual or material comfort but they would rarely go hungry: game was plentiful in the woods, fish teemed in the rivers and lakes, a cow or two would keep them well-supplied with butter, milk and cheese, a pig to slaughter in the autumn would provide meat for many weeks and hams to hang in the smoky chimney hood, a gaggle of geese produced eggs and, from time to time, a useful addition to the broth which always simmered on the hearth. A few sheep provided wool to be spun and woven in the home for their simple clothing and bed-covers; crops of oats, barley and rye would, with luck, be harvested in sufficient quantity to ensure fodder for their horses, ale for the household brew, and flour for baking the haver-bread which featured so largely in their diet.[7] The woods around them offered, in season, a rich variety of herbs, greens, berries and edible fungi as well as ample stores of fuel. For the young, the fit, the enterprising and the fortunate, life need not always have seemed a constant, dreary struggle but to others it must have been nasty, brutish and short.

In the late 16th century events in the distant capital of Queen Elizabeth's England sent an unexpected ripple into this primitive corner of her realm. Fleeing from the penal restrictions placed on all those whose religious loyalties still adhered to the 'Bishop of Rome', there arrived in Patterdale a Sussex family, retainers of the Catholic Howards, who for the next 250 years were to exercise a dominion in the valley which was as tyrannous and as capricious as that of any whimsical despot. Within a generation the Mounsey family had bought Patterdale Hall and acquired the sobriquet of 'The King and Queen of Patterdale' and their home was known as 'The Palace'.[8]

Mystery surrounds the elevation of the Mounseys to royal dignity. James Clarke, writing in 1787, asserted that they had enjoyed the title 'time out of mind' because of 'their neither ever having paid any rents or done any homage, fealty or service to the King' and because of 'their superiority to their neighbours'. Another explanation, related by several 18th-century guidebooks, is that the honour was bestowed (by whom is never made clear) in recognition of the part alleged to have been played by John Mounsey in 1648 when a band of marauding Scotsmen were repulsed at the 'Battle of Stybarrow Crag', a skirmish in which the 'heroism' of Mounsey is open to question. John Housman believed the pre-eminence of the Mounseys was 'on account of them possessing more property than any of their neighbours', an opinion shared by the Reverend William Gilpin who was so taken by the comfortable life led by the ruler of this little kingdom that he mused romantically that if he 'were inclined to envy the situation of any potentate in Europe, it would be that of the King of Patterdale'.[9]

Joseph Budworth, rambling in the district 10 years later, presents us with a less flattering portrait of the Mounseys. In 1795 the reigning Mounsey was 93 years of age and so had lived long enough to have attracted numerous stories concerning his exploits and eccentricities. From his 'palace' this 18th-century Mounsey operated as a sharp businessman with profitable interests in charcoal manufacture, slate quarries, timber sales, hiring ponies, sheep farming, and renting fields and houses for 'entertainments'. This enterprising capitalism was accompanied by an unappealing miserliness exemplified by his meanness towards the poor on the grounds that as he never got anything from them why should he give anything to them? Budworth recounted a local belief that the Mounseys had amassed a fortune of £40,000 – probably no more than a figure to represent wealth beyond the imagination of the Patterdale peasant of 200 years ago. Nor was Mounsey's reputation enhanced by his amorous propensities which, regrettably, Budworth, the son of an anglican vicar, felt unable to elaborate on: 'The stories of his amours are more funny to hear than it would be decent to relate.' As an old man, Mounsey's main eccentricity seems to have been an insatiable appetite for China tea, by that time well established as one of the marks of gentility; although one suspects that the withdrawing-rooms of Jane Austen's society did not witness the avid quaffing of 10 to 14 cups of the beverage in thirsty succession – all with copious quantities of sugar.

Mrs. Mounsey, the 'Queen of Patterdale', also had a thirst, but of a rather different kind. Budworth followed her to an alehouse where she indulged in 'one of her moderate fits of drinking' in the course of which she struck and abused her husband, swore that a maid had put a spider in her ale, offered her grand-daughter to Budworth's friend for 300 guineas and finally threatened to overwhelm Budworth himself with a kiss – a fate from which he promptly fled, concluding that he 'had seen quite sufficient of Patterdale royalty'. The 'Queen' received more sympathetic understanding from Dorothy Wordsworth who wrote in her *Journal* that Mrs Mounsey was 'formerly a very nice and tidy woman' and 'had been brought to drinking by her husband's unkindness and avarice'.[10]

In 1824 the Mounseys sold their recently rebuilt palace to a Leeds textile manufacturer, William Marshal, who engaged the distinguished architect, Anthony Salvin, to refurbish the Hall in the classical style, to create an elegant residence worthy of a family of successful 19th-century industrialists who sat in the House of Commons and made a positive contribution to the society of their day. The elaborately laid out grounds of Salvin's Hall, with their plantations of conifers and rhododendrons, their terraced gardens, neat lawns and balustrades, knot gardens and herbaceous borders, may have deviated from nature's 'path of simplicity and beauty' rather more than Wordsworth would have approved of, but it would be curmudgeonly prejudice not to concede that, in their maturity, these fine gardens were an enhancement to the valley scene.

Another Patterdale monument to Victorian industrial enterprise, less than two miles from the Hall, at the northern end of the valley, is the Greenside lead mine with its rich vein of galena, worked in the 17th century but not fully exploited until the 19th century. From 1822 onwards the Greenside Mining Company invested heavily in new shafts and machinery and by 1962, when mining ceased, more than three million tons of ore had been raised to yield 250,000 tons of lead concentrates. It was the most profitable mining venture in the north of England, and this despite the immense cost and difficulty involved in transporting the ore to the smelting works at Alston, more than 30 miles away. This was done at first by horse and cart for the entire distance but later partly by rail after the opening of the rail link from Penrith in 1867. The impact of this great mining operation on such a small community must have been overwhelming. Mining and quarrying were traditional and familiar industries in and around Patterdale but this was quite different from any earlier enterprise, with its dams and water-races, its machine houses and crushing mills, its shafts of horrifying depth and its huge heaps of spoil, and an influx of 'foreign' miners whose disturbing effects on the valley were noted by James Clarke as early as 1789. The village of Glenridding did not exist before the 19th century but it grew into a miners' community with rows of terraced cottages more typical of industrial Lancashire than of Lakeland. A flood of effluent from the mine poured into Ullswater creating a delta at the mouth of Glenridding Beck which grew at the rate of 10ft. a year and now projects, like a great proboscis, into the lake, providing convenient landing facilities for the Ullswater steamers. Baddeley's classic *Guide to the Lake District,* first published in 1886, considered the whole mining operation to be a disaster marring 'hopelessly what was once a very beautiful valley'.

A silver mine near Hartsop Hall was worked in the 16th century and yielded 30 ounces of silver per ton of galena and a small quantity of gold. Some perfect cubes of pale fluorspar embedded in the ore are the only specimens of this mineral found in the Borrowdale Volcanics.[11]

The economic success of 19th-century Britain and British dominance of the world's markets brought improved standards of living to all sections of society, even if the conditions of labour which made it possible were harsh and relentless.

In the late 18th century, however, visitors to Patterdale were less than enthusiastic about the standard of accommodation available. The village inn, then known as *The King's Arms*, now the *Patterdale Hotel*, had a succession of distinguished guests: Joseph Budworth, Ann Radcliffe who commented on her 'low-roofed habitation', Sarah Aust (the Honourable Mrs. Murray) who was 'obliged to pass the night in a chair by the kitchen fire, there not being a bed in the house fit to put myself upon', William Wordsworth and Samuel Coleridge who described it as a 'bad inn', and in 1805 Wordsworth again, this time accompanied by Sir Walter Scott and Sir Humphry Davy who were kept from their sleep by a party of talkative ladies who were occupying their room.[12]

Whatever shortcomings they may have found in the accommodation offered at that time, many of the visitors paid tribute to the quality of the food put before them and the very reasonable bills presented at the end of their stay. Dorothy Wordsworth was clearly impressed by the inn at Patterdale which served them ham, veal cutlets, preserved plums, ale, rum and a 'decent breakfast'. Travellers from the southern counties were particularly intrigued by the haver-bread or clap-bread which accompanied their meals. This was the traditional oatmeal bread made throughout northern Europe for centuries and commonly made in most households in northern Britain until the arrival of cheap and plentiful wheat from North America in the late 19th century. Haver-bread is found today mainly in Norway where it is still widely enjoyed in the form of flatbröd, a thin, crisp bread exactly as described by Celia Fiennes on her journey through the Lake district 300 years ago:

... they mix their fine oat flour with water so soft as to rowle it in their hands into a ball, and then they have a board made round and something hollow in the middle riseing by degrees all round to the edge a little higher, but so little as one would take it to be only a board warp'd, this is to cast out the cake thinn and so they clap it round and drive it to the edge in a due proportion till drove as thinn as paper, and still they clap it and drive it round, and then they have a plaite of iron same size with their clap board and so shove off the cake on it and so set it on coales and bake it; when enough on one side they slide it off and put the other side; if their iron plaite is smooth and they take care their coales or embers are not too hot but just to make it look yellow it will bake and be crisp and pleasant to eat as any thing you can imagine.[13]

39   *Iron Girdle and Brandreth for Haver Bread*

The 'iron plaite' on which the clap-bread was baked was usually a circular griddle, or 'bakstone', made by the local blacksmith and hung over the open hearth or set on an iron tripod known as a 'brandreth'. In earlier days the bakstones were often flat slabs of stone found in certain well-known spots in the countryside: place-names such as Bakestone Barrow, Baxton Gill, Backstones and Beckstones are reminders of this ancient household necessity. Bread-making day was a special occasion in any household, involving a great deal of hard work from very early in the morning. The dough had to be made and 'clapped', the fire had to be steadily maintained throughout the day-long process, and the stacks of bread put to cool and then stored in oak cupboards some of which were elaborately carved. It was usual to bake sufficient bread to last for a month.[14]

The first tourists to descend on Patterdale may have seemed pre-occupied with their material comforts but it was the grandeur of the scenery which left a lasting impression. Poets, painters, guidebook writers, even novelists, have found inspiration here. Some of Wordsworth's more felicitous verse originated in Patterdale, notably the famous daffodil poem – 'I wandered lonely as a cloud', the celandine poem – 'There is a flower, the lesser celandine', 'Airey Force Valley', and his lightly tripping celebration of sunshine after a storm by Brothers Water:

> The Cock is crowing,
> The stream is flowing,
> The small birds twitter,
> The lake doth glitter,
> The green field sleeps in the sun;
> There's joy in the mountains,
> There's life in the fountains,
> Small clouds are sailing,
> Blue sky prevailing;
> The rain is over and gone.

A quite different inspiration came to the sad 20th-century poet, Stevie Smith, whose ghostly poem 'The Frozen Lake' makes Ullswater a haunted lake, the icy grave of drowned lovers and of Arthur's sword Excalibur, a concept far removed from the gentle landscapes of John Glover, the Patterdale artist known as the English Claude, who was almost forgotten here after he emigrated to Tasmania but who was President of the Water-colour Society in 1815 and Founder of the Society of British Artists. Forgotten, too, is the Patterdale writer, Edna Lyall whose novel, *Hope the Hermit*, was once the most widely read work of Lakeland fiction.[15]

It is above all Ullswater that is the jewel in the crown of Patterdale with its magnificent setting in some of the finest mountain scenery in the country, a balance of beauty and composition unrivalled even in the Lake District. Thomas Gray's description of the lake as he saw it in 1768 has fixed for all time the image which visitors come to see and wish to remember:

I went to Ulzwater and saw the lake opening directly at my feet majestic in its calmness, clear and smooth as a blew mirror, with winding shores and low points of land covered with green enclosures, white farmhouses looking out among the trees, and cattle feeding. The water is almost everywhere bordered with cultivated lands gently sloping upwards till they reach the feet of the mountains which rise very rude and awful with their broken tops on either hand.[16]

William Green, half a century later, advised his readers that 'from Gowbarrow to the inn at Patterdale (is) in every respect ... one of the loveliest of the lovely districts bordering the lakes', while William Gilpin, in his diligent quest for the picturesque, declared that 'among all the visions of this enchanting country we had seen nothing so beautifully sublime, so correctly picturesque as this'.[17]

It is doubtful, however, if today many would share the enthusiasm shown by both Green and Gilpin, and by William Hutchinson, for music and gunfire as a means of enhancing visitors' appreciation of the Ullswater scene. Hutchinson in the 1770s relates that the Duke of Norfolk hired out barges on the lake to take tourists to a picnic spot by some sheltered bay where:

> While we sat to regale, the barge put off from the shore to a station where the finest echoes were to be obtained from the surrounding mountains. The vessel was provided with six brass cannon mounted on swivels; on discharging one of these pieces the report echoed from the opposite rocks, where by reverberation it seemed to roll from cliff to cliff, and return through every cave and valley.

The discharge re-echoed 'seven times distinctly' in 'a kind of wondrous tumult and grandeur' to be followed by

> the music of two French horns, whose harmony was repeated from every recess which echo haunted on the borders of the lake; here the breathings of the organ were imitated, there the bassoon with the clarinets ... from the further sounding cliffs, the cornet ... amongst the caverns and the trilling waterfalls, we heard the soft-toned lute accompanied with the languishing strains of enamoured nymphs ... innumerable aerial beings who breathed celestial harmony ... The exquisite softness and harmony which the echoes produced were not to be described.[18]

William Gilpin was equally enthralled by this entertainment and he was especially enraptured by the musical echoes which he found 'exquisitely melodious' like 'a thousand symphonies playing together from every port' transforming the whole lake 'with a kind of magical scene'. William Green went so far as to suggest that 'mountain guides should from their infancy be taught the clarinet, bassoon, flute and horn' in order that this invaluable addition to the attractions of Ullswater should always be assured.[19]

All this contrasts sharply with the lyrical description of Ullswater and Patterdale written by Ann Radcliffe after her visit in 1794.[20] She depicts the reality of the scene with a perceptive appreciation of the way in which the scenery and one's perception of it changes with the contrasting moods of nature. Rugged and romantic mountains set against a dark and stormy sky, lowering and wind-riven, evoke different emotions when seen against a calm and serene egg-shell blue; a violent, storm-tossed lake is an awesome sight compared with the safe and soothing mirror of a quiet summer's day; the wildest tempest which shakes the trees and thunders on the crags is disturbing and exciting and quite unlike the gentle soughing of a breeze. Of all the guidebook writers of her day Ann Radcliffe was perhaps the only one who saw the grandeur of the Lakeland scene as an ever-changing stage-set which could reflect the lives and emotions of humanity.

Ann Radcliffe did well to set her novel *The Mysteries of Udolpho* in Italy rather than in Patterdale but, after all her terrifying adventures, her heroine would have found no more certain way back to sanity than a walk along the shore of Ullswater from Sandwick to Patterdale village, four miles of peace and beauty with, on the one hand, a steep wooded fellside, a tumble of boulders, crag and scree clothed with heather, juniper and silver birch, and on the other hand, the glittering lake, sometimes spread before you in a dazzling expanse to the opposite shore, sometimes glimpsed between rocky outcrops or wooded knolls, its surface broken by white-flecked wavelets driven onwards by the breeze to end their dance in a tiny bay or on the shore of an island.

Much of the story of Patterdale is gleaned from the fleeting impressions of visitors – writers, poets and curious travellers – who, however perceptive their appreciation of the natural beauty to be found here, were outsiders, here today and gone tomorrow, returning to their distant homes to polish their phrases and embellish their reminiscences which posterity would constantly repeat and admire. Too often we forget the generations of ordinary dalesfolk whose lives should form the real story of the Lakeland dales. They left no written records of their thoughts and feelings but they lived closer to nature than anyone. The light on the lake and the shadows on the fellsides, the rising of the moon and the setting of the sun, the sounds of rushing water and the wind in the trees, the flight of birds and the secret life of animals, the signs of the eternal changing of the seasons were, to them, just strands in the fabric of daily life.

Wild daffodils in a wood

15

MARTINDALE

Children no longer go to gather black cherries in Martindale. Old age and winter gales have taken their toll of the trees and few are planted to replace them; but those that remain are still white with blossom to delight the eye at Eastertide. The *Star Inn* took down its sign many years ago; but there are still flourishing farms in the valley and no visitor will find a lack of hospitality. The 20th century has brought changes here, as elsewhere, yet for those who live and work in this secluded Lakeland dale change has been a blessing: they who were once so desperately poor, are now able to enjoy many of the pleasures of life; they who once could only watch and envy the progress of the Earl of Lonsdale's yellow phaeton bearing his wealthy hunting guests to and fro, now welcome the summer tourists bearing unaccustomed prosperity and making few demands. The dalesmen share most of the genuine advantages of modern living without being overwhelmed by its more unattractive features.

To the outward eye Martindale seems virtually untouched by the impact of the modern age; no through road, no industrial scars, no Victorian villas nor luxury hotels, no commercial tourist attractions, no caravan parks nor large camp-sites, no reservoirs nor dark conifer plantations, no shops and no Post Office. Only the bright red lodges in Rampsgill – built to entertain Kaiser Wilhelm II and others of 'Lordy's' hunting guests – might justifiably be included among Wordsworth's 'discordant objects disturbing that peaceful harmony of form and colour which [has] been through a long lapse of ages most happily preserved'.[1] Almost every cottage and farmstead dates from the 17th century, the vicarage is Georgian, the old church is largely Elizabethan, the new church is a triumph of Victorian restraint, and in the latter, appropriately enough, there is striking evidence that, however thoroughly Martindale may seem to retain the image of a pre-industrial age, it is both willing and able to set an example in the best of modern style. In 1975 St Peter's Church acquired five new stained glass lancet windows which must surely rank among the most radiant produced by any artist in the present century. Jane Gray has executed a design of colour and beauty portraying the lives of the four saints traditionally associated with Martindale – St Peter, St Ninian, St Patrick and St Martin – and dedicated to those who lost their lives in the sinking of HMS *Glorious* in the Second World War.

Some eighteen hundred years before this a Roman soldier, tired from the long haul over High Street from Brougham or Ambleside, may have paused by a wayside shrine near the edge of Rampsgill Head, to gaze down at the wooded valley below, a sea of birch and alder forest, the relics of which may be seen on Gowk Hill above Rampsgill Beck, the home of deer and the red stag, of wild cats, foxes, wild boar, martens and innumerable birds. He may have known about the British settlement hidden away over the hill in Bannerdale as well as others close by the Roman highway on the fells near Barton and Moor Divock, but he was in lonely country with no Roman station anywhere near him. The Britons may have made Martindale their hunting ground and venison was, no doubt, a familiar meat to them but the Romans felt more secure on High Street.[2]

40 *St Peter's Church*

The Britons may, indeed, have been well-acquainted with this wooded valley as a source of food but they preferred to live on the higher ground and, as elsewhere in Lakeland, it may not have been until the arrival of the Norsemen in the 10th century that there was any permanent clearing of the land in the valley itself. Norse names dominate almost exclusively here: Boredale (the valley with the 'bur' or storehouse); Fusedale (the valley with the 'fjös' or cow byre); Swinsty (a clearing with a pig-sty); Bonscale (a freeholder's shieling); Sandwick (a sandy 'vik' or creek); Bannerdale (the valley of the holly trees); and so on throughout the length of Martindale. Many of these names first appeared in written form in legal documents of the 13th century and some not until the reign of Elizabeth I but all are of indisputable Norse origin.

Some five hundred years elapsed between the departure of the Romans from Britain and the arrival of these Norse settlers leaving us with the problem of establishing the sequence of events during these sparsely documented centuries. There is a strong historical tradition that the early Christian missionaries were active among the many British and Romano-British settlements which survived into the fifth and sixth centuries throughout the Ullswater hinterland.[3] We cannot say when the Christian faith first came to Martindale nor who first taught the Gospel here: local folklore favours St Patrick in the fifth century but this rests mainly on the dubious theory that it was St Patrick who gave his name to neighbouring Patterdale and on his known admiration for the work of St Martin. A stronger candidate might be St Ninian who is said to have returned from a visit to St Martin's bishopric of Tours fired with enthusiasm to do in Britain what St Martin had done in Gaul, namely to evangelise the remote rural areas and found the institution of monasticism. It now seems beyond doubt that Ninian founded the Candida Casa on the Isle of Whithorn, as Bede asserted, dedicated it to St Martin, and launched a mission into the countryside around the Solway.[4] Perhaps it was he who brought Christianity to the region between Ullswater and the Eden Valley, and also the cult of St Martin to whom are dedicated churches at Brampton and Martindale. Support for this tradition is found in the belief that Ninian's missionaries carved out the cells in the caves at Isis Parlis by the River Eden (just as St Martin's followers did above the Loire) and that the name 'Ninekirks' now given to the isolated church there is derived from Ninian's own name. The mysterious ruins on Boredale Hause known as the Chapel on the Hause have much the same proportions as Ninian's Candida Casa at Whithorn. Some cast doubt on the entire Ninian theory and lend support to the idea that it was, after all, St Kentigern, a century later than Ninian, who brought the Christian Church to the country near the Eamont as he did to the lands near the Derwent.[5]

It would be interesting to discover historical evidence to support the tradition that the first chapel in the dale was, in fact, the 'Chapel on the Hause'. Names were not usually given lightly to such places and the ruins certainly seem to be neither barn nor sheepfold but, once more, the mystery must remain unsolved: we can only agree with Wordsworth that 'the rustic psalmody must have had the accompaniment of many a wildly whistling blast; and what dismal storms must have often drowned the voice of the preacher'.[6] One must also admire the fervour of those who toiled to such a spot for their religious devotions. Whatever the origin of this chapel on the Hause, on one point we may be quite certain: it was not the 'chapel of Martyndale' referred to in an early 13th-century charter nor was it the 'chapel of St Martin' mentioned in a document of 1266. Both were legal grants by William de Lancaster, Baron of Kendal, to Roger, his half-brother, of land and rights 'in the whole of my forest of Martyndale'[7] and the chapel referred to is that at Christy Bridge (formerly Kirkstead Bridge) where a church has stood for over 700 years and the yew trees for almost twice as long. This was the valley church until it was abandoned in 1882 with the dedication of the new church of St Peter, an occasion marked by a great storm which ripped off the roof of St Martin's leaving it open to the elements. For many years it was demoted to the status of a mortuary chapel and suffered from serious neglect but recent generations have devoted great care to the task of restoring and preserving this simple dales chapel. Here men and women have worshipped and children been baptised since it was built in 1633 on a site where a 'capella Sancti Martini' stood for 400 years before that. It is in such places that we may hear 'the articulate and audible voice of the Past' and remind ourselves of our debt to our predecessors and our responsibility to the future. Evensong here on a summer evening is a truly spiritual experience.

A few stones of the medieval chapel may be seen by the south wall and a medieval bell hangs in the open turret, inscribed with a series of Lombardic letters which defied interpretation until earlier this century when they were discovered to represent nothing more profound than the letters of the alphabet in order from A to N. Even the 'new' 17th-century church must have been a rather primitive abode, for we learn that in 1714 the floor was paved with flagstones 'as the growing luxury of the age could no longer tolerate that the feet of worshippers should rest on damp earth'. Luxury also demanded the construction of a porch and this was added at the same time. The chapel once boasted a gallery where the choir sang to music provided by pipes and fiddles which many a dalesman was proud to play for church services, weddings and any seasonal or family celebration in the valley. One would not expect a church such as this to possess valuable treasures or splendid appointments but to reflect the simple lives of a poor community rather than the affluence of a prosperous gentry: so we find here no elaborate adornments but unpretentious pews and pulpit, a lectern carved with the simplest of patterns and a plain altar table, all probably made by local craftsmen in the 17th century.

41   *St Martin's Chapel*

A standing stone inside the church has a long and strange history. It is believed to be a small wayside shrine brought down at some unknown date from the Roman road along High Street. It has deep incisions as if at one time it had been used for sharpening tools or weapons, and a hollowed-out bowl in it has been deepened for use as a holy water stoup. A visitor in 1688 described it as 'a standing stone instead of a Font upon which they place a bason when they Christen their children'. It is not in itself an object of beauty but it is worthy of a moment's reflection for it is now some 1,800 years since it began its career as a religious shrine by the Roman highway on the high moorland above.

We shall probably never know more precisely the history of this stone but, since we are so much involved in the realms of imaginative speculation in the story of this valley, it seems not unreasonable to suppose that the man most likely to have seen a practical use for such a stone was the first 'vicar' of St Martin's, Richard Birkett, who from 1633 to 1699 was priest in Martindale as well as lawyer, clerk and schoolmaster to the whole district. Birkett must have been a remarkable character: he arrived in his cure with only two shirts and the clothes he wore but, having married at the age of 81, he left his widow the sum of £1,200. James Clarke, writing in 1789, sourly comments that 'his penury and avarice were the sole causes of his wealth'. Even so, Clarke was clearly impressed by Birkett's achievements and goes on to relate that 'he transacted most of the law affairs of his parishioners, and was by them, on that account, nicknamed Sir Richard and The Lawyer. Whenever he lent money, he deducted, at the time of lending, two shillings in the pound for interest, and the term of the loan never exceeded a year: he charged for writing a receipt two pence, and for a promissory note four pence; and he used such other acts of extortion as one would scarce believe to have been practised in so contracted a sphere. He likewise taught a school, and served as parish clerk, and in both these offices he likewise showed his wonderful turn for economy and gain; for his quarter-dues from his scholars being small, he had from the parents of each scholar a fortnight's board and lodging; and with the Easter dues, being usually paid in eggs, he, at the time of collecting, carried with him a board, in which was a hole which served him as a gauge, and he positively refused to accept any which could pass through'.[8] Just such a man, one feels, would instinctively have spotted the possibilities of the old stone with its scooped out bowl ready for use as a font in the new but ill-furnished church for which he was responsible.

When Birkett died no-one could be found to replace him – 'on account of the smallness of the stipend', according to Clarke, and for some time the dalesmen who could read 'performed the services by turns', an arrangement which suggests an unexpected level of literacy at that time in so remote a place. As schoolmaster Birkett had obviously done his work well; and he must have been sadly missed for in 1739 the house known as Cote How was assigned 'to the only proper use, benefit and behoof of Martindale School for ever' – a period of time which in the event proved to be less than eternity for by 1801 Cote How was well-established as an inn. Dorothy Wordsworth and her brother William, intrepid travellers both, chose to visit Martindale in the dead of winter and visited the *Star Inn* at Cote How on 29 December 1801 after a stormy expedition to the head of the valley: 'We dined at the public house on porridge with a second course of Christmas pies'.[9]

The foundation of the school may have been partly a result of that community spirit which featured so often in the story of Martindale, a legacy, perhaps, of the many struggles the dalesmen had been forced to undertake to defend themselves against the impositions of exacting landlords. Henry Brierley, in his *Notes on Martindale*, commented that:

The stout co-operation of the Martindale folk in defence of what they believed to be their rights is most marked, and they never seem to have shirked tedious and expensive litigation. Two formal agreements providing for the raising of Funds for mutual protection against aggression are in the Parish Chest.[10]

Law suits were undertaken with remarkable frequency and tenacity over complex matters ranging from encroachments on common land and the right to dig peat to the collection of unauthorised tithes; from 'taking excessive fynes and breakynge of their customes for their widdowes estates' to rights of pasturage and foggage; from charges of bribery in court judgments to the expense of Border Service which, it was alleged, 'on Horse costs £10 per annum with Jack and Lance ... and on Foot ... £4 per annum with Bowes and Arrowes'. A reminder of these litigious days in Martindale is the 'Sessions Road' along which the King's Law Officers travelled on their affairs. It is now a succession of tracks, paths and bridleways, a pleasant walk in the lower part of the valley and over the fell to Pooley Bridge.

Many of the problems of the Martindale tenants arose from the complex tenures which applied to farmsteads situated in a royal forest or baronial deer park. 'The forest looms large on the scene of medieval England. The forest clauses of Magna Carta were deemed to be so important that in the re-issue of 1217 they were taken out of it, and augmented to form a separate charter, the Charter of the Forest.[11] Defiance of the Forest Law was symbolised by Robin Hood who in the 13th century became a folk-hero whose exploits enraged noblemen such as William de Lancaster who in 1230 made a grant to his half-brother, Roger, of 'the whole of my forest of Martyndale from one end to the other, with woodland and cleared land, sward and pasture and soil whatever it be, in water and out, with all its hunting and its game, as well in beast as bird, and with all other belongings and liberties attaching to the aforesaid land and forest'. The interests of the hunt took precedence over any farming interests: only very rarely do we find any concern for the welfare of the tenants and their cattle, sheep and crops. In the words of a 12th-century Treasurer of the Exchequer, the forest was 'the safe mansion of wild beasts' and the inhabitants of Martindale were considered to be remarkably favoured when in 1363 Edward III granted them the right of common pasture in the forest as compensation for the damage done to their crops when these beasts strayed with impunity into the culti- vated fields.

Living under the forest law involved feudal obligations as well as inconvenience for the farmers. Not only did they have to agree not to drive the lord's deer out of their pastures but on the lord's summons they were bound to attend for duty at the hunt. 'On these occasions they have each their district allotted on the boundaries of the chase, where they are stationed to prevent the stag flying beyond the liberty': William Hutchinson, writing in the 1770s, thus reveals the survival into the late 18th century of an obligation referred to in early medieval documents from the abbeys of Shap and Furness. In return for this service the tenantry were provided with a free meal and a quart of ale, while the first to seize the hunted animal received a bonus of the deer's head. James Clarke relates 'that the first buck taken [in a Martindale hunt] was seized by a woman: she, for the sake of his head, laid hold upon him as he stood at bay upon a dunghill, threw him down, and getting upon his neck, held him fast.' A practical housewife who recognised the oppor- tunity of a good bargain when she saw it![12]

By the late 16th century political and economic changes had made drastic inroads on the power of these mighty overlords and also on the extent of the royal forests. Yet in Cumbria the great forests of Inglewood, Copeland and Martindale still covered vast areas and deer were plentiful in them. Queen Elizabeth I granted the manor of Martindale to the Earl of Sussex but took care to reserve the hunting rights to the Crown. Agricultural needs continued to put pressure on the remaining areas covered by the laws of the forest but in the late 19th century the Earl of Lonsdale was still able to offer his guests excellent deer-stalking on his Martindale estates. In more recent times the Hasell family of Dalemain, whose ancestors were much addicted to the hunt and entertained lavishly at Dale Head with legendary huge pasties and plentiful liquor, have done much to ensure the survival of the red deer in Martindale, not now for purposes of sport but primarily to preserve the herd in its natural and historical environment.[13] Many have now escaped from the once protected area on the Nab and may be seen in almost any part of the Lake District.

The long reign of the red deer in Martindale has left no permanent mark on the valley nor did the impact of the Industrial Revolution leave any scars here. A small fulling mill and a short-lived bobbin mill are all that the records reveal while a patch of ground bearing the name 'tentercroft' indicates that woven cloth was once stretched here to bleach and dry. The corn-mill was abandoned in 1850 and only its name remains at Mill How on Sandwick Beck. Far more profound changes have been brought about by the social and economic upheavals of the late 20th century: in particular, the transformation in the pattern of upland agriculture has dramatically reduced the number of working farmsteads and in consequence the total population of the valley has fallen to approximately half the total at the beginning of the century. Wordsworth's wish to see 'the long, narrow, deep cradle-shaped glen' of Boredale 'planted by human hands' has been partly fulfilled but we are less likely than he was to discover 'what grand effect the music of the bugle-horn would have among these mountains ... though well-contented with the quiet everyday sounds – the lowing of cattle, bleating of sheep, and the very gentle murmuring of the valley stream'.[14] Captain Joseph Budworth on his *Fortnight's Ramble to the Lakes* in 1795 was not content with these quiet everyday sounds and recounts that 'In Water Nook [by Howtown Wyke] we fired a small cannon and heard an echo which might have been tolerable' if he had not already heard a louder one 'upon Keswick Lake' – neither an activity nor a sentiment we would consider appropriate to the unspoilt pastoral tranquillity of one of Lakeland's most secluded valleys.[15]

Roe deer

16

THE VALE OF ST JOHN

The Reverend William Gilpin, usually a man of fine perception in his observation of Lakeland scenery, must have slept badly or eaten unwisely on the night before his journey to the Vale of St John. It was, he wrote, a valley 'esteemed one of the most celebrated scenes of beauty in the country, but it did not answer our expectations'.[1] He concedes, rather reluctantly, that 'the ground consisting of patches of fenced meadow, adorned with farm-houses and clumps of trees, was beautifully tumbled about in many parts; but the whole was rather rich than picturesque'. With characteristic integrity and precision he added that he was speaking 'only of the general appearance of the vale: it contains undoubtedly many beautiful scenes, if we had had time to explore them'. And here we have the secret to a proper appreciation of this most unassuming of the Lakeland valleys – it has to be explored, and under many different skies. It is, as Harriet Martineau noted, 'a valley of character and charm from end to end',[2] but its charms and hidden corners, its remarkable changes of colour and light, and its exquisite scenic miniatures, have to be sought out, patiently waited for, and then

42 *Bram Crag Farm*

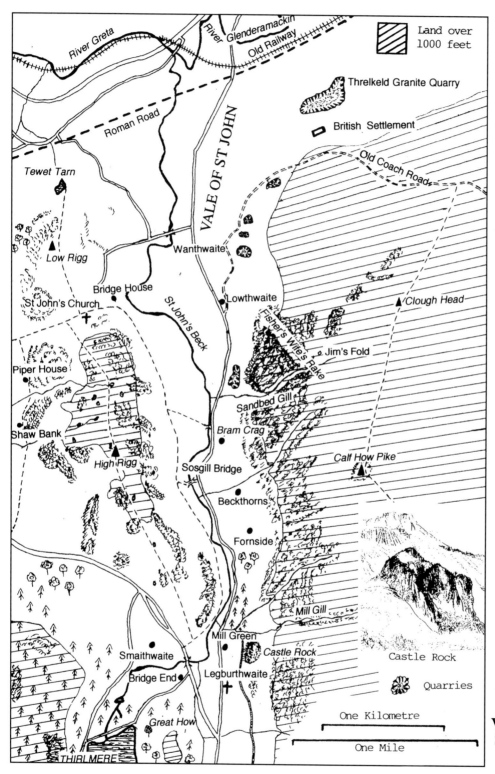

Land over 1000 feet

River Greta

River Glenderamackin

Old Railway

Threlkeld Granite Quarry

Roman Road

British Settlement

Old Coach Road

VALE OF ST JOHN

Tewet Tarn

Low Rigg

Wanthwaite

Clough Head

Bridge House

Lowthwaite

St John's Church

St John's Beck

Fisher's Wife's Rake

Jim's Fold

Piper House

Sandbed Gill

Shaw Bank

Bram Crag

Calf How Pike

High Rigg

Sosgill Bridge

Beckthorns

Fornside

Mill Gill

Mill Green

Smaithwaite

Castle Rock

Bridge End

Legburthwaite

Castle Rock

Great How

Quarries

THIRLMERE

One Kilometre

One Mile

**VALE OF
ST JOHN**

43 *St John's Beck and Blencathra*

appreciated in tranquillity. St John's Vale, as we shall see, is not without its tales of mystery and imagination, nor, indeed, its moments of real drama, but there is truly no need to conjure up visions of Merlin's fiery meteors or of gallant knights storming fairy castles in order to enhance the natural beauty of these five square miles, described accurately, if somewhat prosaically, by William Green, in his *Tourists' New Guide* as 'a most singularly interesting assemblage of the wild and the lovely'.[3]

It was Green who took Gilpin to task for his failure to appreciate the spectacular view of Blencathra framed by the Vale of St John as one approaches from the south: 'How Mr. Gilpin could admire the first sight of Wyburn Water [Thirlmere] as presented from Dunmail Raise in preference to this first sight of St John's Vale cannot easily be accounted for!' Indeed, it can not! for there is no more memorable vista of Lakeland's mountain grandeur than this breathtaking perspective of the snow-covered ridges of Blencathra on a clear winter's day – and it is of much more than passing grandeur at any other time of the year.[4]

Northwards towards this mountain backdrop flow the waters of St John's Beck as they ripple and glide through green pastures between the wooded slopes of High Rigg and the ravines and crags of Clough Head and Watson's Dodd. In its four-mile journey to join the River Glendaramackin at Threlkeld Bridge the beck passes by ancient farmsteads whose names speak clearly of their Norse origins, by the traces of once busy mills, by the scars of many now abandoned quarries, by a former stagecoach road and several elegant packhorse bridges, by a desolate British village now sinking into oblivion among the heather and the rubble of its own decay, and finally it crosses the course of the Roman road from Penrith to Keswick.[5]

The story of the geographical formation of the Vale of St John belongs to the specialist realm of glaciology. The most recent Ice Age in Lakeland occurred some 10,000 years ago when glaciers which were a permanent feature of the highest ground began to spill over once more sending massive, rock-grinding tongues down into the valley heads. The glacier descending from Dunmail Raise which had created the original basin in which Thirlmere lies appears to have divided into two, one fork cutting through the broad valley of Naddle Beck and the other, the more powerful of the two, chiselling out the Vale of St John. The final melting of the ice, therefore, eventually drained into the course now followed by St John's Beck.[6]

Human settlers did not arrive in the valleys until long after the ice had disappeared and it is almost impossible to date the earliest settlements with confidence. Surviving evidence is sparse and often difficult to interpret. The existence of the great Stone Circle at Castlerigg on the high ground above the Naddle Valley is a strong indication that a permanent settlement was established in the area in the Late Neolithic or Early Bronze Age, some 4,000 years ago. Three Cumbrian stone-axes found here also point to the same conclusion; a number of celts, axe-like implements, from the same era have been discovered in St John's Vale as have several small stones with holes bored through them which may have been spindle-whorls or weights for fishing lines. Recent studies have concluded that Castlerigg Stone Circle is one of the oldest in Britain and this would seem to confirm that, possibly as early as 3,000 B.C., it was the ceremonial centre of a community which had settled in the Vale of Keswick, the Naddle Valley and the Vale St John.[7]

The Carles, as Castlerigg Circle is officially known, stands on a dramatic site with sweeping views of the surrounding fells and of the valley below. To the north the scene is dominated by Skiddaw, Blencathra and Lonscale Fell; to the west is a fine panorama of the Derwent fells seen across Derwentwater, and to the south the rugged knolls of High Rigg and Bleaberry Fell. It has been described as 'one of the most visually impressive prehistoric monuments in Britain'[8] and, after Stonehenge, it is the most visited and the most photographed. Thomas Gray was there in 1769 in one of those memorable moments when 'the sun breaking out discovered the most enchanting view I have yet seen, of the whole valley behind me, the two lakes, the river, the mountains in all their glory'. Gray, like Keats 50 years later, believed the Circle to have been a Druidical Temple – 'a dismal cirque of Druid stones' – but whatever the origin and purpose of these remarkable circles may have been, it is quite certain that they had nothing to do with the rituals of the Druids.[9]

Of the 50 stones which stood at Castlerigg when Gray visited the site 38 remain and all but five are still upright. Two tall stones mark the entrance portal on the northern rim with another stone of similar height directly opposite to the south; the tallest stone of all is some two feet higher than these and stands at 7½ft. (2.3m). Within the circle is an unusual rectangle of stones the purpose of which is still unknown. Indeed, the function of the Stone Circle in the culture of the Neolithic people remains an unsolved mystery: that they were of considerable importance is beyond question.

It seems reasonable to suppose that they were tribal meeting points, perhaps for a variety of purposes. They may have been religious temples where certain ceremonies and rituals took place on fixed days in the calendar; they may have been rallying points for social gatherings, games or festivities; they might even have served as trading posts or, like the Norse Thingmounts, as places of assembly where tribal laws and disputes were settled.

Professor Alexander Thom has in recent years propounded the theory that the Stone Circles were centres of megalithic astronomy constructed in accordance with a sophisticated system of mathematical calculations based on a measurement which he dubbed the 'megalithic yard' or 2.72 ft. (83m). The stones at Castlerigg are, according to Thom, precisely placed to coincide with a remarkable number of solar and lunar alignments and he regarded this particular circle as of great significance in terms of his whole theory: for example, a line from the tallest stone through the centre of the circle is aligned with the point of sunset over Skiddaw at the summer solstice. Such alignments enabled certain dates in the yearly change of the seasons to be fixed with a great degree of accuracy.[10]

Another student of Castlerigg, 50 years before Professor Thom, went further along the road of speculation and claimed that 'one of the main purposes of the circle was for the construction of a "Celtic Kalendar" in order to fix feast-days', the principal dates marking the Feasts of Bealtuinn (the Earth God) on 1 May, of Lugunasd (the Sun God) on 1 August, of Samhuinn (the God of Fertility) on 1 November, and of Imbolc (the God of Lambing-time) on 1 February. The summer and winter solstices were also important dates in this calendar and could be calculated with the appropriate alignments within the circle.[11]

All this has yet to be convincingly authenticated – and it may be difficult ever to do so – but merely to contemplate such possibilities adds to the sense of awe inspired by this extraordinary achievement by a people of whose culture we understand so little. It is not at all difficult to agree with one modern authority on our megalithic circles: 'Of all the superb rings in the Lake District', he wrote, 'the Castlerigg Stone Circle is the most exciting and the most mysterious.'[12]

Two miles due west of Castlerigg, at the northern end of St John's Vale, are the ruins of a much later British settlement, at Threlkeld. This, too, occupies a dramatic site with a wide view over the River Glendaramackin across to the dark, precipices of Blencathra, a mountain which, despite all the Norse incursions around it, has retained its Celtic name. There is now very little to instruct the untutored eye among the disorderly mounds of stones which are all that remains of numerous hut circles and the boundary walls of tiny fields. Much was plundered to build the new walls of the enclosures which followed the agricultural changes 200 years ago and excavation has revealed little of the history of this once extensive Celtic homestead. The discovery of a beehive-type rotary quern points to occupation in the first century and it seems likely that this community flourished as part of the Romano-British economy but, after the Roman withdrawal, could not survive on its unfavourable north-facing site and dispersed to the more prosperous settlement which had grown up in the valley below.[13]

Further destruction of the hut-circles at Threlkeld was caused by the 19th-century expansion of the nearby microgranite quarry. In the 1860s vast quantities of stone came from here to provide material for the construction of the Penrith, Keswick and Cockermouth Railway, and, 30 years later, 80,000 tons a year were quarried for the

Thirlmere Waterworks operation. During the same period innumerable flagstones were made for paving the rapidly growing towns of industrial Lancashire. Other quarries in the valley, notably at Wanthwaite and Bramcrag, enjoyed a similar prosperity and all have left their scars on the landscape. The story of the Threlkeld Quarry from its opening in the 1870s to its closure in 1982 may be experienced at the Threlkeld Quarry and Mining Museum which has a fine collection of artefacts from the industry including several locomotives and earth-moving machines as well as a display of quarrying tools, the smithy and an excellent geology room with numerous 'hands-on' rock specimens.

Whatever earlier folk may have passed this way – Neolithic, Celt or Roman – it was the 10th-century Norsemen who, as in other Lakeland dales, left an enduring mark on the Vale of St John. It was they who established farmsteads whose names are a permanent memorial to their labours: Smaithwaite, Legburthwaite, Lowthwaite, Wanthwaite, Stanah, Sosgill, Fornside, Birkett, Beckthorns and Shundraw.

It seems that in St John's Vale a Norseman named Leggr had some kind of stronghold at Legburthwaite, and that Forni, who gave his name to Fornside and is recorded in 1302, was the son of Ljotolfr whose name occurs 20 years earlier as the master of Castel Lyndolf. This is none other than Castle Rock, the craggy bastion guarding the southern entrance to the valley, an imposing wall of rock which has long had a place in the annals of rock-climbing, archaeology and romantic literature.

Castle Rock and the legends associated with it fascinated the guidebook writers. Even the staid Mr. Hutchinson whose sedate prose described the Vale of St John, rather uninspiringly, as 'a very narrow dell, hemmed in by mountains, through which a small brook makes many meanderings', imagined that he could see in this formidable pile of rock 'the appearance of an ancient ruined castle ... a massive bulwark [which] shews a front of various towers and makes an awful, rude and gothic appearance, with its lofty turrets and ragged battlements'.[14] Eighty-five years and innumerable guidebooks later the usually rational and sagacious Miss Harriet Martineau believed it looked 'as like as may be to a scene of witchery'.[15] Certainly this southern end of the valley had a long literary tradition as the scene of great events which acquired a romantic credibility when the eminent archaeologist and historian, W.G. Collingwood, established the reality of Ljotolfr and his son, Forni, and discovered on Castle Rock itself the remains of substantial walls, almost a metre thick, which he believed to be the remnants of a series of buildings remarkably similar to 11th-century Viking constructions in Iceland. In particular, he drew a parallel with Borgarviki in Northern Iceland, also built on a defensible rock. Perhaps there was some kind of fortified house here, and out of its mysterious history were created an enchanted castle and all the tales of medieval romance.[16]

The central figure in it all is, almost inevitably, King Arthur who, with his band of knights, apparently frequented these parts as regularly as they did Camelot, Caerleon, Cornwall and the Vale of Avalon. Was it not here by Castle Rock that Sir Gawain met the Green Knight to fight their duel by the Green Chapel? And was it not the great king himself who journeyed here from 'merry Carlisle' (while Queen Guinever 'smiled', in his absence, on brave Sir Lancelot) to seek out the lovely, treacherous Gwendolen?

The full story is told in Sir Walter Scott's famous verse, *The Bridal of Triermain*, a long narrative poem which enshrines all the important elements of 19th-century romantic poetry and medieval chivalry. The final assault on the ramparts of Castle Rock by Sir Roland de Vaux, followed by his triumph over many obstacles to win the fair Gwyneth (the daughter of King Arthur and Gwendolen) firmly places this 'banner'd castle, keep and tower' well within the realms of belief for those who wish to believe.[17] But any visitor with starry eyes should heed Scott's warning:

'Tis now a vain illusive show,
That melts whene'er the sunbeams glow
Or the fresh breeze hath blown.

In his description of the mighty upheavals in the natural world which preceded de Vaux's display of knightly valour Scott may have been referring to a catastrophe which struck the valley some 60 years before he wrote 'Triermain', a disaster which figured in most of the *Guides to the Lakes* published in Scott's time.

On the night of 22 August 1749, the Vale of St John was inundated by a torrential storm which devastated fields and farmsteads and swept away the mill at Legburthwaite so that 'not one stone was left upon another: even the heavy millstones were washed away; one was found at a considerable distance; but the other was never found'. James Clarke, visiting the area 40 years later, was told that 'About one in the morning rain began to fall, and before four such a quantity fell as covered the face of the country below with a sheet of water many feet deep', and, near to Wanthwaite, 'thousands of prodigious stones are piled upon each other to a height of 11 yds.; many of these stones are upwards of 20 tons weight each ... the fields at Fornside exhibited nothing but devastation'. This was clearly one of those violent manifestations of the forces of nature which have, from time to time, been visited on the inhabitants of Lakeland and which never fail to fascinate tourists from gentler climates.

One of the few houses to escape destruction in 1749 was an inn at Legburthwaite known as *Lame John's*, now no more, but doubtless well-known to the most famous native of St John's Vale, John Richardson. Mason, schoolmaster, dialect writer and poet, Richardson was born at Piper House and lived from 1817 to 1886, acquiring a distinguished reputation well beyond his own valley. A mason by training he put his skills to good use quite early in life by building the present church of St John while still in his twenties, and then for 22 years he was schoolmaster to the young folk of the neighbourhood at the school nearby, a task which enabled him to develop his interest in the Cumberland dialect and his talents as a dialect poet. From his writings we have a first-hand account of the custom of 'barring-out' the schoolmaster at Christmas and Midsummer:

It use to be than, when t'time com for brekkin' up
for t'Cursmas or Midsummer hellidays, 'at when t'maister
went heam tull his dinner, we use to bar up aw t'dooers
an' windows, an' wuddent let im in agean.

A bargain was struck that if the master could not get into the school again then the pupils would have no work set for the holidays; but, if he did manage to get in, they were the recipients not only of holiday tasks but 'mebby a good hiden to be gaen on wi'.

Richardson's poetry is composed in the Cumberland dialect and while it is, therefore, an enthusiast's literature, his rustic verses are full of charm and humour and an affectionate understanding of human nature. Perhaps the best-known are 'It's nobbut me', a delightful ballad-like tale of country courtship, and 'Robin Redbreast', a poignant, whimsical comment on human frailty.[18]

Robin Redbreast

When winter winds blow strang and keen
An' neets are lang an' cauld,
An' flocks o' burds, wi famine team't,

Come flutteren into t' fauld;
I hev a casement, just ya pane,
'At Robin kens reet weel,
An' pops in menny a time i t'day,
A crumb or two to steal.

At furst he's shy an' easy flay't,
Bit seunn he bolder gits,
An' picks aboot quite unconsarn't.
Or heer an' theer he flits.
An' when he gits his belly full,
An's tir't o' playin' pranks,
He'll sit quite still, on t'auld chair back,
An' sing his simple thanks.

Bit when breet spring comes back ageann,
An' fields ur growen green,
He bids good day, an' flees away,
An' than na mair he's seen;
Til winter comes ageann wi' frost,
An' driften snow, an' rain,
An' than he venters back ageann,
To leuk for t'oppen pane.

Noo, burds an fwok ur mickle t'seamm,
If they be i' hard need;
An' yan hes owt to give, they'll come,
An' be girt frinds indeed.
Bit when theer nowt they want to hev,
It's nut sa lang they'll stay,
Bit just as Robin does i' t'Spring,
They'll seun aw flee away.

Richardson left as his memorial the church of St John the Baptist and his grave is in the churchyard. The earliest reference to a church here is 1554 but it is probable that there was a chapel on this site long before then. Situated on the pass between High Rigg and Low Rigg, Richardson's church stands on a once well-frequented road leading from the Vale of St John to the Naddle Valley. The church was built in 1845 and although it was restored half a century later it still retains its original plan with the nave and chancel all in one and a tiny tower at the west end. Inside it is warm, colourful and welcoming. William Hutchinson has a curious reference to an old seat in the church 'with the date 1001 on the back of it'. He adds that there is a tradition that this seat was formerly in the chapel 'on St Herbert's Island' in Derwentwater – probably an error for Lord's Island as no chapel is known to have existed on St Herbert's Island – but nothing further has been discovered about this seat. It was no longer in the church in 1889 when informed speculation cast doubts on the authenticity of the date which seemed highly unlikely and may have been a carver's mistake for 1601.

John Richardson achieved renown as mason and poet and he left a tangible legacy for subsequent ages to enjoy. Two other individuals from the valley, of whom we know nothing, also achieved a kind of immortality by giving their names to specific locations on the local map, names which have become familiar to all who walk these fells. One is 'Jim' of 'Jim's Fold', a spot high above Wanthwaite Crags; the other is 'Fisher's Wife' who, it would seem, gave her name to the precipitous rake leading up to Jim's Fold.

The view from Fisher's Wife's Rake is, indeed, impressive but a far easier and much better way to appreciate both the pastoral scene of the whole valley and also the mountain panorama is to walk along the terrace above St John's Beck, turn up the old road to visit the church, and return by the long ridge of High Rigg.

44 *St John's Church*

The first stage from Smaithwaite Bridge to the church is a pleasant, easy stroll of just over two miles with many delightful viewpoints. The brief climb up from the church and the ridge-walk are a little more strenuous but the rewards are immense – spectacular views, exhilarating walking, varied terrain, and innumerable idyllic spots to rest and enjoy (*pace* the Reverend William Gilpin) 'one of the most celebrated scenes of beauty in the country'.

Curlew

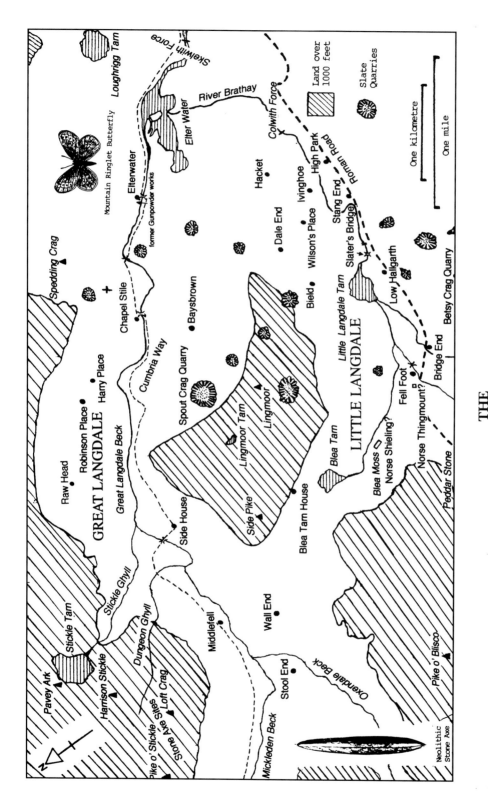

THE
LANGDALES

Land over
1000 feet

Slate
Quarries

One kilometre

One mile

Loughrigg Tarn

Skelwith Force

River Brathay

Elter Water

Colwith Force

Mountain Ringlet Butterfly

Elterwater

Hacket

Ivinghoe

High Park

Stang End

Roman Road

Spedding Crag

Dale End

Wilson's Place

Slater's Bridge

Chapel Stile

former Gunpowder works

Low Hallgarth

Robinson Place

Harry Place

Baysbrown

Bield

Little Langdale Tarn

Betsy Crag Quarry

Raw Head

Cumbria Way

Spout Crag Quarry

LITTLE LANGDALE

Bridge End

GREAT LANGDALE

Great Langdale Beck

Lingmoor Tarn

Lingmoor

Blea Tarn

Blea Moss

Norse Shieling?

Fell Foot

Stickle Tarn

Side House

Side Pike

Blea Tam House

Norse Thingmount?

Peddar Stone

Pavey Ark

Harrison Stickle

Stickle Ghyll

Dungeon Ghyll

Middlefell

Wall End

Pike o' Stickle

Stone Axe

Loft Crag

Stool End

Mickleden Beck

Oxendale Beck

Pike o' Blisco

Neolithic
Stone Axe

N

17

THE LANGDALES

Lingmoor Fell rises gently from the reedy meadows which fringe the western shores of Elterwater. At first its flanks are adorned with the awesome depths and working debris of quarries notable for the most beautiful of all green slates, and with delectable woods where oak, ash, birch and hazel mingle with holly, yew and larch and abandoned rhododendron groves. These give way to sheep-cropped fellside pastures embellished with rocky knolls, ancient junipers and patches of bracken – and everywhere reminders of the quarries which have always contributed so much to the economy of the Langdales. The unfolding views of the valleys below and of the whole of southern Lakeland make every step of the ascent a delight but the summit itself is sheer joy. Set on an unmistakable eminence and surrounded by a sea of purple heather with a small, glittering tarn like an island in its midst, this is by far the best introduction to the glories of the Langdales. From the summit cairn it is clear that Lingmoor Fell is isolated from other fells and forms a crescent-shaped mass whose geographical 'function is to divide Great Langdale from Little Langdale; the wide, curving sweep of the former to the north, the latter gentler and more secluded to the south'. And to the west, enclosing the head of each valley is an array of majestic mountains among the finest in Lakeland – the long, dark wall of the Coniston Fells across Little Langdale and the bastions of Crinkle Crags, Bowfell, Great End, Esk Pike, Gimmer Crag, and magnificent in the foreground the Langdale Pikes themselves, Pike o' Blisco, Pike o' Stickle, Loft Crag and Harrison Stickle. This is the place, on a bright and clear summer solstice, to put to the test Wordsworth's claim that 'at the calm close of summer's longest day' the sun sets between two 'lusty peaks'.[1]

Lingmoor Fell terminates in a steep descent towards Blea Tarn with its fringe of pine trees and blazing rhododendrons and it is here that the two Langdales which were separated at Elterwater are re-united as the road which encircles Lingmoor Fell like a necklace completes its circuit.

It is in 'these craggy regions, these chaotic wilds' that we may trace evidence of prehistoric man's activity in the Langdale valleys. The long-held belief that, except for the years of the Roman garrisons, the Lake District was virtually unknown to mankind until the arrival of the Norsemen was dispelled in the early 1870s with the discovery of a Neolithic village settlement at Ehenside Tarn near Beckermet in West Cumberland. Among the substantial quantity of household tools found there was a number of stone axes manufactured from the grey-green rock of the Borrowdale Volcanic type characteristic of the central fells some twenty or so miles away. The search for the source of these axes was rewarded in 1947 when a major 'stone-axe factory' was discovered on the steep scree slopes of Pike o' Stickle high above Great Langdale. Other sites were later identified on Loft Crag, Harrison Stickle and Thunacar Knott and also on Great End and Scafell. Dating processes have given the period 2730 to 1550 B.C. as the most likely age of these tools and this corresponds closely to the dates given for the various axes, chisels, adzes and other artefacts from Ehenside. It is possible to imagine that these men whose home was at Ehenside spent the lighter and warmer summer days chipping away at the rough-wrought axes on the crags, returning home to grind and polish them in the winter. No polished axes have been found on the 'shop-floor' but sand and stone would be readily available nearer the coast. These axes were highly regarded and examples have been found in various parts of the British Isles and also in countries on the European continent as far away as Poland. The efficiency of tools such as these was effectively demonstrated some years ago when three men using Neolithic stone axes cleared 600 square yards (approximately 500 square metres) of Danish birch forest in four hours. Tools which could do this could also plough the soil, build houses and boats, and fashion implements for farm and household use; could, in short, transform the standard of human life. The Langdale stone-axe factory probably continued in production for about a thousand years until stone was replaced by bronze in the manufacture of tools and weapons, a significant span of time in the story of human civilisation.[2]

Archaeology has been less successful in revealing the true origin and purpose of two historical sites at the head of Little Langdale. On the east side of Blea Moss, some 500 metres south-east of Blea Tarn, are two ruined enclosures of considerable antiquity. It has not yet been possible to establish with any degree of certainty either the age or the function of these structures but it seems reasonable to conjecture that these remains were the foundation walls on which timber huts or byres were built, and that this could have been the site of a Norse seter or summer shieling. We know from the evidence of Norse farming customs in north Scotland that Norse settlers in Britain continued the system of summer transhumance which was customary in their Scandinavian homeland. This aimed to conserve the limited amount of grazing available in the valley bottom by transferring stock to higher upland pastures during the summer months. In the late spring the women and young girls took the cattle, sheep and goats up to the shielings and spent the summer there tending the animals, making cheese, spinning wool, harvesting the hay, and occasionally visiting their loved ones down in the valleys. William Camden, travelling here in the 16th century, tells us that this way of life still persisted in the northern counties, and if one imagines the conditions which must have prevailed in the early days of the Norse clearances of the first tiny fields, it is not difficult to visualise that these ruined enclosures on Blea Moss – and elsewhere as in Mickleden, and on Seat Sandal and Troutbeck Tongue – could once have been a Lakeland version of an upland shieling or seter.[3]

Another archaeological mystery lies a short distance away in the field behind Fell Foot Farm. This is a rectangular flat-topped mound with steps cut into two sides. It measures approximately 150 feet by 95 feet (45.7m x 30m) and rises on average some 9 to 10 feet (approx. 3m) but its once clear outline has in recent years suffered from lack of protection from farming activities. It is situated close by the line of the Roman road through Little Langdale and at the junction of the road over to Great Langdale. Controversy has surrounded this unusual structure for many years and archaeological investigation has failed to reveal any helpful information concerning its origins, but its appearance and situation have led to a supposition that it could be a Viking 'Thing Mount', the meeting place of the Council or Assembly which once determined the laws and judgments of the community of the Langdales. The name 'Thing' is still given to the modern Parliamentary Assemblies of Scandinavia and Iceland while in the British Isles we have retained the Tynwald (Norse: 'thing-völlr') of the Isle of Man and its ancient meeting place on Tynwald Hill. In the open-air meetings of the Norse Thing all men could attend who were of age to bear arms; anyone who refused to accept and obey any judgments given was outlawed, and in a small community that could mean only exile or death. Written records clearly indicate the extent of the power of these assemblies: laws were promulgated on every aspect of the life of the community, from murder and arson to boundary marks and infringement of grazing rights, from public morality to charges of turning a neighbour's butter sour, and from religious observance to the propriety of dubious love songs. Final approval to any decision was expressed by a great shout and clash of spears on shields. In the quiet of an early morning here on this mysterious mound at Fell Foot one may be forgiven a flight of imagination which conjures up such a scene and such a sound, however slender the historical evidence may be.[4]

Fell Foot farm is one of the 40 farmhouses in the Langdales which were built in or just before the 17th century in an era of expansion and prosperity for the yeomen farmers of Lakeland and the country as a whole. For almost 300 years upland farming traditions continued little changed and ensured a simple but modestly comfortable standard of living as the reward for a life of hard work and dedication. But the dramatic social and economic upheavals of the 20th century have steadily undermined this economy and the whole future not only of upland farming but of the appearance of the landscape itself is now being questioned.[5/6]

Fortunately the work of conservation bodies such as the National Park Authority, the National Trust and the Friends of the Lake District should ensure that in 2064 visitors to Langdale ought still to be able to share the pleasure so eloquently expressed by Eliza Lynn Linton in 1864:

> Every step of the way is lovely ... These wooded lanes are things to remember for ever, especially if seen in the Autumn time, when the yellow leaves are scattered in showers of gold on the ground, and the sunlight slanting through the trees brings out all the hues and tones possible to nature.[7]

The abandonment of the smallest farms began in the earliest years of the 20th century and gathered pace after the two World Wars; as farms were amalgamated long-established families left the valley and the population went into a steady decline. For a time employment could be found in the slate quarries and the gunpowder works but from the 1930s these, too, could no longer be relied upon. The latter closed in 1933 and although slate quarrying continued to prosper at a few sites many quarries also closed. The copper mines of Wetherlam and Tilberthwaite barely survived into the 20th century. It was inevitable that with such fundamental changes in the economy there should be not only a sharp decline in the native population but a steady increase in the number of 'off-comers' who have acquired farmhouses, barns and cottages for use either as holiday homes or as permanent residences. The population of the valleys reached a peak of 846 in 1911, fell to 563 fifty years later and in 1991 was only 389 with 38 per cent of properties occupied as 'second homes'. These bare statistics reflect the transformation which has taken place in the way of life in the Langdales following the decline of employment in the farming and quarrying industries and the end of the manufacture of gunpowder.

Slate quarrying is the oldest and the most important of all the industries of the Lake District. It is also the least well-documented: this may be because until the mid-20th century almost all the slate produced was used locally and so few records were kept, but in recent times there has been a significant demand for the attractive and extremely durable blue and green-stone Lakeland slates as building material in other parts of the

45   Slate-rivers at Tilberthwaite Quarry, late 19th century

country and in many places overseas. The carborundum polishing process has given a further boost to the industry and for those who are able to afford the comparatively high cost of building and ornamentation in this material the result is one of the most beautiful and impressive of architectural adornments. To contrast the alluring green-stone elegance of St Catherine's College, Oxford, with the dreary drabness of almost any modern concrete structure is a telling lesson in aesthetic appreciation and sense of timeless durability.

The great spoil-heaps, the vast gaping holes, the tunnels and shafts, the cutting, riving and polishing sheds and the massive blocks of newly quarried slate, which every walker in the Langdales is familiar with, are in themselves clear indicators of the contribution made by these valleys to this industry. At Spout Crag, Thrang Crag, Tilberthwaite and Hodge Close were some of the most important green slate quarries in the whole district, employing several hundred workers who have their monument not only in the changes they brought about in the landscape but in great public buildings as far apart as the National Library in Edinburgh, the Bank of Canada in Montreal, the *Observer* offices in London and in the palaces of wealthy and discerning sheiks through-out the Middle East. So promising did the future of this industry seem in 1960 that it was considered a judicious economic enterprise to bring down as large a quantity of rock as possible in one blast: at the Spout Crag Quarry in Great Langdale 11 tons of explosive dislodged 250,000 tons of rock, a record for a single blast. But even then a long shadow was being cast over this confidence in a certain future, for not only was slate now becoming more and more uncompetitive in price in an age when short-term economics was fast becoming the new orthodoxy, but the concept of landscape conservation was taking root as one of the principal purposes of the National Park within the boundaries of which all the green-stone quarries operate. The first (1961) review of the Lake District Planning Board's Development Plan, while giving the industry positive encouragement, nevertheless sounded a warning note that unrestricted future expansion was unlikely to find unqualified approval:

> It is the policy of the Lake District Planning Board to encourage the working of the Park's mineral resources, not only in order to help in maintaining a true and diverse economy, but also to ensure a continued supply of indigenous building materials so important to the continuity of the traditional landscape ... The encouragement of mineral workings must, however, involve some compromise with the Board's other duty to protect the landscape.

This added to the harsh facts of economic competition has left the Burlington blue slate with the lion's share of the market rather than the green-stone slates of Langdale.[8]

The explosive which brought down a quarter of a million tons of rock at Spout Crag was dynamite. This had replaced gunpowder in the early decades of the 20th century as a safer and more readily controlled means of blasting the massive blocks of slate from the quarry face. Until the 1930s Langdale had its own gunpowder manufactory at Elterwater, one of the seven sites in South Westmorland which from 1764 to 1937 produced explosives for the quarrying industry and for the armed forces, and by 1914 provided half the total requirement for the whole country.

The gunpowder works at Elterwater were founded in 1824 by David Huddleston, a Kendal banker, who saw opportunities presented by the demand from many local slate quarries and from the Coniston and Little Langdale copper mines, both about to enter a period of expansion and profitability. Huddleston acquired a triangular site of some twenty acres with the Great Langdale Beck on its western boundary to provide water-power for the many mills and turbines required in the complicated process of manufacture. To supplement this supply he constructed the dam at Stickle Tarn as a reservoir but this was not an unqualified success as a result of constant leakage on the three-mile course to the works. In the peak years of production (1860-1918) the Elterwater factory employed over 50 people and packed 20 tons of gunpowder every week. At first this was taken by horse and cart to a quay at the head of Windermere and dispatched by boat to Lakeside and thence to the port of Greenodd for shipping to the rest of the country or to West Africa and other foreign destinations. After the opening of the railway to Windermere in 1846 there was a regular consignment of three or more cartloads delivered to the station each day.

The essential ingredients for the manufacture of gunpowder are saltpetre, sulphur and charcoal. The latter was made, for this purpose, from alderwood or from savin (*juniperus sabina*), and supplies were readily available within the locality, but the saltpetre came from India, Chile and Italy, and the sulphur from Italy and Sicily, imported through the ports of Milnthorpe and Greenodd. Each stage of the manufacturing process − mixing, pressing, granulating, glazing, drying, moulding, and packing into strong oak barrels each holding 100 lbs of gunpowder − was accompanied by the hazard of explosion. The columns of the *Westmorland Gazette* in these years have frequent reports of accidents and fatalities: 71 workers were killed at the Westmorland gunpowder sites and of these 13 were at Elterwater. The use of dynamite as the blasting agent quickly reduced many of these hazards but soon afterwards the control of the industry passed to Imperial Chemical Industries who in 1928 concentrated production at Ardeer in Scotland. The Elterwater works, among others, were closed, leaving an abandoned and unemployed workforce and a dangerous site which had to be totally razed and cleansed by fire to remove all trace of explosive powder. Very little now remains of the whole complex operation and the site itself has been converted into a Timeshare Estate with well-appointed chalets and facilities of every kind. Most of the many thousands who speed along the nearby road into Great Langdale each year would be surprised to learn that on this pleasant wooded spot there once stood an important and hazardous industry.[9]

It is, indeed, along the modern highway into Great Langdale that most of today's tourists make their way as they seek out the famous vistas of the Langdale Pikes or jostle for a parking space from which to begin a day's enjoyment on the popular peaks so easily accessible from the valley head. But Little Langdale has been a busy highway throughout recorded history. The Romans drove their Tenth Iter (Highway Ten) along the banks of the River Brathay from their fort at Ambleside to Little Langdale and thence along the valley and over Wrynose and Hardknott Passes to Eskdale and down to the sea at Ravenglass. Succeeding generations followed where they had shown the way. Roman cohorts were succeeded by land-hungry Norsemen who had come by sea from Ireland or from the Western Isles; medieval drovers herding their cattle to distant markets came this way, to be joined later by packhorse trains and freight wagons carrying slate, copper, coal, wool, farm produce, tobacco, sugar and rum; and 20th-century car-borne tourists grind their way over Hardknott, Wrynose or Blea Moss to negotiate the hazards of the twisting, narrow, valley lane which has now replaced the Roman road. It is as a busy highway that much of Little Langdale's history has been made.

The exact course taken by the Tenth Iter built towards the end of the first century is now almost impossible to determine. Investigations by eminent archaeologists during the 20th century offer a rough guide but agricultural activity and erosion by the waters of the Brathay have destroyed almost every trace of the road. In 1921 R.G. Collingwood produced a fairly detailed reconstruction of the route as he believed it to have been, an exercise in informed imagination which thirty years later Professor I.A. Richmond, using the rather stricter standards of a later archaeological discipline, found wanting at many points. In 1959 Professor Ivan Margary's study attempted to re-state much of Collingwood's route and, while much uncertainty still remains, the essential difference between the opposing views is simply analysed: did the Romans follow the valley bottom all the way along the south bank of the river or did they choose a slightly higher level? The existence of a good walking track along much of the upper route makes this by far the easiest line to take today.[10]

From the summit of the Skelwith Bridge – Coniston road a steeply terraced descent took the Romans down to Colwith Bridge. From here there is a green lane between walls and through the woods to High Park Farm and Stang End in the vicinity of which Professor Margary describes traces of a metalled causeway as the remains of the 'agger' or raised foundation of the road. This disappears into the river where the banks have been eroded. Henceforward, we may follow Collingwood's road along the present track to Hall Garth, to Bridge End and over the river to Fell Foot or try to imagine Richmond's preferred route along the river bank just a short distance below. It is an academic point of no great significance if the object of the journey is rather to enjoy the exquisite natural beauty of the scenery all around. For those who insist on placing a foot on Roman terra firma it is necessary to climb the modern road to Wrynose as far as the Pedder Stone, just one kilometre from Fell Foot. This stone forms a natural bench which provided a resting-place for the pedlars and chapmen who travelled the roads selling their wares in the valley communities and in the lonely farmhouses. They were a much-valued link with the outside world. Here, slightly to the north of the present road, the Roman road emerges from obscurity on a narrow eroded terrace, and rounding Great Horse Crag it continues on a curving course to cross Wrynose Beck a few metres upstream from the modern bridge, and then follows a causeway over five metres wide to just south of the Three Shire stone. The gradients here are notably less difficult than those on the modern road![11]

We may never know precisely how far this path diverges from the actual line of the Roman road through Little Langdale but we have the consolation of the certain knowledge that it is very close to it, and that this was one of the most important roads in the Roman network in Britain. One indication of the status of a Roman road is its relation to the prestigious Imperial System of Posts: in north-west Britain only Carlisle and Ravenglass were nominated as terminal points in this system, the former at the end of the main north-south route, the latter at the end of the Tenth Iter and a major supply port.

It is well-known that the Romans took every opportunity to exploit the mineral deposits of their British province wherever they might occur and it seems highly likely that they were the first to mine the iron and copper ore in the Langdale and Coniston fells. The haematite deposits by Red Tarn near Cold Pike are close to their road over Wrynose; the Tilberthwaite, Greenburn and Bonsor copper mines are accessible to the road through Little Langdale; a number of ancient bloomeries have been identified in the area; but there is, as yet, no firm evidence that any of these were actually worked in Roman times. That they were extensively worked in later times is well recorded and, indeed, very visible both above and below ground. A lively account of a visit to Tilberthwaite copper mines is given in a Victorian gentleman's notes on the Coniston district: A. Craig Gibson's *The Old Man ... or Ravings and Ramblings* (1849) describes in detail his remarkable guided tour of the mines and his observations of the work in progress.[12]

Thomas Robinson assures us that 140 years before this

> Langdale and Cunningston mountains do abound most with iron veins, which supplies with ore and keeps constantly going a Furnace in Langdale, where great plenty of good and malleable iron is made, not much inferior to that of Dantzick.[13]

Robinson here was almost certainly referring to one of the most important of the iron forges in Langdale – at Hacket above Colwith Force in Little Langdale. The forge here was operating in 1608 processing ore from both Red Tarn and Rossett Gill. A sledway was constructed down the gill to facilitate the transport of the ore. When the forge ceased to operate, in the late 18th century, it was producing some 30 tons of iron each year and was also refining iron from Backbarrow, near Newby Bridge.

All these worthy activities in the Langdales had a darker side too. The ancient road to Ravenglass had other uses than the transport of legitimate trading goods. The unique status of The Island of the Kingdom of Man exempted it from the import duty regulations which prevailed throughout the mainland and with the rapid extension of trade with the Carribean and the American colonies it was not long before a group of adventurers saw the possibilities of a lucrative smuggling operation from the Isle of Man through the small ports of West Cumberland. Ravenglass thus became the recipient of regular cargoes of duty-free brandy, rum, sugar, tobacco, tea and lace, smuggled across in unobtrusive scout-boats, stored in concealed cellars, secret rooms and hidden lofts in Ravenglass and in stone caches specially constructed underground in the surrounding fields. From here the goods were distributed throughout the north-west along planned routes with 'safe houses' and storage facilities on the way. The most direct but the most hazardous of these routes was via Hardknott, Wrynose and Little Langdale. To reduce the risk of ambush by vigilant excisemen smuggled goods were carried under cover of darkness and it was reckoned that a distance of twelve miles or thereabouts was as much as could be safely travelled in one night. Thus a secure hiding place was required at this distance along the whole journey: Fell Foot farm at the head of Little Langdale fitted this exactly and this seems to lend substance to the many smugglers' tales attached to the story of this ancient farm.[14]

A new stimulus – and additional spice – was given to this 'running trade' with the mid-18th-century restrictions imposed on the distilling of Scotch whisky. According to popular legend illicit stills were at work in many hide-outs in the fells and among their most notorious operators was one Lancelot or 'Lanty' Slee, an Irishman born in Borrowdale in 1802. He lived at Low Arnside, near the Coniston road above Little Langdale, worked in the Tilberthwaite slate quarries, and distilled and distributed his 'mountain dew' in the hours of darkness. It is believed that he had several stills in remote places but the best known is that in Betsy Crag Quarry above Little Langdale Tarn. Slee was apprehended by the law on several occasions and given brief gaol sentences after trials which were reported as excellent entertainment. He always returned to his secret 'worms' and continued to provide his customers with his high quality whisky at 10 shillings a gallon until his death at Greenbank in Little Langdale in 1878.

A short distance from Greenbank is Iving Howe, a house where, when Lanty Slee was a stripling of 16, poetry and politics became involved in an unedifying conspiracy which demonstrated to the full the corruption of parliamentary elections in the days before the Reform Acts of the 19th century. In the 1818 Election William Wordsworth campaigned energetically for the Tory candidate, Sir William Lowther, whose father was the poet's most important patron. In order to qualify for the right to vote under the pre-Reform electoral arrangements it was necessary to be a freeholder of certain types of property. Wordsworth accordingly devised a scheme whereby eight of his relatives and friends would acquire small tenements on the Iving Howe Estate and so qualify for votes in the forthcoming election. All were, of course, favourable to the Lowther cause and their votes no doubt played a small part in securing the return of Sir William to Parliament for the constituency of Westmorland. For once, it was left to Wordsworth's wife, Mary, to show appreciation of the beauty of the place: while William's letters at the time are solely concerned with the political advantages of purchasing the estate, Mary wrote in one of her letters from Iving Howe: 'An hour ago a bargain was struck in this house for a beautiful freehold in Langdale ... a sweet sunny place with beautiful rocks ... yew trees and hollies'.[15]

There is always something new to discover in Langdale. The sheer beauty of the place is a poem in itself, and like all good poetry it has many levels of enjoyment and appreciation. This the eye can perceive and the heart enjoy but the lively and enquiring mind will wish to delve more deeply, perhaps into the geology of the volcanic rocks with their alternating beds of tuffs and lava flows which form the bare bones of the natural scene and to ask why Great Langdale is unique among the Lakeland valleys in its unusual twisting changes of direction. The spoil-heaps and derelict quarries and mines prompt questions on the industrial history of these valleys and the life and skills of the men who worked there, at the quarry face or deep underground. Was it these slate workers who built the picturesque Slater's Bridge by Little Langdale Tarn or did it acquire its name from the local medieval family of Sleyther?

Curiosity about the abundance of juniper bushes in these valleys will reveal that they were at one time protected and even planted, as 'savin' or juniper charcoal was

46   *Slater's Bridge, Little Langdale*

found to be the most suitable fuel for use in the manufacture of gunpowder: almost 100 kilograms of wood were consumed to produce 50 kilograms of gunpowder.

Both curiosity and energy are required to seek out some of the botanical rarities of Langdale – the lichens and mosses of Raven Crag and Hell Gill and, at a lower level, the bright yellow flowers and orange seed-pods of the bog asphodel, the pink bells of the bog rosemary or the purple spikes of orchids.

Here, too, there is much to learn and admire about the flight of the raven, the kestrel and the peregrine or, in the sun-dappled woods, the ways of the redstart, tree pipit and pied flycatcher. Buzzards, sparrowhawks and barn-owls nest in these valleys and the Lakeland golden eagles are also seen from time to time. Red deer and roe deer frequent the woodlands where the red squirrel still maintains a foothold and the badger flourishes. Whooper swans still come to Elter Water as they did when the lake was first given its name, recorded in 1157 as Helterwatra, the lake of the swans. A bonus for those who climb the Pikes could be a sighting of the Small Mountain Ringlet Butterfly which has one of its Lakeland colonies on these crags, while those who are content to wander through the meadows along the Cumbrian Way might contemplate the curious differences between the breeds of sheep hereabouts, the Herdwick, the Rough Fell and the Swaledale, or to speculate on the origin of such names as Pavey Ark, Pye Howe, and Tilberthwaite.[16]

Some might be intrigued to learn that the Robinson who gave his name to Robinson Place was an Elizabethan yeoman, that Harry of Harry Place was the Harrison who gave his name to the Stickle, that the Spedding of Spedding Crag was one of Wordsworth's

47   *The Nick Stick seat, Great Langdale*

political pawns and that a Wilson from Wilson Place went on from Little Langdale to manufacture the famous Kendal Mint. An observant eye will note the unusual bee-boles at Raw Head or the stone seat by the roadside opposite Robinson Place, a landmark of some importance only a few generations ago; for this was the spot where at hiring time farmers and labourers met to exchange tallies or notched sticks, each retaining an identical half of the stick as evidence of the contract agreed upon. The 'Nick Stick Seat' was also used as the meeting point for landowners and tenants on 'rent-days'. There is, indeed, almost no end to the avenues of knowledge to be pursued in these two valleys, so rich is their heritage.[17]

Red squirrels

GLOSSARY

Glossary of some of the dialect words in the extracts from Sarah Yewdale's memories:

barns	=	children, bairns	med hae hard	=	might have heard
beeaken	=	baking	mickle	=	much
Cannelmas	=	Candlemas (2 February)	mud	=	ought to be
chapel garth	=	church yard	ran through yan's sel	=	wore oneself out
chimley	=	chimney	rannel balk	=	the beam over the
clad	=	clothed			fire-place
clippen	=	shearing time	rarely	=	specially
coonten beuk	=	book of sums	reet	=	right
coos	=	cows	seeal	=	a sale
Cursmas	=	Christmas	seeam	=	same
Darren	=	the River Derwent	sic	=	such
deeal	=	dale	sic scrows	=	such a hubbub,
deuaan	=	able to do			excitement
donn't up	=	dressed up	skeul	=	school
drusser	=	a dresser or sideboard	snell	=	raw, chilly
dud sae	=	did so	statesman	=	a name generally
fadder	=	the person who gave away			used to denote the
		the bride			independent yeoman
fakes	=	antics			farmers or the freehold
flicks	=	flitches			and customary tenants
fwok	=	folk			who achieved prosperity
gang	=	going			in the Lakeland valleys
gart	=	big			in the 17th and 18th
geavelock	=	an iron crowbar			centuries
inkle	=	linen	towt	=	taught
laal	=	little	wad hae gaen	=	would have gone
lang sen	=	long since, in the old days	wedder	=	weather
larnen	=	learning, education	woo' an t' line	=	wool and flax
leeved	=	lived	wosseln	=	wassailing
maistly	=	usually			

NOTES

Chapter 1

1. Brown, John, *Description of the Lake at Keswick* (1767), reprint (1985) pp.5-6.
2. Radcliffe, Ann, *Observations during a Tour to the Lakes ...* (1795), p.465.
3. Walker, Adam, *A Tour from London to the Lakes* (1785). A comprehensive survey of the literary references to Borrowdale and the Vale of Keswick is given in Lindop, G., *A Literary Guide to the Lake District*, 1993, Part Two, pp.164-209.
4. Gray, Thomas, *Journal to the Lakes ...* (1775), 3 October 1769.
5. Proceedings of the Prehistoric Society, No 55 (1989).
6. Allan, M., *The Roman Route across the Northern Lake District* (1994).
7. Gambles, R., *Lake District Place-names* (1994).
8. Collingwood, W.G., *Lake District History* (1928), p.64.
9. Gilpin, W., *Observations...*(1786), p 195.
10. Johnson, Susan, 'Borrowdale, its Land Tenure and the Records of the Lawson Manor', *CWAAS (NS)* (1981), pp.63-71.
11. Gilpin, W., *op. cit.*, p.205.
12. Robinson, T., *A Natural History of Cumberland and Westmorland* (1709), p.75.
13. Topographical details of Moses' Trod are given in Wainwright's *Western Fells* (Great Gable 7-8). G. Sutton, *Fell Days*, 1948, pp.143-147, has a note on Gable Hut.
14. Hutchinson, W., *op. cit.*, has comments from numerous contemporary guidebooks on the wad mines in the 18th century, pp.212-220. A detailed recent study is Tyler, I., *Seathwaite Wad and the Mines of Borrowdale* (1995).
15. The plans for this railway may be seen at the County Record Office, Carlisle, Ref: Q/R2/1/154.
16. Johnson, Susan, *Conserving Lakeland*, No. 19, 1992 (Friends of the Lake District).
17. Clarke, James, *Survey of the Lakes...* (1787), p.154.
18. Riving is the process of reducing blocks of slate to small slabs about 2in. (5cm.) thick and then splitting or riving these along the line of cleavage with a wedge-shaped hammer, thus producing slate about one quarter of an inch (6mm.) in thickness. These were then trimmed by a slate 'dresser' and graded according to size and quality. For a detailed study of the Honister Quarry see Tyler, I., *Honister Slate* (1994).
19. Friar's Crag owes its name to the pilgrimages made by the monks of Lindisfarne to St Herbert's Island. This was their embarkation point.
20. Martineau, Harriet, *Complete Guide to the Lakes* (1885 edn.), p.75.
21. Symons, G.J., *The Floating Island of Derwentwater* (1888).
22. Ratcliffe, D.A., *Borrowdale Woods*, in Pearsall, W.H. and Pennington, W. (eds), *The Lake District* (1973).
23. Budworth, J., *A Fortnight's Ramble to the Lakes* (1795), reprint 1990, pp.69-70.
24. Bailey, J. (ed), *Borrowdale in the Old Time: as Gathered from the Conversation of the late Sarah Yewdale, Queen of Borrowdale* (1869).

Chapter 2

1. Wordsworth, W., *Guide to the Lakes* (1835) (OUP edn. 1973, p.26). Budworth, J., *A Fortnight's Ramble to the Lakes* (1792), p.203. Gilpin, W., *Observations ...* (1786), p.218. Linton, E. L., *The Lake Country* (1864), p.195, has an interesting description of Newlands.
2. Haskett-Smith, W.P., 'Fountains Abbey and Cumberland', *CWAAS (NS)* (1921).
3. Marshall, J.D., *Old Lakeland* (1971) Chapter 2: The Lakeland Yeoman. Dickinson, W., *Cumbriana* (1876), has a rhyming dialect account of the farming year.
4. 'Sir Daniel Fleming's Notebook', *CWAAS (NS)* (1928).
5. Heaton, H., *The Yorkshire Woollen and Worsted Industries* (1920), p.344.
6. Monkhouse, F. J., 'Some Features of the Historical Geography of the German Mining Enterprise in Elizabethan Lakeland', *Geography* Vol. 28, p.107 (1943).

7. Donald, M.B., *Elizabethan Copper*, (1955), p.12.
8. Fisher-Crosthwaite, J., 'The German Miners in Keswick', *Transactions of the Cumberland Association for the Advancement of Literature and Science*, Vol. 8 (1882).
9. Donald, M.B., *op. cit.*, Chapter 6 gives details of the legal proceedings.
10. Historical MSS Commission: Kendal MSS, Rep. 10, App. Pt. IV, p.304.
11. Hammersley, G., *Daniel Hechstetter the Younger: Memorabilia and Letters 1600-1639: Copper Works and Life in Cumbria* (1988).
12. Collingwood, W.G., *Elizabethan Keswick* (1912).
13. The stope and feather were implements used to extract ore from the vein: two thin pieces of iron (feathers) about six inches long and half-an-inch wide, flat on one side and rounded on the other; a thin, tapering wedge (the stope) of the same length and width. A hole was driven into the rock with an iron bar (the jumper) and into this the feathers were driven with their flat sides together and parallel with the cleavage of the rock. The stope was then hammered between them to split the rock.
14. Bouch, C.M.L. and Jones, G.P., *The Lake Counties 1500-1830* (1962), pp.120-127. Nicolson, J. and Burn, R., *The History and Antiquities of the Counties of Westmorland and Cumberland* (1777), Vol. 2, p.69.
15. Sandford, E., *A Cursory Relation of all the Antiquities and Families of Cumberland* (1675).
16. Adams, J., *Mines of the Lake District Fells* (1988), pp.47-48.
17. Postlethwaite, J., *Mines and Mining in the Lake District* (1913), pp.59-96. See also Adams, J., *op. cit.* Part 1.
18. Clarke, J., *Survey of the Lakes* ... (1787), p.84.
19. Pearsall, W.H. and Pennington, W., *The Lake District* (1973), Chapter 8.

Chapter 3

1. Wordsworth, William, *Guide to the Lakes*, 1835, Oxford edition (1906), p.13.
2. West, Thomas, *Guide to the Lakes* (1778), p.131.
3. Nicholas Size in his novel *The Secret Valley* makes much of this and he is partially supported by the *Victoria County History* which affirms that the family of Bueth or Boet held its own against the Norman invaders. Even so, historical probability and lack of evidence weigh heavily against the story. See also his *Shelagh of Eskdale*, pp.16-18.
4. Size, N., 'A Click Mill at Buttermere', *CWAAS (NS)* (1936).
5. Alfred Wainwright, 200 years later, described 'the long cascade of Sour Milk Gill' as 'the attraction everybody remembers Buttermere by'. (Red Pike 2).
6. Gilpin, William, *Observations on the Mountains and Lakes* ... (1786), p.223.
7. Clarke, James, *Survey of the Lakes* ... (1789), pp.84-86.
8. Aust, Sarah (The Hon. Mrs S. Murray), *A Companion and Useful Guide* ... (1796), p.19. Gray, Thomas, *Journal in the Lakes* (1775), p.28.
9. The height of the waterfall at Scale Force, the highest in Lakeland, depends on the source of one's information. Joseph Budworth's 200 feet is reduced to 172 feet by Hunter Davies's *Good Guide to the Lakes* and to 160 feet by Harriet Martineau. John Murray's *Handbook* measured it at 156 feet, John Wyatt's *Walks Guide* at 130, Molly Lefebure at 125 and the Automobile Association at no more than 100. The National Park's own *Guidebook* declares it to be 120 feet. Wordsworth cautiously described the fall as 'immense', 'a lofty chasm with a lofty though slender fall of water'. The path to the force has greatly deteriorated since Samuel Coleridge and George Eliot and Eliza Lynn Linton came this way, but it is still a popular attraction.
10. Budworth, Joseph, *A Fortnight's Ramble to the Lakes* (1795), p.217 seq.
11. Mary's story has been retold many times, most recently by Melvyn Bragg in his novel *The Maid of Buttermere* (1987).
12. Clarke, James, *Survey of the Lakes* ... (1789), p.84.
13. Murray, John, *Handbook to the Lakes* (1867), p.59.
14. The Church was built in 1841. Henry Holiday's fine stained glass dates from 1893. A recent addition is a memorial tablet to Alfred Wainwright whose life-story has been told by Hunter Davies in his *Wainwright: the Biography* (1995).
15. Wainwright, A., *The Western Fells* (Fleetwith Pike).
16. Martineau, Harriet, *A Complete Guide to the English Lakes* (1858), 1974 edition, p.122.
17. Tyler, I., *Honister Slate* (1994), has a detailed account of the Honister Quarry and also lists 100 species of herbaceous plants and ferns which flourish in the inaccessible gullies and on the screes of Honister Crag.
18. Lindop, G., *A Literary Guide to the Lake District* (1993), p.211.
19. Collingwood, W.G., *The Lake Counties* (1932), p.101.

Chapter 4

1. Gilpin, W., *Observations* ... (1786 edn.), Vol.2, p.7.
2. *Ibid.*, p.4.

3.   Ramshaw, D. and Adams, J., *The English Lakes* (1993), p.18.
4.   Winchester, A.J.L., *Landscape and Society in Medieval Cumbria* (1987), pp.143-149.
5.   Winder, F.A., 'The Winders of Lorton', *CWAAS (NS)* (1912).
6.   Bogg, E., *Two Thousand Miles of Wandering in the Border Country, Lakeland and Ribblesdale* (1898), Part 2, p.193.
7.   *Ibid.*, p.194.
8.   Bradbury, J.Bernard, *A History of Cockermouth* (1981), gives a concise history of the town.
9.   Marshall, J.D., *Old Lakeland* (1971), Chapter 9 'The Bobbin Makers'.
10. Gambles, R.H., 'The Spa Resorts and Mineral Springs of Cumbria', *CWAAS (NS)* (1993).
11. Hankinson, Alan, *A Century on the Crags* (1988), p.31.
12. *Ibid.*, p.30.
13. Stagg, John, 'The Bridewain', printed in *The Cumberland Minstrel* (1821).
14. Bogg, E., *op. cit.* p.193.

Chapter 5

1.   Linton, E.L., *The Lake Country* (1864), pp.227-8.
2.   The detailed plans for this railway are in the County Record Office, Carlisle, Ref: Q/R2/1/153-155. The campaign of opposition to the scheme is recounted in Rawnsley, E.F., *Canon Rawnsley, An Account of his Life and Work* (1923), p.53.
3.   Pennington, W., *The Lake District – A Landscape History* (1973), p.126.
4.   Fletcher, W. and Fell, C.I., 'Stone-based huts and other structures at Smithy Beck, Ennerdale', *CWAAS (NS)* (1987).
5.   Dickinson, W., 'The Wild Deer of Ennerdale', *Cumbriana* (1875).
6.   West, T., *Guide to the Lakes*, 6th edition (1778) p.297.
7.   Linton, E.L., *The Lake Country* (1864), p.227.
8.   Wordsworth, W., 'The Brothers' – a tale of two brothers from Ennerdale, one of whom fell to his death while asleep on Pillar Rock.
9.   Wainwright, W., *The Western Fells* (1966), Pillar 2.
10. The story is told in detail by Dickinson, W., *Cumbriana* (1875).
11. McIntire, W.T., 'Pearl Gathering in the Lake District', *CWAAS (NS)* (1941). Ritchie, C.I.A., *Cumbrian Pearls, Cumbria* (Dalesman), May 1987.
12. A comprehensive account of the Patricksons' lawsuits and details of their genealogy may be found in *CWAAS (NS)* (1925).
13. West, T., *op. cit.* p.299.
14. The Friends of the Lake District published a full account of the campaign in 1982 under the title 'A Tale of Two Lakes'.
15. Linton, E.L., *op. cit.* p.226.

Chapter 6

1.   Wordsworth, W., *Guide to the Lakes*, Oxford edition (1973), pp.22-23.
2.   Wastwater is 258 ft. (78.6m) deep. The lake bed is 58 ft. (18m) below sea-level.
3.   The quotations are from A. Wainwright's *Western Fells and Southern Fells*.
4.   Hoskins, W.G., *The Making of the English Landscape* (1955), p.84.
5.   Liddell, W.H., 'The Private Forests of South West Cumbria', *CWAAS (NS)* (1960).
6.   Elliott, G.G., 'The Enclosures of Aspatria', *CWAAS (NS)* (1960).
7.   Marshall, J.D., 'The Domestic Economy of the Lakeland Yeoman, 1660-1749', *CWAAS (NS)* (1973).
8.   Clarke, James, *A Survey of the Lakes* (1787), p.98.
9.   Ryder, M.L., 'The History of Sheep Breeds in Britain', *Agricultural Review*, 12 (1964).
10. Parkinson, R., 'The Old Church Clock' (1843) – quoted in Lindop, G., *A Literary Guide to the Lake District* (1993), p.245.
11. Ellwood, T., 'The Mountain Sheep and their Marking', *CWAAS (OS)* (1899).
12. Ellwood, T., 'Numerals formerly used for sheep-scoring in the Lake Country', *CWAAS (OS)* (1877).
13. Martin, J.D., 'Wasdale Hall', *CWAAS (NS)* (1976).
14. McIntire, W.T., 'Pearl Gathering in the Lake District', *CWAAS (NS)* (1941). Ritchie, C.I.A., 'Cumbrian Pearls, Cumbria' (Dalesman) May 1987. See also 'Ennerdale', supra p.44.
15. Linton, E.L., *The Lake Country* (1864), p.207.
16. Wilkinson, T., *Tours to the British Mountains* (1824), p.223.
17. Lefebure, M., *The English Lake District* (1964), p.117.
18. Rollinson, W., *The History of Man in the Lake District* (1967), p.68.

Chapter 7

1. Symonds, H.H., *Walking in the Lake District* (1933), p.201.
2. Wainwright, A., *The Southern Fells*, Whin Rigg 3 (1960).
3. Winchester, A.J.L., 'Deserted farmstead Sites at Miterdale Head', *CWAAS (NS)* (1978).
4. John Wesley, *Journal*, 18 April 1761, Vol. IV p.448, Epworth Press (1936).
5. Rushes were known as 'sieves' in Cumberland, a derivation from the Norse 'sef'.
6. The truth of this tale has never been established and there are, consequently, several versions of it. Alice Rea's *The Beckside Bogle* is the best-known early account (1884). A modern attempt to reconstruct the story is in Dudley Hoy's *English Lake Country* (1969) but, unfortunately, no details are given of the newspaper report and this has not yet been traced. The ruins of Sword House (the reputed site of *Nanny Horns Inn*) were investigated in 1978 – see Note 3 above.
7. I am indebted to Dr. Angus Winchester for elucidation of the Miterdale tolls.
8. For details and diagrams of the stone circles see Waterhouse, J., *Stone Circles of Cumbria* (1985), pp.53-61.
9. 'Pighill' is derived from the Middle English word 'pightel' meaning an 'enclosure'. It survives here in Pickle Coppice, a plantation near to Low Place.
10. See Garnett, F.W., *Westmorland Agriculture 1800-1900* (1912) for further details.
11. Parker, C.A. and Fair, M.C., 'Bloomery Sites in Miterdale and Eskdale', *CWAAS (NS)* (1922).
12. See Smith, B., 'The Glacier Lakes of Eskdale, Miterdale and Wasdale', in the *Quarterly Journal of the Geological Society*, No. 88 (1932).
13. The name 'La'al Ratty' is believed to refer to a Mr. Ratcliffe, the first engineer to work on the construction of the line.
14. The mill is open to visitors every day except Saturday from April to October.
15. Fair, M.C., 'An ancient ford of the River Mite', *CWAAS (NS)* (1929).
16. Camden, W., *Britannia*, 1586 ed. (1806)Vol. 3 p.42. See references to Cumbrian pearl-fishing in the chapters on Ennerdale, (pp.44) and Wasdale (pp.55).
17. Dr. Niko Tinbergen, Nobel prizewinner, did much of his research on the Ravenglass Reserve.
18. See Birley E, 'The Roman Fort at Ravenglass', *CWAAS (NS)* (1958); Caine, C., 'The Fair at Ravenglass', *CWAAS (NS)* (1921).

Chapter 8

1. *The Hardknott National Forest Guide* (1949), p.31.
2. Richmond, I.A., 'The Roman Fort at Hardknott', *Hardknott National Park Guide* (1949), p 16. Collingwood, R.G., 'Hardknott Castle', *CWAAS (NS)* (1928).
3. Birley, E., 'The Roman Fort at Ravenglass', *CWAAS (NS)* (1958). Collingwood, R.G., 'Roman Ravenglass', *CWAAS (NS)* (1928). Knowles, C. and Jackson, W., 'Walls Castle Ravenglass', *CWAAS(OS)* (1876).
4. Bellhouse, R.L., 'Excavations in Eskdale – the Muncaster Roman Kilns', *CWAAS (NS)* (1960-61).
5. Richmond, I.A., 'The Roman Road from Ambleside to Ravenglass', *CWAAS (NS)* (1949). Margary, I., *Roman Roads in Britain* (1973), p.389 seq.
6. Smith, B., 'The Glacier Lakes of Eskdale, Miterdale and Wasdale', *Quarterly Journal of the Geological Society*, No. 88 (1932), pp.57-83.
7. Collingwood, R.G., *Roman Eskdale*, p.9.
8. A description of Barnscar as it appeared a hundred years ago is given in Dymond, C.W., 'Barnscar, An Ancient Settlement in Cumberland', *CWAAS (OS)* (1891).
9. See Gambles, R., *Lake District Place-names* (1994).
10. The discovery and investigation of the ancient upland shielings of the Lake District is a long-term archaeological exercise which has only just begun.
11. As in a Commission appointed to enquire into property ownership in 1163.
12. See references in the article on the Eskmeals bloomery sites by Cherry, J., in *CWAAS (NS)*(1966). Fair, M.C. and Parker, C.A., 'Bloomery Sites in Eskdale and Wasdale', *CWAAS (NS)* (1922-25).
13. *Victoria County History: Cumberland*, Vol.2, p.422.
14. Forty tons of nuts a year were exported through Broughton-in-Furness in years of good harvest in the 19th century.
15. Fair, M.C., 'A Relic of Packhorse Days in Eskdale', *CWAAS (NS)* (1922).
16. The mill has been restored and is now open to the public as a working museum every day except Mondays, but including Bank Holidays, Easter to end of September.
17. The nearby *King of Prussia Inn* was renamed in a spirit of patriotic enthusiasm during the First World War but its new name, *The Tatie Garth*, was itself replaced by the less original name of the King George IV. The inn does, however, have the distinction of being able to offer more than one hundred brands of whisky.
18. For full details of the history of the line see Davies, W.J.K., *The Ravenglass and Eskdale Railway* (1968).
19. Davies, W.J.K., *op. cit.*, p.34.

20. Davies, W.J.K., *op. cit.*, p.96.
21. Winchester, A.J., 'Peat Storage Huts in Eskdale', *CWAAS (NS)* (1984).

Chapter 9

1. The initials 'W.F.' inscribed on this stone are those of William Field who in 1816, as Bridge Master and High Constable of Cartmel, ordered the stone to be carved and erected to mark the boundary of Cumberland, Westmorland and Lancashire. It was not, in fact, put up until after his death in 1860.
2. Linton, E.L., *The Lake Country* (1864), p.246.
3. Murray, J., *Handbook to Cumberland, Westmorland and the Lakes* (1869), p.47.
4. Green, W., *Guide to the Lakes* (1819), vol.1 p.322.
5. Richmond, I.A., 'The Roman Road from Ambleside to Ravenglass', *CWAAS (NS)* (1949).
6. Linton, E.L., *op. cit.*, p.251.
7. Murray, J., *op. cit.*, p.46.
8. Wordsworth, W., 'Duddon Sonnets' Nos. X and XIII.
9. *Ibid.* No. XVIII.
10. Chaucer, Geoffrey, *Prologue to the Canterbury Tales*, lines 479-83.
11. Woodforde, James Rev., *Diary*, 14 September/3 December (1776).
12. Murray, J., *op. cit.*, p.46.
13. Dawes, Robert, *Effective Primary Instruction* (1857), p.7.
14. *Annual Register* (1760).
15. Linton, E.L., *op. cit.*, pp.247-8.
16. Martineau, Harriet, *Complete Guide to the English Lakes* (1858), (1974 edn. p. 101).
17. Fair, M.C., 'Two Medieval Diptychs from Cumberland', *CWAAS (NS)* (1928).
18. Collingwood, W.G., 'Ulpha Old Hall', *CWAAS (OS)* (1899).
19. Daniel Paterson included the road by Frith Hall as a coach route in his comprehensive *Road Book* published in numerous editions in the early years of the 19th century.
20. An experienced besom-maker could produce more than four hundred besoms in a day's work.
21. Fair, M.C., 'Notes on the History of Ulpha', *CWAAS (NS)* (1950).
22. Fell, A., *The Early Iron Industry of Furness and District* (1908), p.45.
23. An illustration of one of these quays is printed in *The Lake District at Work* (1971), p. 83, by J.D. Marshall and M. Davies-Shiel.
24. Mart, J.N., *Transactions of the Newcomen Society*, vol.18 (1937-8).
25. The restoration of this industrial monument was given a Heritage Award in 1992. Access to it is by a gate a short distance from the Duddon Bridge Road Junction.
26. Two of Cumbria's famous men had their homes near Askam: the artist George Romney was born at Dalton-in-Furness and Thomas West, historian and author of the first *Guidebook* to the Lakes, lived at Tytup Hall.
27. Marshall, J.D., *Furness in the Industrial Revolution* (1958), p.180 seq.
28. Harris, A., '*Cumberland Iron – the story of Hodbarrow Mine, 1855-1968*', a Monograph in Mining History, No.2 (1970).
29. Harris, A., *op. cit.*, p.115.
30. Harris, A., *op. cit.*, p.116. Harris, A., 'Millom – A Victorian New Town', *CWAAS (NS)* (1966).
31. Winchester, A.J.L., 'The Castle Household and Demesne Farm at Millom in 1513-14', *CWAAS (NS)* (1983). Cowper, H.S., 'Millom Castle and the Hudlestons', *CWAAS (NS)* (1924). (This article has a detailed description of the castle as it was in 1924.)
32. Dickinson, R.W., *The Agriculture of the County of Lancaster* (1815).
33. Linton, E.L., *op. cit.*, p.143.
34. Wordsworth, W., 'Duddon Sonnets', No. XXXIV.
35. Butler, W., 'Townfields of Broughton and Subberthwaite-in-Furness', *CWAAS (NS)* (1929).

Chapter 10

1. From *Stray Walks* by John Clare, *Selected Poems and Prose*, Oxford (1966).
2. A Viking sword was found some years ago at the foot of Whitbarrow Scar. It is now in the Kendal Museum. See Hutton, F.R.C., 'Witherslack Church and Manor', *CWAAS (NS)* (1901) pp.193-4 and Cowan, J.D., 'Viking Burials in Cumbria', *CWAAS (NS)* (1948).
3. Cowper, H.S., 'Cowmire Hall', *CWAAS (NS)* (1901). Jones, G.P., 'The Deeds of Burblethwaite Hall', *CWAAS (NS)* (1962).
4. See Jones, G.P., *A Short History of the Manor and Parish of Witherslack to 1850*, and Jones, G.P., *A Short Account of Cartmel Fell to 1840*.
5. John Barwick (1612-1664) was born in Witherslack and became a prominent churchman. He was an ardent Royalist during the Civil War and passed secret information to both Charles I and Charles II. He was

imprisoned in the Tower for treason under the Commonwealth but later became a Royal Chaplain. He participated in the negotiations which led to the Treaty of Breda by which Charles was restored to the throne in 1660. Barwick then became successively Dean of Durham and of St Paul's.

6. Cave-Brown-Cave, B.W., *Jonas Barber, Clockmaker of Winster* (1979).
7. See Curwen, J.F., 'St Anthony's Chapel, Cartmel Fell', *CWAAS (NS)* (1912).
8. Machell, Thomas, *Antiquary on Horseback*, 1692, transcribed by Jane Ewbank (1963), p.80.
9. Short, Thomas, *Principle [sic] Mineral Waters*, 1740, pp.55-6.
10. Parson and White, *Directory* (1829).
11. Brogan, H., *The Life of Arthur Ransome* (1984). Hardyment, Christina, *Arthur Ransome and Captain Flint's Treasure Chest* (1984), p.45.
12. Storrs Temple is a National Trust property.
13. Meathop Moss may be visited with a permit from the Cumbria Wildlife Trust.
14. English Place-name Society, Smith.A.H. (ed.), *The Place-names of Westmorland* (1967), 1, 15.

Chapter 11

1. Pearson, W., *Letters, Journals and Notes on the Natural History of Lyth* (1844), p.60.
2. Budworth, J., *A Fortnight's Ramble to the Lakes* (1795), Reprint 1990, p.12.
3. Garnett, F.W., *Westmorland Agriculture 1800-1900* (1912), p.7.
4. Garnett, F.W., *op. cit.*, p.33.
5. Rollinson, W., *Life and Tradition in the Lake District* (1974), pp.102-3.
6. Pearson, W., *op. cit.*, pp.1-23. Rollinson, W., *op. cit.*, p.46 and p.79.
7. Jones, G.P., *A Short History of Crosthwaite and Lyth mainly to about 1830* (1966), pp.17-18.
8. Barnes, J.A., 'Ancient Corduroy Roads near Gilpin Bridge', *CWAAS (NS)* (1904).
9. Machell, Thomas, *Antiquary on Horseback* (1692), transcribed by Jane Ewbank (1963), p.75.
10. Levens Highway Book, Kendal Record Office.
11. Strickland Hornyold, H., *Sizergh Castle* (National Trust Guidebook) (1979/83). Curwen, J.F., *An Historical Description of Levens Hall* (1898). Curwen, J.F., 'Nether Levens Hall', *CWAAS (NS)* (1904).
12. Nicolson, J. and Burn, R., *The History and Antiquities of the Counties of Westmorland and Cumberland* (1777), vol. 1, p.226.
13. Somervell, J., *Water-power mills in South Westmorland* (1930), p.38 seq.
14. Jones, G.P., *op. cit.*, p.71. Jones, G.P., 'The Broad Oak Estate Feoffees', *CWAAS (NS)* (1965).
15. Pearson, W., *op. cit.*, p.78.
16. Ferguson, R.S., *The Early History of The Society of Friends* (1871) with an Appendix printing passages from Joseph Besse's *Sufferings of the People Called Quakers 1650-1689.*
17. Pearson, W., *op. cit.*, p.82.
18. Webster, C., 'Essay on the Farming of Westmorland', *Journal of the Royal Agricultural Society*, vol. 6 (1904), p.33.
19. Jones, G.P., *op. cit.*, p.60 seq.
20. Jones, G.P., *op. cit.*, p.61 seq. Steer, T.P., *Landscape Changes in the Lyth Valley 1770 to the 20th century* (1991). Wood, M.L., *The Reclamation of the Lyth Mosses* (1968), p.20 seq.
21. Pearson, W., *op. cit.*, p.78.
22. Steer, T.P., *op. cit.*, p.37.
23. Garnett, F.W., op. cit., pp.54, 59.
24. Pearson, W., *op. cit.*, p.82.
25. Webster, C., *op. cit.*, p.35.
26. Information on 'candle lettings' related by a native of Lyth now deceased.
27. For an analysis of possible future landscape patterns for upland areas see O'Riordan, T., *Interpreting Future Landscapes* (1992) (Yorkshire Dales National Park).

Chapter 12

1. Dickinson, S., 'Bryant's Gill, Kentmere' in *The Scandinavians in Cumbria* (1985).
2. Fell, C., 'A Viking Spearhead from Kentmere', *CWAAS (NS)* (1956). Fell, C., 'A Note on the Kentmere Boat', *CWAAS (NS)* (1955).
3. Curwen, J.F., 'Some notes respecting Kentmere Hall', *CWAAS (NS)* (1901).
4. Atkin, M.A., 'Medieval Land-use in Kentmere', *CWAAS (NS)* (1991).
5. Martindale, J.A., 'An Ancient British Village in Kentmere', *CWAAS (NS)* (1901).
6. I am grateful to Mr. M. Davies-Shiel for information on the chopwood kilns. See also his articles in *CWAAS (NS)* (1972) and (1974).
7. Somervell, J., *Water-power Mills in South Westmorland* (1930), p.6. Yuen, R., *The Kentmere Lead Mines* (1969). Scott, J., ed., *A Lakeland Valley Through Time, A History of Staveley, Kentmere and Ings* (1995).

8. Somervell, J., *op. cit.* The mills are listed in Wainwright, A., *Three Westmorland Rivers* (1979).
9. Watts, D.G., 'Water-power and the Industrial Revolution', *CWAAS (NS)* (1967). Marshall, J.D. and Davies-Shiel, M., *The Industrial Archaeology of the Lakes Counties* (1969), Chapter 3.
10. Marshall, J.D., *Old Lakeland* (1971), Chapter 9, 'The Bobbin Makers'.
11. Weston, G.F., 'Burneside Hall', *CWAAS (OS)* (1881). Machell, T., *Antiquary on Horseback* (1692), ed. Ewbank, J. (1963), p.101.
12. The text of Braithwaite's poem 'The Fatall Nuptiall' is printed in an article by W.G.Collingwood in *CWAAS (NS)* (1913), p.151 seq.
13. Cowper, H.S., 'Notes on Richard Braithwaite of Burneside', *CWAAS (NS)* (1922). Atkinson, G., 'Richard Braithwaite', in *Worthies of Westmorland* (1850), vol.2. Braithwaite, R., *Barnabae Intinerarium*, ed. Penguin Books (1932).
14. Curwen, J.F., 'The Castle Dairy, Kendal', *CWAAS (NS)* (1916). Curwen, J.F., 'Kendal Castle', *CWAAS (NS)* (1908). A detailed study of Kendal Castle will be found in the Westmorland Volume of the *Royal Commission on Historical Monuments* (1936), pp.122-4. Bingham, R., *Kendal, A Social History* (1995). Nicholson, C., *Annals of Kendal* (1861). Curwen, J.F., *Kirkbie Kendal* (1900). Marshall, J.D., 'Kendal in the late 17th and 18th centuries', *CWAAS (NS)* (1975). Nicholls, A.R., *Kendal Town Trail* (1986). *RCHM Westmorland* has a detailed description of Holy Trinity Church, pp.119-22.
15. Wainwright, A., *Three Westmorland Rivers* (1979), p.61. Gambles, R., 'A Gracious and Sociable Custom', in *Lakescene,*(July 1991).
16. Potter, T., 'The Watercrook Excavations 1974-5', in 'The Romans in North-West England', *CWAAS Research Series*, vol. 1 (1976).
17. Wilson, P.N., *The Gunpowder Mills of Westmorland and Furness* (1964). Wilson, P.N., *A Short History of the New Sedgwick Gunpowder Mills* (National Trust) (n.d.).
18. Newmarsh, R., *Mary Wakefield* (1912).
19. Curwen, J.F., *An Historical Description of Levens Hall* (1898). Greenwood, W., 'The Redmans of Levens Hall', *CWAAS (NS)* (1903).
20. Hornyold Strickland, H., *Sizergh Castle* (1983). Washington, S.H. Lee, 'The Early History of the Stricklands of Sizergh', *CWAAS (NS)* (1942).
21. The name of the river is said to be derived from a British word *cunetju* which is believed to indicate that the waters were 'sacred'. See Ekwall, E., *English River-names* (1928)

Chapter 13

1. Murray, John, *Handbook to the Lakes* (1867), p.105.
2. Wordsworth, William, *Guide to the Lakes* (1835) (Oxford ed. 1906) Section Third.
3. Murray, John, *op. cit.,* p.xxix.
4. Murray, John, *op. cit.,* p.xxvi.
5. Curwen, J.F., *Records relating to the Barony of Kendale* (1926), p.150, quoting from the *Kendal Order Book* for 3 May 1717.
6. Marshall, J.D., *Old Lakeland* (1971), pp.84-5.
7. See Gambles, R., *Lake District Place-names* (1994).
8. Manby, J., 'Westmorland Slate at Buckland (Berkshire) and Bath, 1754-59', *CWAAS (NS)* (1992). David, R.G. and Brambles, G.W., 'The Slate Quarrying Industry in Westmorland', *CWAAS (NS)* (1992).
9. Somervell, J., *Waterpower Mills in South Westmorland* (1930), pp.26-36. Revegill is behind the house known as Kilnstones which was once an outpost of Shap Abbey and later a resting-place for travellers and packhorses.
10. I am grateful to Mr. M. Davies-Shiel for information on Long Sleddale's potash kilns and fulling mills.
11. Watson, J., *Annals of a Quiet Valley* (1894), p.47. The valley school was in the building next to the church. An account of life there during the Second World War was written by the schoolmistress, Olwen Harris – *The School in the Fells* (1969).
12. *Royal Commission on Historical Monuments* (Westmorland) (1936), pp.157-8.
13. Ward Humphry, Mrs., *Robert Elsmere* (1888), p.3.

Chapter 14

1. Wordsworth, William, *Guide to the Lakes*, Oxford edn. (1973), p.126.
2. *Ibid.* p.127.
3. Wordsworth, William, *The Prelude*, Book 1.
4. Fiennes, Celia, *The Journeys of Celia Fiennes* (1695), ed. Morris, C. (1947). Budworth, J., *A Fortnight's Ramble to the Lakes* (1795), p.82. Clarke, J., *Survey of the Lakes* (1789), pp.32-3. Gray, Thomas, *Journal in the Lakes* (1775), 1803 edn., p.31.
5. Gilpin, William, *Observations ...* (1795), vol.2, p.65.
6. Hartsop Hall was sold to the Lowther family in 1425 and they held it until 1943 when it became the first

farm property in Britain to be accepted by the Treasury in lieu of death duties.

7. A mill is recorded in Patterdale in 1217.
8. Parson and White, *Directory of Cumberland and Westmorland* (1829).
9. Clarke, J., *op. cit.*, p.32. Gilpin, W., *op. cit.*, vol.2, p.64. Housman, J., *A Topographical Description of Cumberland and Westmorland* (1800), p.79.
10. Budworth, J., *op. cit.*, p.88 seq. Wordsworth, Dorothy, *Journal* for 22 December 1801.
11. Shaw, T., *Mining in the Lakes Counties* (1972), pp.76-90 and pp.92-8.
12. Aust, Sarah (The Hon. Mrs. S. Murray), *A Companion and Useful Guide ...* (1799), p.19. Lindop, G., *A Literary Guide to the Lake District* (1993), pp.312-3.
13. Fiennes, C., *op. cit.*, pp.193-4.
14. Examples of iron griddles, bakstones, brandeths and bread cupboards may be seen in the Abbot Hall Museum of Lakeland Life and Industry in Kendal.
15. Lindop, G., *op. cit.*, pp.311 and 321.
16. Gray, T., *op. cit.*, 1 October 1769.
17. Green, W., *The Tourists' New Guide to the Lakes ...* (1819), p.322. Gilpin, W., *op. cit.*, vol. 2, p.52.
18. Hutchinson, W., *An Excursion to the Lakes ...* (1773), 1786 edn. pp.65-7.
19. Gilpin, W., *op. cit.*, pp.60-2. Green, W., *op. cit.*, p.324.
20. Radcliffe, Ann, *Observations during a Tour to the Lakes* (1794).

Chapter 15

1. Wordsworth, William, *Guide to the Lakes* (1835), Oxford edn. (1973) p.72.
2. For a detailed account of the Bannerdale settlement see the *Royal Commission on Historical Monuments: Westmorland*, pp.166-7.
3. Fell, C., *Early Settlement in the Lakes Counties* (1972), Chapter 4.
4. Ralegh Bradford, C.A., *Transactions of the Dumfries and Galloway Society* (1950). Jackson, K.H., *St Ninian's Church at Whithorn, ibid.* (1949).
5. Thomas, A.C., *Christianity in Britain 300-700: The Evidence from North Britain* (1967).
6. Wordsworth, William, *op. cit.*, p.125.
7. Both documents are printed in *CWAAS (NS)* (1910).
8. Clarke, James, *Survey of the Lakes* (1789), p.35.
9. Wordsworth, Dorothy, *The Journals of Dorothy Wordsworth*, ed. E. de Selincourt (1941) vol.1, p.97.
10. Brierley, Henry, *Notes on Martindale* (1907), p.110. (This is a rare book of which only 20 copies were printed.)
11. Poole, A.L., *Domesday Book to Magna Carta*, Oxford History of England (1951), pp.29-30.
12. Clarke, James, *op. cit.*, p.34.
13. Macpherson, H.A., *A Vertebrate Fauna of Lakeland* (1892), p.62.
14. Wordsworth, William, *op. cit.*, p.124.
15. Budworth, Joseph, *A Fortnight's Ramble to the Lakes* (1795), p.270.

Chapter 16

1. Gilpin, William, *Observations on Mountains and Lakes &c.* (1786), vol.2, p.32.
2. Martineau, Harriet, *A Complete Guide to the English Lakes* (1858), 1974 edn. p 62.
3. Green, William, *The Tourists' New Guide to the Lakes* (1819), p.424.
4. Gilpin's disgruntlement with the Vale of St John even included disapproval of Blencathra which he thought 'disagreeable', 'displeasing' and 'grotesque'.
5. Allan, M., *The Roman Route across the Northern Lake District* (1994).
6. Millward, R. and Robinson, A., *The Lake District* (1970), p.49.
7. Burl, A., *The Stone Circles of the British Isles* (1976), p.56 seq.
8. Waterhouse, J., *Stone Circles of Cumbria* (1985), p.45.
9. Keats, John, *Hyperion*, Part III, lines 34-7. The Druids belong to a much later era than the Stone Circles – see Piggott, S., *The Druids* (1968).
10. Thom, A., *Megalithic Sites in Britain* (1967) and *Megalithic Lunar Observations* (1971).
11. Anderson, W.D., 'Some Recent Observations at the Keswick Stone Circle', *CWAAS (NS)* (1915). Waterhouse, J., *op. cit.*, pp.45-6.
12. Burl, A., *op. cit.*, p 39; Waterhouse, J., *op. cit.* pp.45-6.
13. Hay, T., 'The Threlkeld Settlement', *CWAAS (NS)* (1943).
14. Hutchinson, W., *An Excursion into the Lakes ...* (1773), p.121.
15. Martineau, H., *op. cit.*, p.62.
16. Collingwood, W.G., 'The Castle Rock', *CWAAS (NS)* (1916). In his novel *Thorstein of the Mere* Collingwood describes a Norse Thingstead at Legburthwaite which he also made the site of a decisive battle between the Norsemen allied with Dunmail, Chief of the Cumbrians, and the Saxon army of King Eadmund.

17. Bartholomew's map names the rock as 'Castle Rock of Triermain' but the Ordnance Survey, unromantically correct, prefers simply 'Castle Rock'.

18. John Richardson's verses and other writings were published in two volumes under the title *'Cummerlan' Talk, being Short Tales and Rhymes in the Dialect of the County* (1871) and (1876).

Chapter 17

1. Wordsworth, W., *The Excursion*, lines 717 seq.

2. Plint, R.G., 'Stone Axe Factory Sites in the Cumbrian Fells', *CWAAS(NS)* (1962). Bunch, B. and Fell, C., 'A Stone Axe Factory at Pike of Stickle, Great Langdale' in *Proceedings of the Prehistoric Society* (1949 and 1989). Fell, C.I., 'The Cumbrian Stone Type of Polished Stone Axe and its distribution in Britain', *Proceedings of the Prehistoric Society* (1964). Fell, C.I.,'The Great Langdale stone axe factory', *CWAAS(NS)* (1951). For a more general discussion of stone axes see Cole, S., *The Neolithic Revolution* (1961).

3. Cowper, H. S., 'A contrast in Architecture', *CWAAS(NS)* (1901).

4. Cowper, H.S., 'The Law Ting at Fell Foot', *CWAAS(OS)* (1890). The place-name 'Thengeheved' (Thing-mound) is recorded from Swindale *c.*1200 but this is now lost.

5. Dewdney, J.C., Taylor, S.A. and Wardhaugh, K.G., *The Langdales: A Lakeland Parish*, Durham University Occasional Papers (1959).

6. Professor Timothy O'Riordan has made a special study of this problem, *Interpreting Future Landscapes* (1992), published by the Yorkshire Dales National Park.

7. Linton, E.L., *The Lake Country* (1864), p.255.

8. The slate-quarrying industry of the Lake District has a notably short bibliography: Postlethwaite, J., *Mines and Mining in the Lake District* (1913). Bridge, J.N., 'The Slate-quarrying Industry in the Lake District', *Journal of Durham University Geographical Society* (1963/64), pp.14-20. Rollinson, W., *Life and Tradition in the Lake District* (1974), Chapter 12. David, R.G. and Brambles, G.W., 'The Slate Quarrying Industry in Westmorland', *CWAAS(NS)* (1991/92). Tyler, I., *Honister Slate* (1994).

9. Details of the gunpowder industry in South Westmorland are given in Wilson, P.N., 'The Gunpowder Mills of Westmorland and Furness', *Transactions of the Newcomen Society*, Vol. 36 (1964), and in Marshall, J.D. and Davies-Shiel, M., *Industrial Archaeology of the Lake Counties* (1964), pp.75-88, which has a reconstructed map of the works at Elterwater.

10. Collingwood, R.G., 'The Roman Road from Ambleside to Wrynose', *CWAAS(NS)* (1921). Richmond, I.A., 'The Roman Road from Ambleside to Ravenglass', *CWAAS(NS)* (1949). Margary, I., *Roman Roads in Britain* (1973), pp.389-91.

11. 'Pedder' is derived from the dialect word 'ped' which was the pannier in which the pedder or pedlar carried his wares.

12. Gibson, A. Craig, The Old Man ... or Ravings and Ramblings (1849), pp.88-99. Craig Gibson also visited the Hodge Close quarry which he describes on pp.132-33.

13. Robinson, Thomas, *A Natural History of Westmorland and Cumberland* (1709).

14. Fell Foot farm has panelling, plasterwork, oak beams and fireplaces dating from the Tudor and Jacobean period but the building is probably much older than this. It was bought in 1707 by Fletcher Fleming, one of Sir Daniel Fleming's many sons, who placed his coat of arms over the doorway. This heraldic design is not easily seen in detail but it comprises the Fleming fret with a cross moline (for the eighth son) and a serpent nowed (knotted) with vine leaves in its mouth. The Flemings retained the farm until 1735. Harriet Martineau's *A Complete Guide to the English Lakes* (1858) described it as 'the house of entertainment whence the packhorse calvacade began the ascent, or where they stopped to congratulate themselves on having accomplished the descent'.

15. Iving Howe is usually referred to as Ivy How by the valley folk.

16. Pavey Ark owes its unusual name to a 13th-century lady, Pavia, 'Daughter of William', who was, in some way, associated with a mountain pasture-land (or 'ergh') in this vicinity. The word 'ark' is most probably a corruption of 'ergh'. Pavey Ark thus seems to mean 'Pavia's hill pastures'. Pye Howe is derived from the Old English 'piot', a magpie, and from the Old Norse 'haugr', a hill: 'magpie hill'. Tilberthwaite appears in 1196 as 'Tildesburgthwait', the 'thwaite' or 'clearing' near Tilli's 'burh' or fort.

17. Bee-boles are discussed by Walker, P. and Crane, E., 'Bee-shelters and bee-boles in Cumbria', *CWAAS(NS)* (1991). For the 'nick-stick' see a note by Bevan, W., *CWAAS(NS)* (1989). Much fascinating detail on Langdale may be found in the reminiscences of a local inhabitant: Buntin, T. F., *Life in Langdale* (1993).

BIBLIOGRAPHY

Adams, J., *Mines of the Lake District Fells* (1988) 1988)

Allan, M. *The Roman Route across the Northern Lake District* (1994)

Aust, S., (The Hon. Mrs. Murray), *A Companion and Useful Guide to the Beauties of Scotland and the Lakes* (1796)

Bailey, J., ed., *Borrowdale in the Old Time: as Gathered from the Conversation of the late Sarah Yewdale, Queen of Borrowdale* (1869)

Baines, E., *Companion to the Lakes* (1829)

Baldwin, J. and Whyte, I.D., *The Scandinavians in Cumbria* (1985)

Bingham, R., *Kendal, A Social History* (1995)

Bogg, E., *Two Thousand Miles of Wandering in the Border Country, Lakeland and Ribblesdale* (1889)

Bott, G., *Keswick, The Story of a Lake District Town* (1994)

Bouch, C.M.L. *Prelates and People of the Lake Counties* (1948)

Bouch, C.M.L. and Jones, G.P., *The Lake Counties 1500-1830: a Social and Economic History* (1961)

Bradbury, J.Bernard, *A History of Cockermouth* (1981)

Bradley, R. and Edmonds, M., *Interpreting the Axe Trade: Production and Exchange in Neolithic Britain* (1993)

Bragg, M., *The Maid of Buttermere* (1987)

Bridge, J.N., *The Slate-quarrying Industry in the Lake District* (1963-4)

Brierley, H., *Notes on Martindale* (1907)

Brogan, H., *The Life of Arthur Ransome* (1984)

Brown, John, *A Description of the Vale and Lake at Keswick, 1753* (1767)

Brunskill, R.W., *Vernacular Architecture of the Lake Counties* (1948)

Budworth, Joseph, *A Fortnight's Ramble to the Lakes in Westmorland, Lancashire and Cumberland* (1792)

Buntin, T.F., *Life in Langdale* (1993)

Burl, A., *Stone Circles of the British Isles* (1976)

Camden, William, *Britannia* (1586)

Carruthers, F.J., *Lore of the Lake Country* (1975)

Cave-Brown-Cave, B.W., *Jonas Barber, Clockmaker of Winster* (1979)

Clarke, James, *A Survey of the Lakes of Cumberland, Westmorland and Lancashire* (1787)

Cole, S., *The Neolithic Revolution* (1961)

Coleridge, S.T., *Collected Letters*, ed. Griggs (1956-71)

Collingwood, R.G., *Roman Eskdale* (1929)

Collingwood, W.G., *Elizabethan Keswick* (1912)

Collingwood, W.G., *The Lake Counties* (1932)

Collingwood, W.G., *Lake District History* (1925)

Collingwood, W.G., *Thorstein of the Mere* (1895)

Curwen, J.F., *An Historical Description of Levens Hall* (1898)

Curwen, J.F., *Kirkbie Kendall* (1900)

Curwen, J.F., *Records Relating to the Barony of Kendale* (1926)

Davies, Hunter, *Wainwright: The Biography* (1995)

Davies, W.J.K., *The Ravenglass and Eskdale Railway* (1968)

Davies-Shiel, M., *Watermills of Cumbria* (1978)

Denton, Thomas, *Perambulation of Cumberland and Westmorland* (1667-8)

de Quincey, Thomas, *Recollections of the Lakes and the Lake Poets* (1839)

Dewdney, J.C., Taylor, S.A., and Wardhaugh, K.G., *The Langdales: a Lakeland Parish* (1959)
Dewdney, J.C. and Wardhaugh, K.G., *The Newlands Valley* (1960)
Dickinson, S., ed., *The Scandinavians in Cumbria* (1985)
Dickinson, W., *Cumbriana* (1875)
Donald, M.B., *Elizabethan Copper, the History of the Company of Mines Royal* (1955)
Ekwall, E., *English River-names* (1928)
English Place-name Society, *The Place-names of Cumberland* (1950-2)
English Place-name Society, *The Place-names of Westmorland* (1967)
Eversley, R., *Wasdale, a Celebration in Words and Pictures* (1981)
Fell, A., *The Early Iron Industry of Furness and District* (1908)
Fell, C., *Early Settlement in the Lake Counties* (1972)
Ferguson, R.S., *The Early History of the Society of Friends* (1871)
Fiennes, Celia, *The Journeys of Celia Fiennes*, ed. Morris, C. (1947)
Fisher-Crosthwaite, J., 'The German Miners at Keswick', *Transactions of the Cumberland Association for the Advancement of Literature and Science* (1882)
Friends of the Lake District, *A Tale of Two Lakes* (1982)
Gambles, R., *Lake District Place-names* (1994)
Gambles, R., *Out of the Forest: the Natural World and the Place-names of Cumbria* (1989)
Gambles, R., *The Borders of Lakeland* (1994)
Garnett, F.W., *Westmorland Agriculture, 1800-1900* (1912)
Gell, William, *A Tour in the Lakes made in 1797*, ed. Rollinson, W. (1968)
Gibson, A.C., *The Old Man ... or Ravings and Ramblings* (1849)
Gilpin, William, *Observations Relative chiefly to Picturesque Beauty made in the year 1772 on several parts of England; particularly the Mountains and Lakes of Cumberland and Westmorland* (1786)
Gray, Thomas, *Journal in the Lakes* (1775)
Green, William, *The Tourists' New Guide to the Lakes* (1818)
Hammersley, G., *Daniel Hechstetter the Younger: Copper Works and Life in Cumbria* (1988)
Hankinson, A., *A Century on the Crags* (1988)
Hardyment, C., *Arthur Ransome and Captain Flint's Treasure Chest* (1984)
Harris, A., *Cumberland Iron – the Story of Hodbarrow Mine, 1855-1968* (1970)
Heaton, H., *The Yorkshire Woollen and Worsted Industries* (1920)
Hervey, G.A.K. and Barnes, J.A.G., *Natural History of the Lake District* (1970)
Hilton, A., *Hermit of Eskdale* (n.d.)
Hindle, P., *Roads and Trackways of the Lake District* (1984)
Hodge, E.W., *Enjoying the Lakes: from Post-chaise to National Park* (1957)
Hodgson, J., *Westmorland as it was* (1822)
Hornyold Strickland, H., *Sizergh Castle* (1983)
Hoskins, W.G., *The Making of the English Landscape* (1955)
Housman, John, *A Descriptive Tour and Guide to the Lakes, Caves, Mountains and other Natural Curiosities in Cumberland, Westmoreland, Lancashire and a Part of the West Riding of Yorkshire* (1800)
Hoy, D., *English Lake Country* (1969)
Hughes, E., *North Country Life in the 18th Century: vol.2, Cumberland and Westmorland 1700-1830* (1965)
Hutchinson, William, *An Excursion to the Lakes in Westmorland and Cumberland; with a Tour through part of the Northern Counties in the years 1773 and 1774* (1776)
Hutchinson, William, *The History of the County of Cumberland* (1794)
Jenkins, R., *The Society for the Mines Royal and the German Colony in the Lake District* (1939)
Jones, G.P., *A Short History of Crosthwaite and Lyth mainly to about 1830* (1996)
Jones, G.P., *A Short History of the Manor and Parish of Witherslack to 1850* (1969)
Lefebure, M., *The English Lake District* (1964)
Lefebure, M., *Cumbrian Discovery* (1977)
Leland, John, *The Itinerary of John Leland: Part IX*, ed. Smith, L.T. (1964)
Lindop, G., *A Literary Guide to the Lake District* (1993)
Linton, Eliza L., *The Lake Country* (1864)
Little, E. A., *Chronicles of Patterdale* (1961)

Lyall, Edna (Ada Ellen Bayly), *Hope the Hermit* (1898)

Lysons, D. and S., *Magna Britannia: vol. 4 Cumberland* (1816)

Machell, Thomas, *Antiquary on Horseback*, 1692, transcribed by Jane Ewbank (1963)

MacPherson, H.A., *A Vertebrate Fauna of Lakeland* (1892)

Mannex, P.J., *History, Topography and Directory of Westmorland* (1849)

Mannex, P.J. and Whellan, W., *History, Gazetteer and Directory of Cumberland* (1847)

Margary, I.D., *Roman Roads in Britain* (1957)

Marr, J.E., *Geology of the Lake District* (1916)

Marshall, J.D., *Old Lakeland* (1971)

Marshall, J.D., *Furness in the Industrial Revolution* (1958)

Marshall, J.D. and Davies-Shiel, M., *Industrial Archaeology of the Lake Counties* (1969)

Marshall, J.D. and Davies-Shiel, M., *The Lake District at Work* (1971)

Marshall, J.D. and Walton, J.K., *The Lake Counties from 1830 to the Mid-twentieth Century* (1981)

Martineau, Harriet, *A Complete Guide to the English Lakes* (1858)

Mason, A.E.W., *A Romance of Wasdale* (1895)

Mills, A.D., *The Place-names of Lancashire* (1976)

Millward, R. and Robinson, A., *The Lake District* (1970)

Monkhouse, F.J., 'Some Features of the Historical Geography of the German Mining Enterprise in Elizabethan Lakeland' (1948) *(Geography,* vol.28*)*

Morris, W.P., *Records of Patterdale* (1903)

Moseley, F., *Geology of the Lake District* (1990)

Murray, John, *Handbook to Cumberland, Westmorland and the Lakes* (1867)

Newmarsh, R., *Mary Wakefield* (1912)

Nicholls, A.R., *Kendal Town Trail* (1986)

Nicholls, A.R., *Explore Kendal* (1996)

Nicholson, Cornelius, *Annals of Kendal* (1832)

Nicholson, J. and Burn, R., *The History and Antiquities of the Counties of Westmorland and Cumberland* (1777)

Nicholson, N., *The Lakers: the First Tourists* (1955)

Nicholson, N., *Portrait of the Lakes* (1963)

Nicholson, N., *The Lake District: an Anthology* (1977)

O'Riordan, T., *Interpreting Future Landscapes* (1992)

Orrel, R., *Saddle Tramp in the Lake District* (1979)

Otley, Jonathan, *A Concise Description of the English Lakes and Adjacent Mountains* (1823)

Parker, C.A., and Collingwood, W.G., *The Gosforth District* (1904)

Parson, W. and White, W., *Directory of Cumberland and Westmorland* (1829)

Patterson, E.M., *Blackpowder Manufacture in Cumbria* (1995)

Pearsall, W.H. and Pennington, W., *The Lake District: a Landscape History* (1973)

Pearson, William, *Letters, Journals and Notes on the Natural History of Lyth* (1844)

Pennant, Thomas, *A Tour in Scotland and a Voyage to the Hebrides in 1772* (1774)

Pevsner, N., *The Buildings of England: Cumberland and Westmorland* (1967)

Postlethwaite, J., *Mines and Mining in the Lake District* (1913)

Prehistoric Society, *Proceedings,* volumes for 1949, 1964, 1989

Radcliffe, Ann, *A Journey made in the Summer of 1794 to which are added Observations during a Tour of the Lakes of Lancashire, Westmorland and Cumberland* (1795)

Ramshaw, D. and Adams, J., *The English Lakes* (1993)

Ransome, Arthur, *Swallows and Amazons, Swallowdale, Pigeon Post, Winter Holiday* (1930s)

Rawnsley, E.F, *Canon Rawnsley: an Account of his Life and Work* (1923)

Rea, A., *The Beckside Bogle* (1884)

Richardson, John, *Cummerlan' Talk* (1871)

Richmond, I.A., *The Roman Fort at Hardknott* (1949)

Robinson, John, *Guide to the Lakes* (1819)

Robinson, Thomas, *An Essay towards a Natural History of Westmorland and Cumberland* (1709)

Rollinson, W., *A History of Man in the Lake District* (1967)

Rollinson, W., *Life and Tradition in the Lake District* (1974)

Rollinson, W., *A History of Cumberland and Westmorland* (1978 and 1996)

Rollinson, W., *Lakeland Walls* (1972)
Royal Commission on Historical Monuments in Westmorland (1936)
Ryder, M.L., 'The History of Sheep Breeds in Britain', *Agricultural History Review* (1964)
Sandford, E., *A Cursory Relation of all the Antiquities and Families of Cumberland* (1675)
Scott, J. ed., *A Lakeland Valley Through Time: a History of Staveley, Kentmere and Ings* (1995)
Scott, Walter, *The Bridal of Triermain* (1805)
Seatree, G.A., *Lakeland Memories* (1923)
Shackleton, E.H., *Lakeland Geology* (1966)
Shaw, W.T., *Mining in the Lake Counties* (1970)
Short, Thomas, *An Essay towards a Natural, Experimental and Medicinal History of the Principle Mineral Waters* (1740)
Short, Thomas, *A Treatise on Cold Mineral Waters* (1766)
Size, N., *Shelagh of Eskdale* (n.d.)
Size, N., *The Secret Valley* (1929)
Smith, B., 'The Glacier Lakes of Eskdale, Miterdale and Wasdale', *Quarterly Journal of the Geological Society*, No 88 (1932)
Somervell, J., *Waterpower Mills in South Westmorland* (1930)
Somervell, J., *Waterpower and Industry in Westmorland* (1938)
Stagg, John, *The Cumberland Minstrel* (1821)
Steer, T.P., *Landscape Changes in the Lyth Valley 1770 to the 20th Century* (1991)
Sutton, G., *Fell Days* (1948)
Sutton, S., *The Story of Borrowdale* (1961)
Symonds, H.H., *Afforestation in the Lake District* (1936)
Symonds, H.H., *Walking in the Lake District* (1953)
Symons, G.J., *The Floating Island of Derwentwater, its History and Mystery* (1888)
Thom, A., *Megalithic Sites in Britain* (1967)
Thomas, A.C., *Christianity in Britain 300-700: the Evidence from North Britain* (1967)
Transactions of the Cumberland and Westmorland Antiquarian and Archaeological Society: Old Series (1866-1900); New Series (1900-). (Authors and Titles of Articles in these Transactions and the relevant volumes are referred to in the Notes for each chapter)
Transactions of the Newcomen Society (1937, 1938 and 1963) (details in chapter Notes)
Trevelyan, G.M., *The Call and Claims of Natural Beauty* (1931)
Tyler, I., *Honister Slate* (1994)
Tyler, I., *Seathwaite Wad and the Mines of the Borrowdale Valley* (1995)
Wainwright, A., *A Pictorial Guide to the Lakeland Fells* (1955-1966)
Wainwright, A., *Three Westmorland Rivers* (1979)
Walker, A., *A Tour from London to the Lakes* (1795)
Walpole, Hugh, *The Herries Chronicles* (1930s)
Ward, Humphry, M.A., Mrs., *Helbeck of Bannisdale* (1898)
Ward, Humphry, M.A., Mrs., *Robert Elsmere* (1889)
Waterhouse, J., *Stone Circles of Cumbria* (1985)
Watson, J., *Annals of a Quiet Valley by a Country Parson* (1894)
Webster, C., *Essay on the Farming of Westmorland* (1904)
West, Thomas, *A Guide to the Lakes in Cumberland, Westmorland and Lancashire* (1778)
Whellan, W., *The History and Topography of the Counties of Cumberland and Westmorland* (1860)
Wilkinson, Thomas, *Tours to the British Mountains* (1824)
Wilson, P.N., *The Gunpowder Mills of Westmorland and Furness* (1963)
Wilson, P.N., *A Short History of the New Sedgwick Gunpowder Works* (n.d.)
Wilson, W., *Coaching in Lakeland* (1885)
Winchester, A.J.L., *Landscape and Society in Medieval Cumbria* (1987)
Wood, M.C., *The Reclamation of the Lyth Mosses* (1968)
Wordsworth, Dorothy, *The Journals of Dorothy Wordsworth*, ed. E. de Selincourt (1941)
Wordsworth, William, *Guide to the Lakes* (1835), Oxford edn. (1906)
Wordsworth, William, *Poetical Works*, Oxford edn. (1936)
Young, Arthur, *A Six Months Tour through the North of England*, vol. 3 (1770)
Yuen, R., *The Kentmere Lead Mines* (1969)

Index

References to illustrations are given in **bold**